The Military Book Club® Historical Encyclopedia of the United States Marine Corps

HISTORICAL DICTIONARIES
OF WAR, REVOLUTION, AND CIVIL UNREST
Edited by Jon Woronoff

1. *Afghan Wars, Revolutions, and Insurgencies*, by Ludwig W. Adamec. 1996.
2. *United States–Mexican War*, by Edward H. Moseley and Paul C. Clark Jr. 1997.
3. *World War I*, by Ian V. Hogg. 1998.
4. *United States Navy*, by James M. Morris and Patricia M. Kearns. 1998.
5. *United States Marine Corps*, by Harry A. Gailey. 1998.
6. *Wars of the French Revolution*, by Steven T. Ross. 1998.
7. *American Revolution*, by Terry M. Mays. 1998.

The Military Book Club®
Historical Encyclopedia
of the
United States Marine Corps

Harry A. Gailey

The Scarecrow Press, Inc.
Lanham, Md., & London

SCARECROW PRESS, INC.

Published in the United States of America
by Scarecrow Press, Inc.
4720 Boston Way
Lanham, Maryland 20706

British Library Cataloguing in Publication Information Available

ISBN 0-8108-3401-4

for
Adam, Steven, Christopher, Bryan, and Dylan

Contents

Maps

Editor's Foreword

The United States Marines joined the American armed services almost as stealthily as they entered many a fray since then. They were formed as they were needed, and they continued operating because they were needed. Over nearly two centuries they have fought in countless wars and lesser conflicts, often making a decisive difference in the outcome. Marines have frequently been cited for bravery, and the whole corps is known for its valor. Yet, from time to time, questions have arisen as to exactly what the Marine Corps should be doing and even whether it was truly necessary. This is another time of questioning. We have every reason to believe that the marines will remain and will meet the needs of times to come, even if changes and adjustments occur.

This *Historical Encyclopedia of the United States Marine Corps* traces the history of this branch of the armed services, showing how it emerged and how it has evolved. That is presented in the introduction and summarized in the chronology. The dictionary portion then highlights crucial events, including major wars, battles, and interventions in which the marines have been involved. Other entries present significant persons—whether officers or lower ranks—political and geographical terms, weaponry, and equipment. All in all, this is an excellent place to study the role of the Marine Corps, to see why it proved essential in the past, and will doubtlessly be useful in the future. Those who want to know more can explore sources noted in the bibliography.

The present volume in the war series was written by Dr. Harry A. Gailey, who is professor of history at San Jose State University. He has written five books on World War II in the Pacific, the latest being *The War in the Pacific: From Pearl Harbor to Tokyo Bay*. Since the Pacific was the scene of countless operations by the marines, including some of the most punishing and glorious, this experience has given Professor Gailey considerable familiarity with the Marine Corps. It has also revealed the distinctive characteristics and specific qualities that enables him to portray this exceptional corps in a more tangible form that should please specialists and military buffs alike.

Jon Woronoff
Series Editor

Maps

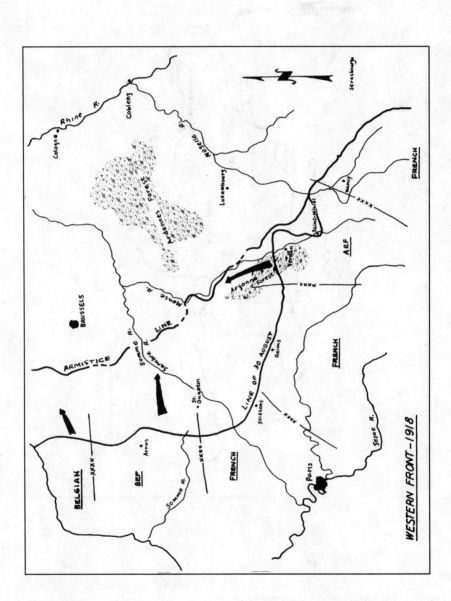

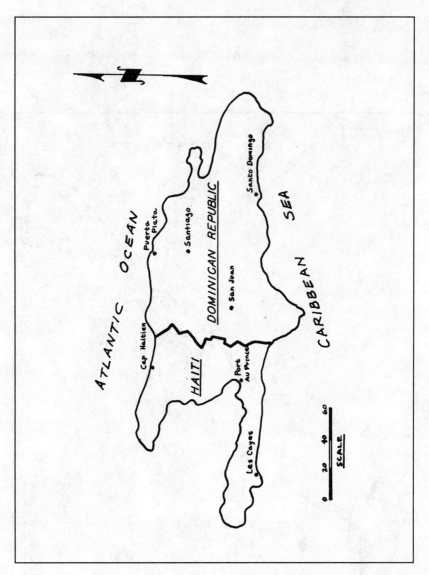

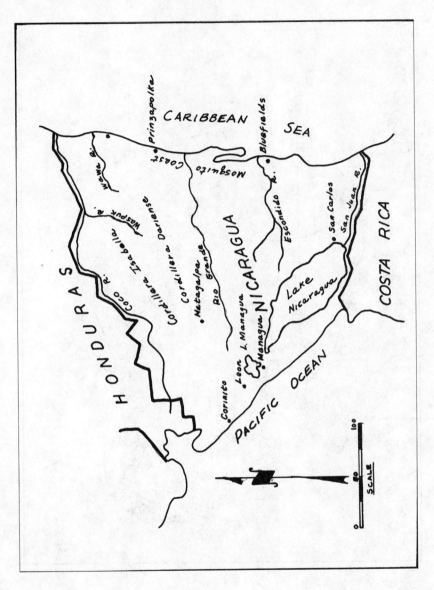

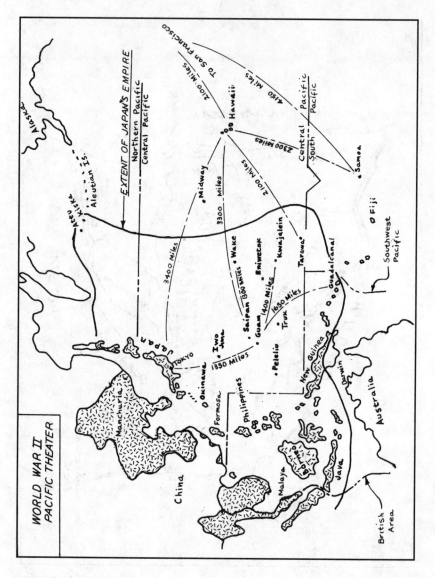

WORLD WAR II
PACIFIC THEATER

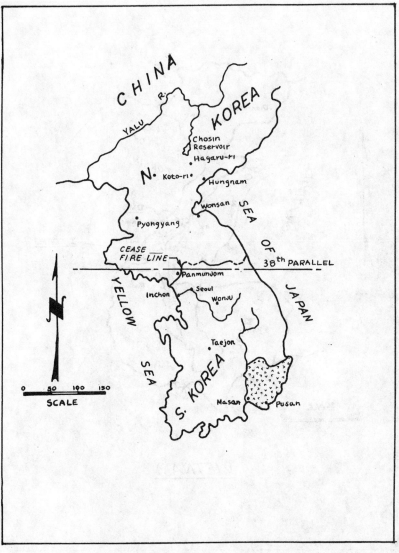

CHINA

KOREA

YALU R.

Chosin
Reservoir

Hagaru-ri

N.   • Koto-ri   • Hungnam

• Wonsan   SEA

• Pyongyang

CEASE
FIRE LINE   38th PARALLEL

YELLOW   • Panmunjom

Inchon   • Seoul
• Wonju

SEA   JAPAN

• Taejon

S. KOREA

Masan   Pusan

OF

0   50   100   150
SCALE

N

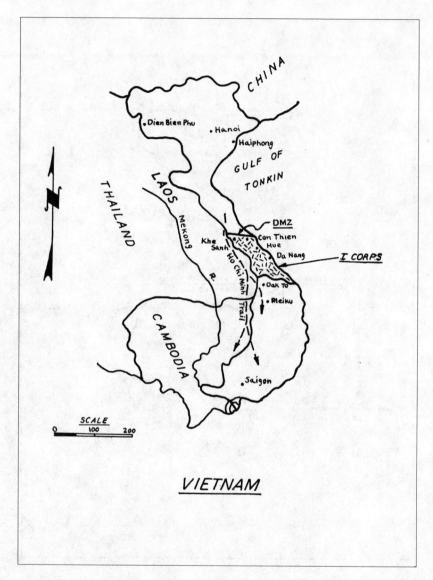

VIETNAM

Abbreviations and Acronyms

A-3	"Falcon," observation aircraft
A-4Y	"Sky Hawk," ground support aircraft
A-6A	"Intruder," attack bomber built by Grumman
A-25	"Helldiver," dive bomber built by Curtiss (same as U.S. Navy's SB2C)
AAV	Assault amphibious vehicle
AIRSOLS	Air Force, Solomons
APC	Armored personnel carrier
ARVN	Army of Republic of Vietnam (South Vietnam)
AV-8	"Harrier," vertical takeoff fighter
BAR	Browning automatic rifle
CH-37	Medium sized helicopter, built by Sikorsky
CH-46	"Sea Knight," large helicopter built by Boeing
CH-53	"Sea Stallion," transport helicopter built by Sikorsky
CINCPAC	Commander in chief, Pacific
CP	Command post
D	Normal designation for invasion day
DMZ	Demilitarized Zone
DUKW	"Duck," six-wheel-drive amphibian
F2A	"Buffalo," fighter aircraft built by Brewster
F2H	"Banshee," single-seat fighter built by McDonnell
F2T	"Black Widow," night fighter built by North American
F4B	"Phantom," large attack fighter built by McDonnell
F4D	"Skyray," single-seat fighter-bomber built by Douglas
F4F	"Wildcat," early marine fighter built by Grumman
F4U	"Corsair," fighter bomber built by Vought
F6F	"Hellcat," single-seat fighter built by Grumman
F8C	"Helldiver," two-seat fighter built by Curtiss
F-18	"Hornet," escort fighter built by McDonnell Douglas
FJ-1	"Fury," jet fighter built by North American
FMC	Food Machinery Corporation
FMF	Fleet Marine Force
H	Designation for the hour of invasion, landing, or attack on an enemy position

HRS	"Chickasaw," small utility helicopter
KC-130	"Hercules," transport built by Lockheed
KIA	Killed in action
LCP	Landing craft, personnel
LCT	Landing craft, tank
LCVP	Landing craft, vehicle personnel
LST	Landing ship, tank
LVT	"Alligator" and later "Water Buffalo," landing vehicle, tracked
LVTP	Landing vehicle, tracked personnel
M-1	Model 1; refers to many items (i.e., Garand rifle, Carbine, Abrams tank)
M-1	"Garand," .30-caliber semi-automatic rifle
M-1A1	"Abrams," main battle tank during 1980s and 1990s
M2HB	Model 2, Browning heavy .50 caliber machine gun
M-3	.45-caliber submachine gun
M3A1	Antitank gun
M3/M5	"Stuart," light tank
M-4	"Sherman," medium tank
M-26	"Pershing," main battle tank developed during WWII
M-60	7.62 air-cooled machine gun
M-60A3	Main battle tank during 1960s and 1970s
M1903	.30-caliber rifle
M1911	.45-caliber pistol
M1917A1	.30-caliber water-cooled machine gun
M1919A4 and A6	.30-caliber air-cooled machine gun
M1921	"Thompson," .45-caliber submachine gun
M1941	Johnson .30-caliber rifle
M1941MG	Johnson-designed machine gun
MACV	Marine Amphibious Corps Vietnam
MAF	Marine Amphibious Force
MAG	Marine Air Group
MAGTF	Marine Air Ground Task Force
MarDiv	Marine Division
MBT	Main battle tank
MEB	Marine Expeditionary Brigade
MEF	Marine Expeditionary Force
MEU	Marine Expeditionary Unit
MIA	Missing in action
MPF	Marine Prepositioning Force
NASA	National Aeronautics and Space Agency
NATO	North Atlantic Treaty Organization

NVA	North Vietnamese Army
OAS	Organization of American States
P-40	"Tomahawk," fighter plane built by Curtiss
PBJ	"Mitchell," twin-engined bomber built by North American
PBY	"Catalina," long-range patrol plane built by Consolidated
PW-9	Single-seat pursuit plane built by Boeing
R4D	"Skytrain," cargo transport built by Douglas (Army C-47)
RCT	Regimental Combat Team
ROK	Republic of Korea (also refers to South Korean Army)
ROTC	Reserve Officers Training Course
RVN	Republic of Vietnam (South Vietnam)
SB2C	"Helldiver," dive bomber built by Curtiss
SBD	"Dauntless," scout bomber built by Douglas
SOP	Standing operating procedure
TBF	"Avenger," torpedo bomber built by Grumman
TBM	"Avenger," torpedo bomber built by General Motors
UH-34	"Sea Horse," utility helicopter built by Sikorsky
VC	Viet Cong, Vietnamese Communist
VMF	Marine Fighter Squadron
VMSB	Marine Scout Bomber Squadron
V/STOL	Vertical take-off and landing aircraft
WIA	Wounded in action

Chronology

1775	2d Continental Congress authorizes Continental Marines.
1776	Futile attack on Fort Montague by Continental forces. Small marine units support General Washington's army at the Battle of Princeton.
1783	Disbanding of Continental Marines.
1798	Congress approves creation of United States Marine Corps.
1805	Undeclared war with Barbary pirates. Attack on Port of Tripoli. Derna captured.
1812–13	Naval actions against British.
1813	Battle of Bladensburg.
1814	Action at Nuka Hiva in Marquesas Islands.
1815	Battle of New Orleans (8 January). Marine units were the core of General Jackson's army.
1832	Landing at Kuala Batu, Sumatra.
1834	Action of Congress for "Better Organization of the Marine Corps."
1836	Seminole War was directed against the major Indian tribe in Florida.
1846	Mexican War begins. Marine units capture Tampico (November). Marines involved in defense of San Diego and the battle of San Pascual.
1847	Marines aid in capture of Veracruz (March). Assault of Chapultepec Castle, the key to the capture of Mexico City (September). Marines and sailors capture Mazatlan (November).
1852–54	Actions in Panama.
1855–58	Landings in Fiji Islands.
1858	Capture of John Brown by marine units at Harpers Ferry (October).
1861	Civil War begins with firing on Fort Sumter. First Battle of Bull Run. Capture of Fort Clark and Cape Hatteras in North Carolina.
1862	Marines occupy Saint Augustine, Florida (March). Marines land in New Orleans (April).

1863	Failed assault on Fort Sumter (September).
1865	Attack on Fort Fisher, North Carolina (January).
1871	Destruction of Han River forts in Korea.
1882	Congressional act decreeing that all marine officers be appointed from Annapolis graduates.
1891	Establishment of School of Application.
1898	Spanish-American War—marines land in Cuba and capture Cuzco Well (May).
1899	Philippine insurrection. Action against rebels at Novalita, Luzon.
1900	Boxer Rebellion in China led by anti-Western groups. Defense of the foreign legations at Peking (June–July). Major actions against Moros on Samar, Philippines (August–November).
1903	Marines land at Colon in Panama (October). Some units remained there until the canal was completed in 1914.
1904	Roosevelt Corollary to Monroe Doctrine announced (December).
1909	Provisional regiment sent to restore order in Nicaragua; withdrawn in 1910.
1911	First marine qualifies as a pilot.
1912–13	Marines return to Nicaragua and fight several small actions against rebels.
1913	Marine Advance Base Force created consisting of two regiments, each with specific objectives (December).
1914	Landing at Veracruz, Mexico, and capture of city (April). World War I begins (August). Landing at Port au Prince, Haiti, to secure treasury (December).
1915	Bloody uprising against government of Haiti (July). Marines involved in action against rebels. Haitian Constabulary established. Marines withdrawn in 1916.
1916	Civil war in Santo Domingo. Marine brigade puts down rebellion in north. Dominican Constabulary established. National Defense Act expanded size of Marine Corps to 15,000 men.
1917	U.S. declares war on Germany (6 April). Rapid expansion of the corps formed into two regiments, the first of which sailed for France as part of the American Expeditionary Force.
1918	Marines land in Cuba to help stabilize the government. In France, 4th Brigade created by joining two marine regiments comprising one-half of 2d Division. 2d Division blocks German attack west of Chateau-Thierry

(June). Marine Brigade leads counteroffensive at Belleau Wood. 1st Aviation Force composed of four squadrons arrives in France (18 July). Brig. Gen. John Lejeune appointed commander of 2d Division. 2d Division attacks Germans at Saint-Mihiel (September). In Meuse-Argonne, marines capture key position at Blanc Mont (2 October). Elements of 2d Division operating in Argonne Forest (November); one regiment had forced crossing of Meuse River the day before the Armistice. Brigade posted to Rhineland for occupation duty.

1919   Endemic disorders in Haiti. Marine Brigade and constabulary fight a number of actions against the rebels. Active fighting ceased in May 1920. Marine units removed from Cuba. 4th Brigade returned to United States from France in fall; disbanded in August.

1924   Marine units removed from Santo Domingo.

1927   Civil war again in Nicaragua. A battalion of marines landed (January). Action against Sandinista rebels.

1933   Expeditionary Force redesignated Fleet Marine Force, divided into Atlantic andPacific sections.

1934   Publication of *Tentative Manual for Landing Operations.*

1939   World War II begins in Europe (September).

1940   Strength of Marine Corps stands at 37,000 men.

1941   Japan attacks Pearl Harbor (7 December). United States declares war the following day. Germany declares war on the United States (11 December). Guam invaded (8 December); small marine garrison surrenders. Initial Japanese assault on Wake Island (11 December) beaten off; second attack (23 December) overwhelms the Marine Defense Battalion.

1942   Surrender of 4th Marines with Japanese victory at Bataan, Philippines (May). Attack by marine pilots from Midway during crucial naval battle (June). 1st Division upgraded from a brigade sailed for South Pacific; arrived in New Zealand (26 June). Landing of elements of 1st Division on Guadalcanal and Tulagi Islands in southern Solomons (7 August). Women authorized in Marine Corps (November).

1943   Marine Raiders landed on New Georgia Island (July) and cooperated with army troops in capture of island. Raiders raid Makin Island in Gilbert chain (August). 3d Division lands at Empress Augusta Bay on Bougainville (November). 2d Division assaults Betio Island in the Tarawa Atoll of the Gilbert Islands (November). 1st

Division lands at Cape Gloucester, New Britain (December).

1944   4th Division seizes Roi-Namur Islands in the Kwajalein Atoll in the Marshall Islands (February). One marine and an army regiment take the three major islands in the Eniwetok Atoll (late February). Saipan in the Mariana Islands is assaulted by the 2d and 4th Divisions (15 June). 3d Division, 1st Provisional Brigade, and army's 77th Division land on Guam (21 July). Tinian seized by the 2d and 4th Divisions (July). 1st Division assaults Peleliu (15 September).

1945   4th and 5th Divisions assault Iwo Jima (19 February). 1st, 2d, and 6th Divisions as a part of X Army invade Okinawa (1 April). European War ends (8 May). Pacific War ends with formal surrender of Japan (2 September). Marines of V Corps occupy Kyushu while III Corps units move into northern China.

1946   Deactivation of 3d, 4th, 5th, and 6th Divisions.

1947   Creation of Department of Defense. Status of corps remains questionable.

1948   Further reduction in size of the Marine Corps. Women integrated into corps as regular marines (June).

1950   North Korean army invades South Korea (25 June); United Nations responds by labeling the Communists as aggressors, and President Truman commits U.S. forces to Korea. 1st Provisional Brigade and three squadrons of fighter bombers leave for Korea (July). 5th Marines committed in Naktong Bulge area of Pusan perimeter (2 August). 1st and 5th Marines land at Inchon, the port of Seoul, as part of X Corps (15 September) and later take Seoul. 1st Division reaches the Chosin Reservoir near the Yalu River by mid-November. Chinese troops cross the Yalu (25 November) and force marines into a winter retreat to the port of Hungnam.

1951   As part of IX Corps, the 1st Division participates in Operations Killer and Ripper (February and March). 1st Division helps stop Chinese spring offensive (April).

1952   Marines take over guarding Panmunjom. Intense fighting for "Bunker Hill" (August) and the "Hook" (October).

1953   Marines hold hills code-named "Berlin," "East Berlin," "Reno," and "Carson" against heavy attacks.

Truce agreed upon (27 July) and the Korean "peace-keeping" ends.

1956   A battalion of marines land at Alexandria, Egypt, to cover evacuation of civilians.

1958   Three battalions of marines ordered to Lebanon to support the Lebanese government (mid-July).

1962   Marine helicopter squadron ordered to Vietnam (April). Cuban Missile Crisis (October). Marine garrison at Guantanamo Bay brought up to regimental strength.

1965   Full-scale civil war in Dominican Republic; four battalions of marines land on island (late April). 9th Expeditionary Brigade lands at Da Nang (early spring) By August four regiments and four air groups are operating in central Vietnam. 7th Marines in Operation Starlight attack Viet Cong near Chu Lai.

1966   1st Division arrives in Vietnam joining 3d Division to defend I Corps. Amphibious attack against enemy south of Chu Lai (January). Heavy fighting by 1st Division near Hue (February). Operation Texas, a helicopter assault against North Vietnam Army at An Hao (March). A sea and air assault mounted in Ngan Valley (July). Operations against NVA in highlands of western Onang Tri Province (September).

1967   Marines defend area immediately south of DMZ at Con Thien, Gio Linh, and Khe Sanh. Heavy frontal attack at Con Thien (May) beaten off; counterattack takes NVA's bunker complex. NVA retreats across DMZ. Building of McNamara Line; fails to halt NVA invasions across DMZ. Operation Buffalo batters an NVA regiment (5 July). Regimental size attack on Con Thien broken by artillery (10 September).

1968   Battle for Khe Sanh, key base of McNamara Line, begins (21 January); lasts for 77 days. Tet offensive begins (30 January) when the NVA attacks every major city in South Vietnam; NVA division destroyed at Da Nang. Heaviest fighting during Tet at the old city of Hue; enemy initially captures much of the city. ARVN units and 5th Marines recapture most of city. Six marine battalions trap and destroy an NVA regiment near Laotian border (November).

1969   1st Division strikes hill country west of Da Nang and launches a major amphibious landing into Batangan Peninsula. The 3d Division launches Operation Dewey

Canyon in Da Krong Valley. 9th Marines withdraw as a part of phased withdrawal at midyear. Continual search-and-destroy missions in Que Son Valley and south of Da Nang. Second phase of troop withdrawal begins (September). All of 3d Division relocated outside Vietnam in a month.

1970   Last major offensive, "Pickens Forrest," undertaken with marines in support of ARVN forces.

1971   Only the 1st Marines are left in Vietnam (February), and these are ordered out by midyear.

1972   Marine Air Groups continue to operate in support of ARVN forces.

1973   Peace agreement signed in Paris (27 January), ending direct U.S. participation.

1974   34th Marine Amphibious Unit (MAU) sent to Cyprus to provide protection for U.S. citizens.

1975   The last NVA offensive begins (March); 9th Amphibious Brigade is ordered to Vietnam to help evacuate civilians (April). 31st Marine Amphibious Unit is sent to Cambodia to oversee evacuation of U.S. citizens (April). A U.S. ship, *Mayaguez*, is seized by Cambodia (12 May).

1979   The shah of Iran is overthrown. The U.S. embassy is stormed; 60 U.S. citizens, including marine guards, are taken prisoner (November).

1980   An attempt to rescue hostages in Iran fails (April).

1982   Civil disturbances in Lebanon. Commitment of marine peacekeepers.

1983   Marines in Lebanon under fire. Suicide bomber attacks barracks in Beirut; 241 marines killed (October). Marine and army units sent to Grenada (October).

1984   Last marines withdrawn from Lebanon (26 February).

1989   Operation Just Cause, directed at unseating General Noriega from power in Panama, launched (December).

1990   Iraqi conquest of Kuwait. Operation Desert Shield begins (August). 1st Marine Expeditionary Force (MEF) arrives (September). 2d MEF arrives (December).

1991   Operation Desert Storm begins (18 January) with air strikes into Iraq. Marines assault Kuwait City. Gulf War ends (27 February).

1992   Marine units dispatched to Somalia (December).

1994   Marine units sent to Haiti (September).

Introduction

Early History

Naval warfare during the 18th century was fought largely with heavily armed vessels operating in close quarters, in many cases grappled together. Boarding parties from each ship would attempt to take control of the decks of the enemy ship. To counter such maneuvers, armed men would be stationed along the rigging and on the masts. At first sailors were given this task, but during the many wars between France and Britain, a new specialized force of men better trained in the use of firearms was developed. The direct ancestor of the United States Marine Corps was the British Royal Marine Corps formed in 1664. Very soon these elite sea soldiers were being used for amphibious operations, going ashore in longboats to attack enemy positions under the protective guns of the ships offshore. From the beginning of Marine Corps operations there was an ambivalence. Were they to be used primarily on board ships or in land operations? For the marines of the new United States, this question of function would become crucial with the passage of time.

The Continental Congress in the fall of 1775 decided to create a Continental Navy and thus it was natural to provide a Marine Corps. On 10 November Congress passed a resolution creating two battalions of marines. During the Revolutionary War (q.v.), marines were part of the crew of every major U.S. ship and fought well in a series of battles against the Royal Navy including actions with John Paul Jones on board the *Ranger* and *Bonhomme Richard*. They were also tested in amphibious actions. Two hundred marines were landed in March 1776 on New Providence Island in the Bahamas. They captured the town and neighboring fort before returning to the ships with the precious cargo of gunpowder for the Continental Army. In December three companies of marines joined Gen. George Washington and later participated in the attacks on Trenton and Princeton. In late July 1779 marine units performed well in the abortive attempt to seize a British-held fort on Penobscot (q.v.) Bay. However, by 1781 only a few marines were left in the all-volunteer force, and they were no longer needed since the navy had been reduced to only one ship. Even before peace in 1783, the Continental Marines (q.v.) had disappeared.

The undeclared war with France was the major reason for the revival of a marine organization. New ships had been built and there was a need for a quota of marines for each ship. On 11 July 1789, the true birthday of the corps, Pres. John Adams approved the bill establishing a Marine Corps. The number of men in the proposed corps was to be only 500 privates. The small size of the corps continued until World War I, limiting the role that it would play in major U.S. wars. Headquarters for the new organization was established in Philadelphia. The uniforms (q.v.) were blue and were surplus from Gen. Anthony Wayne's Legion and became by chance the first dress blues.

The main duty of the Marine Corps during the French conflict in the Caribbean was as a part of ships' crews. The one land action was when 90 marines and sailors captured Puerto Plata, a French held harbor in Santo Domingo. Peace with France did not mean an end to difficulties facing the new nation. First there was a conflict with the Barbary pirates when a small contingent of marines in a multinational force captured Derna (q.v.) in North Africa, an action that became "the shores of Tripoli" in the Marine Hymn (q.v.). Further conflict with Britain led to the War of 1812 (q.v.). Marines participated in each of the major naval confrontations, served on the Great Lakes, defended the capital at Bladensburg (q.v.), and 300 marines were the cadre enabling Gen. Andrew Jackson to defeat the British at New Orleans (q.v.).

After the war the minuscule corps was reduced once more and resumed the role of shipboard troops. The navy in the 1820s patrolled the pirate-infested waters of the Caribbean, and from time to time marines were landed to overawe the Spanish administration of the islands. They were involved in landings in the Falkland Islands to free three U.S. ships. In February 1832 marines and sailors were put ashore in Samoa (q.v.) and in bloody fighting overcame the pirates based there and forced them to relinquish a captured U.S. ship. In 1834 an act of Congress for the "Better Organization of the Marine Corps" modified the original 1798 act and specifically made it subordinate to the navy. The authorized strength was raised to 1,224 enlisted men. This did little to change the pattern established for use of the corps. Throughout the rest of the century marines were involved in showing the flag and protecting U.S. interests in all parts of the globe. Two hundred marines were present when Commodore

Matthew Perry forced the opening of Japan for trade in 1854. Other punitive landings were made in Panama (q.v.) in 1852 and 1854, Fiji (q.v.) in 1855 and 1858, and at Canton in 1856. A major victory was achieved in Korea in 1871 when marines were landed to end the threat to U.S. ships posed by the Han River forts (q.v.).

The Marine Corps participated in only a small way in the major wars of the 19th century. In the Seminole War (q.v.) the marines were placed under army command and the commandant took half the corps to Florida. However, they were involved in only one battle in 1837 and most marines returned to Washington after that. During the Mexican War (q.v.), a few marines participated in the California rebellion and later in occupying towns in Baja. The most significant action was supporting Gen. Winfield Scott's army in raids on Gulf Coast ports. Later a marine battalion joined the main force of 11,000 men before Mexico City and was involved in the storming of Chapultepec (q.v.) Castle on 13 September 1847. The 1,800-man corps lost most of its junior officers in early 1861 as the nation drifted into the Civil War, but most senior officers remained loyal and soon enlistments increased the ranks to over 4,000, the largest size in the corps' history. The corps was underutilized during the early phases of the war despite the bravery shown by a hastily put together battalion at Bull Run in July and the capture of Fort Clark the following month.

Most marines during the war served on board ships blockading Confederate ports and from time to time landing to secure specific objectives. In March 1862 a battalion with the South Atlantic Squadron landed and seized St. Augustine, Florida, without a fight. Other marines of the West Gulf Squadron that had forced its way into the mouth of the Mississippi River went ashore as an advance party and seized New Orleans in April. In September of the following year 150 marines in an ill planned venture by the navy attempted to capture Fort Sumter (q.v.) in Charleston Harbor. They failed after suffering one-third casualties. A final use of the corps during the war was also a fiasco because of a flawed plan and poor timing. On 15 January 1865 marines and sailors made a direct seaborne assault on Fort Fisher (q.v.) in North Carolina while the army attacked from the landward side. Although the army captured the fort, the sailors and marines suffered heavy casualties on the beach. During the entire war the corps had only 450 casualties, fewer than in a serious skirmish before a major battle, and its actions did not add luster to its reputation.

After the war the size of the corps was reduced, and its duties reverted to providing personnel for naval ships and protecting U.S. embassies around the world. The growing importance of the

United States in world trade was mirrored by the many petty conflicts involving American interests in all parts of the globe. In addition, the instability of many of the governments in the Caribbean and Latin America imposed a burden on the United States as the protector of the Western Hemisphere. The corps was called on again and again to carry out such forward policies long before the Monroe Doctrine was expanded by Pres. Theodore Roosevelt. In this period marines were landed in China and also three times in Korea and Hawaii. Conditions in Nicaragua (q.v.) brought marine landings four times and twice each in Panama (q.v.), Haiti (q.v.), and Mexico. Landings were also made in Japan, Samoa, Argentina, Chile, and Colombia. Thus, while the fate of the corps was being debated in Congress, small units were being overutilized by showing the flag in all parts of the world.

U.S. economic and humanitarian aims with regard to the Caribbean region culminated in the short-lived Spanish-American War (q.v.), which began in April 1898. The month after the war began Congress raised the authorized strength of the Marine Corps to 3,073 men with a wartime augmentation of 1,525 men. Marine units were active in both the Philippine and Cuban areas. After Commodore George Dewey's naval victory at Manila Bay, a marine detachment on 3 May secured the key city of Cavite. In Cuba (q.v.) a marine battalion on 10 June was landed inside Guantanamo (q.v.) Bay 40 miles east of Santiago. Setting up a defense line, the marines withstood a number of counterattacks on their positions over the next three days. On the 14th two companies seized the Spanish water supply and routed the defenders. This was the last action for the corps in Cuba since the Spanish at Santiago capitulated on 17 July.

The peace treaty with Spain formalized on 12 August ceded the Philippines to the United States. This was viewed as a betrayal by Filipino patriots who believed the war had been fought for their independence. On Luzon Island a revolt began in February 1899. In conjunction with the army, reinforced marine units were active against the insurgents southwest of Cavite and in the area north of Manila Bay. These successful marine operations were halted because of a new crisis, the Boxer Rebellion (q.v.), in China. There anti-Western revolutionaries had threatened to drive all non-Chinese from the country. These activists, called Boxers in the West, supported by the empress, seized most of Tientsin (q.v.) and besieged the Legation Quarter in Peking (q.v.). A small contingent of marines in May 1900 joined a melange of other foreign troops and arrived in Peking. This small group of 56 marines was at the center of the fighting in defense of the embassies until relieved on 14 August by a multinational force. Most of the marines in the Philippines were ordered to China. By early July there was a full regiment near Tientsin, a city that had to be taken before order could be restored in Peking. With U.S. army units and British marines leading the way, Tientsin was captured on 13 July, and the way was opened for the quick relief of Peking.

Within a month of the relief of Peking, the regiment was ordered back to the Philippines. The Luzon rebellion had been quashed, but the Moros on Samar (q.v.) were not yet ready to accept U.S. rule. Thus, in November 1901, 300 marines were sent to the island to aid the army units there. In a campaign of attrition, the marines burned and killed their way through Samar; by the time the action was concluded in January, only a small cadre of Moros continued to resist.

Critics and Reform

From its inception in 1798, the Marine Corps' role in U.S. defense plans has been ambiguous. At first one of the major questions involving the corps related to which branch, the army or the navy, should control its activities. Very soon a significant number of critics wanted it abolished completely. President Andrew Jackson surprisingly was no friend of the corps. In 1829 he recommended to Congress that the corps be merged with either the artillery or infantry. In 1831 the secretary of the navy recommended that it either be discontinued or that the corps be definitely assigned to the army or the navy. Three years later an act of Congress made the corps an integral part of the navy although the president could, if conditions dictated, place it under army jurisdiction.

Attacks on the corps were not seriously resumed until after the Civil War. In June 1866 the House of Representatives directed the Committee on Naval Affairs to consider abolishing it since its functions duplicated that of the army. The committee emphatically supported continuance of the corps. Rather than defend the corps, many senior officers in the navy were critical, and some even led the attack and had some justification. Despite heroic actions throughout the world, the corps did have many deficiencies, not the least of which was the age of its senior officers. Absence of retirement benefits kept many in the service past the point where they were fit for field command. A further problem was the nature of recruitment. Without specific requirements for competence, many of the junior officers had received their commissions because of their political connections and viewed service in the cities as a social rather than a military commitment. The size of the corps after the Civil War remained relatively stable at 3,000 men, but during emergencies recruits were hastily mustered into service and rushed into action with only rudimentary training. These problems indicated that a revamping of the corps was sorely needed. That impetus to change came from the navy.

The attack against the corps as a separate entity was renewed in the 1880s. This coincided with the transition in naval planning from a simple defense-oriented strategy to one of controlling the seas, and it was a period when new, larger, big gun ships were being built. Many naval officers viewed their marine counterparts as unnecessary—merely idlers on board ship. They claimed that the new ship design made the presence of marines on board superfluous. The Greer Board on Organization and Tactics examining the condition of the navy and its future was also hostile to the corps. Although not totally agreeing with the more extreme critics, the government moved to improve the quality of marine officer training. The 1882 Appropriation Act spelled out that future officer appointments were to be made from graduates of the Naval Academy. Although in times of expansion nonacademy officers were appointed, those who attended Annapolis remained the centrum of the officer corps.

During 1888–89 several of the older senior marine officers retired, thus allowing for the promotion of younger men who recognized the need for upgrading of training. The new commandant, Lt. Col. Charles Heywood (q.v.), in 1891 sent a proposal to the secretary of the navy for a School of Application to make junior officers more competent in their various command roles. The proposal was approved and put into effect immediately with a small class reporting in May. The curriculum included infantry tactics, gunnery, torpedoes, and field service. Particularly stressed was the servicing of the secondary batteries of guns aboard the new battleships and cruisers, a task that the marines had assumed and would continue for the next half-century. The following year noncommissioned officers were included. The School of Application was an initial step toward the professionalization of the corps, which would later be reflected in the creation of the Basic School and attention given to specialized training for senior officers. Although during the next half-century the corps remained small and was primarily light infantry, the officers and men became more professional, and their arms and equipment were comparable to the army's.

From Panama to World War II

The pattern of interference in the domestic affairs of Caribbean and Central American states continued during the first quarter of the 20th century. It became an official policy of the United States after the announcement of the Roosevelt Corollary (q.v.) to the Monroe Doctrine whose intention was to interfere directly when the corrupt and inefficient governments might lead to European interference. The Marine Corps became the primary agent for this policy, which was continued by Roosevelt's successors. In the first of these actions, marine units were sent to Panama in 1903 to protect the new government there while the canal was being built. Another very troubled area was Santo Domingo (q.v.). Marines were dispatched there in 1904, and some stayed for three years. Further disturbances there in 1916 brought the marines back, and they remained until 1920. The neighboring state of Haiti was even more challenging. A marine detachment was landed in December 1914 to protect the government from rebel forces. By mid-1915 over 2,000 marines were deployed, and in a series of small engagements, they ended the rebel threat. Marines were also landed in Cuba in 1906 preliminary to the formation of a provisional government headed by an American. Only after order was restored were they withdrawn in 1909.

The most troublesome area was Nicaragua. In 1909 a regiment of marines arrived to support the government. Order was restored, but the marines had to be sent back in 1912 to defeat another uprising. Peace between the factions resulted in over a decade of peace, but in 1926 a number of dissidents rebelled against the government. The most important were the followers of Augusto Sandino. Marine ground and air units and local constabulary spent the next six years attempting to pacify the rebels. The last units were not withdrawn until 1933. The corps was also called upon to avenge the slight to the U.S. flag in April 1914 as well as to counter German influence in Mexico. A marine brigade landed at Veracruz (q.v.), and in four days the city was captured. This was a diplomatic coup for Pres. Woodrow Wilson since the action helped overthrow a government hostile to U.S. interests.

The event that changed the future direction of the Marine Corps was World War I (q.v.). Even before U.S. entry in April 1917, the size of the corps had grown to 15,500 men, and within days of the declaration of war volunteers increased its size to 31,000 enlisted men. The first regiment sailed for France in June, and by early 1918 all marine units in France formed the 4th Brigade. Joined with two army regiments, it became the 2d Division.

Clothed in army uniforms and using army weapons, the brigade thus became a part of a land army. The performance of the brigade first at Belleau Wood (q.v.) on 6 June 1918 driving the Germans from their positions helped halt the drive on Paris. The following month further German attacks were halted at Chateau-Thierry (q.v.), and in September the 2d Division, now commanded by Marine Gen. John Lejeune (q.v.), pinched off the Saint-Mihiel (q.v.) salient. Moved eastward to support the French, the division took part in the Meuse-Argonne (q.v.) campaign, the final allied offensive of the war. Over 32,000 marines served in France, and marine losses amounted to 12,300. Although the size of the corps was greatly reduced after the war, its missions now could include acting as a land army.

World War I had not clarified, but rather confused, the purpose or mission of the corps. Many senior naval officials still viewed it as superfluous to modern naval warfare. The army leaders during and after the war were deeply suspicious of the value of the corps despite the performance of the 4th Brigade. They considered that the only missions that the corps could perform well were small-scale Banana War (q.v.)–type engagements and argued that army light infantry could be utilized for these. In truth, the corps had little preparation for large-scale actions before World War I. Its officers had not been trained well enough in combined arms, and few, even in the interwar years, would attend the more advanced schools that the army considered a prerequisite to higher command. The corps had no integral motor transport system, engineers, or combat logistical services. The major task in the interwar years for marine planners was to better define and expand the role of the corps and to create a balanced field force to carry out the desired mission.

One area of improvement was in the selection and training of officers. Until World War I, there was a lack of a logical officer candidate and reserve system. Many of the officers necessary for the expansion of the corps had come from the noncommissioned ranks or had received field commissions. During the interwar years, the corps reached out to universities with ROTC programs to select candidates who would volunteer for regular commissions. In 1935 a Platoon Leaders Class was established at Quantico (q.v.) and soon afterward at San Diego. Those reservists who attended two six-week classes would be given reserve commissions upon receiving their degrees. Finally, in 1940 a Reserve Officer Course of three months' duration was created and became the prime source for officers after Pearl Harbor. The policy of allowing Annapolis graduates to choose the Marine Corps was continued. By the early 1930s, so many of the top one-quarter of the graduates were choosing the corps that the policy was changed to allowing only 5 percent of the graduating class to so choose. Combined with using the advanced schools of the corps and army, the leadership cadre of the corps had improved greatly by 1941.

In attempting to better define the role of the Marine Corps, the planners in the 1930s, viewing the Pacific as a probable theater of operations, began to refine amphibious warfare techniques. In 1933 the Marine Expeditionary Force was redesignated the Fleet Marine Force (q.v.) and made an integral part of the navy. This was further divided into an Atlantic and a Pacific segment. The Atlantic Fleet Force was located at Quantico, while the Pacific was based at San Diego. The 1st Brigade at Quantico was composed of an infantry regiment, a 75mm artillery battalion, antiaircraft battalion, companies of engineers, a chemical warfare unit, a tank company, and an aviation group. This organization was duplicated in the 2d Brigade located at San Diego. In 1939 defense battalions within the Fleet Marine Force were authorized. These units, authorized to have 1,000-man complements, were created to defend advanced naval bases and were equipped with antiaircraft and larger-caliber guns. The most famous of these units were those in 1941 charged with the defense of Wake (q.v.) and Midway (q.v.) Islands.

During the 1930s, debate within the corps and with the navy continued over the evolving doctrine of amphibious operations. In 1934 the corps published a *Tentative Manual for Landing Operations*. This was revised and republished by the navy in 1938 entitled *Landing Operations Doctrine, U.S. Navy*. Three years later the army issued an almost identical work, FM-31–5, *Landing Operations on Hostile Shores*. Thus, by the beginning of World War II the planning done by the corps had an effect far beyond what was initially envisioned at the start of the debate on the future role of the corps. Furthermore, the corps took the lead in helping design larger and better landing craft and in 1940 adopted the "Alligator," the first of a new generation of landing vehicles. From 1935 onward there were fleet landing exercises testing in practice the theories enunciated in the manuals concerning ship-to-shore actions, naval gunfire support, combat loading, and command relationships.

World War II and Beyond

The reversal of fortune of the Allied forces in Europe in the early stages of World War II (q.v.), and the growing support of Britain by the United States caused a reversal of the former isolationist position with regard to the armed services. A peacetime draft was approved in 1940, and there was a rush to provide arms and equipment for the armed forces. The authorized size of the as yet all-volunteer corps was expanded so that by November 1940 its strength stood at 37,000 men. The Japanese attack on Pearl Harbor united the country as never before, and thousands of men rushed the recruiting offices to volunteer. By January 1942 the size of the corps had reached 73,600, and it continued to grow, partially because after 1943 draftees were allowed to choose the marines. There were 367,000 marines by January 1944, and the corps reached its peak of 444,000 men by the close of the war.

Great organizational changes also took place during the early stages of World War II. Already in 1941 the East and West Coast Brigades had been upgraded to divisions patterned after the army's triangular division. The 1st Division was located at Quantico and the 2d at San Diego. The 3d Division was activated in September 1942, the 4th in August 1943, the 5th in November 1943, and the last, the 6th, was created in September 1944. All saw action in the Central Pacific theater. In 1941 larger organizations were created—the Amphibious Corps, Atlantic, and Amphibious Corps, Pacific. These later evolved into I, III, and V Amphibious Corps for Pacific operations. The corps also experimented with special light infantry units called Raiders and with parachute battalions.

More important than these experiments was marine aviation, which became so important in tactical support of the ground forces during the war. Marine pilots in DH-4s (q.v.) and Jennyies (q.v.) had been involved in the suppression activities in the Caribbean and Central America during the 1920s. However, even when air units were included in the Fleet Marine Forces in 1933, there were still only a few planes and pilots. By 1941 when the air units were organized into two wings each supporting a division, there were only 251 planes of all types in the corps. The number of planes and pilots were rapidly increased after the war began and ultimately organized into the 1st, 2d, and 3d Combat Wings. The 4th Wing was a defensive unit based in Hawaii, and the 9th was the training element. By 1944 the 4th dropped its defense title and became simply the 4th Air Wing.

The theories of amphibious warfare were soon put to the test in the South Pacific theater. Beginning with Guadalcanal (q.v.), marine divisions were the spearhead of the Allied offensives against Japan as Adm. Chester Nimitz implemented the prewar Orange Plan. The 1st Division at Guadalcanal held that key island and administered the first major defeat to the Japanese army in early 1943. From there the marines and navy moved to capture a foothold in the northern Solomon Islands (q.v.) as the 3d Division landed on Bougainville (q.v.) in November 1943. Later the 1st Division was used by General Douglas MacArthur to seize Cape Gloucester (q.v.) on New Britain and in September 1944 to secure his flank by assaulting Peleliu (q.v.).

The outer Japanese defense ring in the Gilbert Islands (q.v.) was broached by the 2d Division's capture of Tarawa (q.v.) in September 1943. The next step was to obtain air and naval bases in the Marshall Islands (q.v.) with the capture of Kwajalein (q.v.) and Enewetok (q.v.). By mid-1944 the overwhelming superiority of the U.S. forces had forced the Japanese in the Mariana Islands (q.v.) into a desperate defensive posture. The 2d and 4th Divisions were involved in the capture of Saipan (q.v.) and Tinian (q.v.), while the 3d and the 1st Brigade with army assistance liberated Guam (q.v.). These islands became the site of the great bomber bases that ultimately allowed the B-29s to devastate Japan.

Iwo Jima, the next target for the marines, was a small volcanic island needed as bases to provide escort fighters for the B-29s. Three marine divisions, the 3d, 4th, and 5th, landed in February 1945 and captured the island in the most desperate fighting in the corps' history. Okinawa (q.v.) in the Ryukyu chain was the last offensive for the corps in the Pacific. As a part of X Army, the 1st and 6th Divisions played a vital role in the capture of the island and the destruction of more than 100,000 Japanese troops. The next objective was to be the invasion of Japan. The plan was for all available marine units to be utilized in landings on Kyushu beginning in November 1945. Japan's surrender fortunately made this strategy unnecessary. At war's end some marine units were posted to North China and others to Korea, but most were transported home for demobilization. In this greatest of all wars, the corps had been the primary factor in the Central Pacific offensives and had suffered 86,940 casualties.

The five years between the end of the war and the Korean conflict saw drastic reductions in the corps, with the Fleet Marine Force limited to only eight battalions and the air arm cut to 12 squadrons. During the debates over unification, culminating in the establishment of the Defense Department, the corps was shunted aside and the commandant was precluded from sitting with the Joint Chiefs of Staff even when they discussed policies directly related to the corps. However, the hostility toward the corps shown by high-ranking officials all but disappeared after the North Koreans attacked South Korea on 25 June 1950.

The decision to intervene as the key member of the United Nations showed how inadequate the depleted U.S. armed force had become. By the end of July all of South Korea had been occupied except a small area around the port of Pusan (q.v.). In Washington the commandant ordered all marine reservists to active duty, and the understrength 1st Division left for Korea on 12 July. General MacArthur used it first to plug holes in the perimeter defense and then as the cutting edge for his plan to defeat the North Koreans. As a part of X Corps, the marines landed on 15 September at the port of Inchon (q.v.) and fought their way through to the capital, Seoul. This success combined with the breakout by army and South Korean forces from the perimeter all but destroyed the North Korean army. Shifted to the east, the marines drove the enemy back to the Yalu River, the border with China. On 25 November they were struck at the Chosin Reservoir (q.v.) by three Chinese divisions. All but trapped in the dead of winter, they fought their way back to the coast and safety. During the rest of the war, the division was shifted from place to place and took part in all the major actions until the final unsatisfactory armistice of July 1953. The police action had cost the lives of 4,262 marines.

While marines were fighting in Korea, the struggle to define the future role of the corps went on in Washington. Senator Paul Douglas and Congressman Mike Mansfield, both former marines, in January 1951 introduced legislation that clarified the size and role of the corps. Although the final act did not provide for the four divisions and four air wings of the initial bills, it did authorize three of each in the active structure. It also provided that the commandant should have equal status with the military heads of the other branches and should sit with the others of the Joint Chiefs when matters concerning the corps were discussed. The decade following Korea also saw the improvement of weaponry and equipment used by the corps, particularly in the air wings. The numbers of helicopters were increased, and further training in their use was instituted with the long range aim of giving marine landing units more flexibility. This was done in conjunction with the navy, which converted a number of old escort carriers to Landing Platform Carriers for helicopters. In 1962 the corps adopted the M-14 rifle chambered for the NATO 7.62 cartridge as well as the new M-60 machine gun (q.v.).

This period also saw the return of using the corps for intervention in the affairs of other states when vital interests of the United States were at stake. In October 1956 a battalion of the 3d Marines was landed at Alexandria (q.v.), Egypt, to cover the evacuation of civilians. Two years later Pres. Dwight Eisenhower committed three battalions of marines to Lebanon (q.v.) for three months to shore up the shaky democratic government there. Another operation in April 1965 intervened in the Dominican Republic (q.v.) to ward off a suspected communist takeover. A marine battalion was the spearhead of the much larger army affair. Ultimately elements of two landing units were involved totaling 8,000 men before all U.S. troops were replaced by a multinational force. By then the greatest trial in marine history was beginning halfway around the world in Vietnam (q.v.).

The United States had inherited from the French the self-imposed task of defending South Vietnam from a Communist takeover by the insurgent Viet Cong (q.v.) and the army of North Vietnam. Direct involvement began slowly by sending military advisers. Marines were among the first such advisors. Weakness of the military-controlled government in the south combined with U.S. fears of losing containment meant the commitment of more troops and equipment. After the Gulf of Tonkin Resolution by Congress in August 1964, the United States became deeply involved in its longest, most frustrating war. Ultimately the bulk of the U.S. armed forces—over one-half million men—were committed to Vietnam. The Marine Corps contributed two divisions and most of its fixed wing and helicopter aircraft, all operating under the tactical leadership of the army. By the end of 1965 the marines had assumed responsibility for I Corps' area composed of the five northern provinces, which included defense of the Demilitarized Zone (DMZ) (q.v.).

Tactics during the long conflict varied only slightly. Political considerations as defined by the president and secretary of defense precluded crossing the DMZ or entering Cambodia even when the enemy used these areas as safe havens. Under army control the marines had to adopt the standard "search and destroy" methodology and abandon their ideas of pacification. Operating out of the major base of Da Nang (q.v.) and from a series of strong points, marines by ground transportation, helicopters, or, rarely, in amphibious vehicles would seek out enemy concentrations. The corps never had enough troops to hold many of the areas after the Viet Cong or North Vietnamese had been driven out. Once the marines left, the enemy would soon drift back. Over the years marines near the DMZ were constantly involved in blunting North Vietnamese attacks. The most famous of these defenses was the 77-day siege of Khe Sanh (q.v.) in 1968 where the outnumbered marines held off numerous attacks by the enemy.

The most crushing defeat suffered by the communists was during the Tet (q.v.) offensive of 1968 when in a concerted effort regular North Vietnamese units attempted to capture the major cities in Vietnam. Marine units along with South Vietnamese forces drove the enemy from the old city of Hue (q.v.). Although a major tactical victory, the Tet fighting was viewed by the American public as a defeat, and soon afterward clandestine peace talks began and the Nixon administration started to reduce troop levels. By early 1971, long before the final peace accords, most of the marines had left Vietnam. During this long, drawn-out, and ultimately fruitless war, the corps had performed mainly as a land army, and in dozens of small- and large-scale encounters with the enemy had never been beaten. At a cost of more than 100,000 casualties, the corps had once again performed its new role with honor.

The memory of Vietnam and lost opportunities had far reaching effects upon all U.S. military units, but of all branches, the corps was least affected. It had become a specialized land army complete with tanks, heavy artillery, and helicopters. During the next decade the air units were strengthened with new and better planes while maintaining the corps' traditional role for ground support. Reduced in size again, its three divisions, learning from the Vietnamese experience, improved its training with better equipment and tactics, particularly with air mobility. Other changes made the corps an even more effective force. At the most senior level the commandant was a coequal with other members of the Joint Chiefs. Changes in overall strategic planning reserved for the corps the task of amphibious operations. To meet new demands the corps' tactical forces were redesigned to provide more flexible responses.

During the two decades following the Vietnam War, various units of the corps were engaged in a number of small-scale actions reminiscent of the period of intervention prior to World War I. Some of these were for humanitarian reasons; others were for political or diplomatic reasons. In July 1974 a marine unit landed on Cyprus to evacuate civilians caught up in the Greek-Turkish conflict. The following year in May two battalions of marines landed in Cambodia to rescue prisoners taken from the U.S. ship *Mayaguez* (q.v.). The revolution in Iran (q.v.) culminated for the United States in the storming of the embassy in Teheran in November 1979. The marine guards were ordered not to fire and were captured. All attempts to gain their release peacefully failed, which led to an unsuccessful military operation. Marine participation in this rescue attempt was limited to providing the helicopters. Continued violence in the Middle East centering on

Lebanon convinced Pres. Ronald Reagan to send in a Marine Expeditionary Unit (MEU) (q.v.) in the fall of 1982 to help keep peace in Beirut. This exercise ended in the tragic bombing in October 1983 of marine headquarters and the deaths of 241 marines. Despite this loss, the marine contingent stayed until February 1984.

During the same period, marines were involved in more small-scale interventions in the Western Hemisphere. Fears of a communist regime on the small island of Grenada (q.v.) caused President Reagan to commit an army/marine task group to take over the island in October 1983. Panama, which had been controlled by military dictators, had become a haven for drug smuggling, and the head of state was implicated. This combined with a popular movement to overthrow the regime led the U.S. government to intervene militarily. In July 1987 marine units as well as army troops were landed and soon had secured Panama City and captured the dictator, Gen. Manuel Noriega. While the attention of the U.S. military was focused upon Iraq (q.v.) and Kuwait (q.v.), the problem of what to do with the murderous, military regime in Haiti became a growing concern. Finally, after diplomatic pressure caused the resignation of the military junta, a Marine Expeditionary Unit landed in northern Haiti in September 1994 to help maintain order until a civilian government could be installed. A different type of intervention had been mounted in December 1992 when marines were sent to Somalia (q.v.) as a part of United Nations humanitarian efforts. Divided command and a lack of a specific mission caused the United States to evacuate the marine units the following May.

The New Corps and the Gulf War

In many ways, the Marine Corps had remained the same in the near 50 years following World War II. Its missions, however, had been clarified and its leaders recognized as equal partners in the defense scheme of the United States. The three-division, three-wing corps also was integrated. African Americans made up a significant part of the corps. Women also had been given more duties although not admitted to direct combat roles. The equipment had been significantly changed. The standard rifles and machine guns were the same as the army's. The new corps had advanced fighter and helicopter aircraft, the latter having become indispensable to a highly mobile attack group. The corps now had its own integral artillery and tank battalions made up of the latest weaponry. Reflecting the need in the changed world after the Cold War, more emphasis was given to small unit policing and combat actions. Marine units were trained to respond quickly to a crisis anywhere in the world with much of their equipment prepositioned.

Despite the continued use of marines in policing activities, the greatest test facing the corps after Vietnam was the Gulf War (q.v.). In August 1990 Iraqi troops invaded and overran Kuwait and threatened Saudi Arabia. The United States, as a part of a multinational effort, attempted to secure the withdrawal of Iraqi troops. Failing this action, the United States took the lead in building a military coalition to protect Saudi Arabia in Operation Desert Shield (q.v.). Only after the buildup of sufficient supplies and an army of 500,000 men was the recapture of Kuwait (q.v.) begun in Operation Desert Storm (q.v.). The first Marine Expeditionary Brigade (MEB) (q.v.) arrived in Saudi Arabia in August. By the end of October, 30,000 marines were in the area, and this force was soon increased to a total of two divisions and two air wings. Although only a small part of the total buildup, the marines were given the key positions on the right of the Allied line directly in front of Kuwait City. In January 1991, just before the air war began, the two divisions were moved north. Prior to this, marine amphibious exercises had convinced the Iraqis that a seaborne assault was probable which froze over 17 enemy divisions in southern Kuwait. Marine air units participated in the month-long air neutralization of Iraqi targets, and marine artillery pounded the defense belts before Kuwait City. On 30 January the marines in conjunction with Arab troops drove the Iraqis from a key city in Saudi Arabia.

The first offensive began on 24 February with the 1st Division attacking Kuwait City on the right of the Allied line and the 2d driving in from the southwest. Supported by tanks, the ground troops moved rapidly forward, breached the Iraqi defenses, and within two days the marines were within the city and the enemy was trying to escape. The honor of liberating the city went to the Arab units that passed through static marine lines on the 27th. Elsewhere the major action had taken place on the extreme left of the Allied line where the army and British and French units had flanked the Iraqi positions and had forced the enemy back against the Tigris River where they faced total destruction. It was at that juncture that Pres. George Bush ordered a cessation of hostilities on the 28th. This lightning victory had been achieved with minimal loss. The marines had only 24 men killed and 92 men wounded.

Operation Desert Storm had shown again that while the corps was adept at small-unit actions and was a master of amphibious warfare, its units could act effectively as a land army. Thus, in the last decade of the 20th century the corps continued to demonstrate its flexibility, and marines still were proud defenders of their motto, *Semper Fidelis* (q.v.).

The Encyclopedia

A

ABRAMS (M1 and M1A1) TANK. In December 1971 the Defense Department recognized the need to replace the M60 (q.v.) as the nation's main battle tank and initiated contracts for a new, larger, more powerful tank. By 1976 two companies, General Motors and Chrysler, had produced prototypes (XM1). After exhaustive tests, the Chrysler version was accepted, and a target of three years for full development was projected. The M1 tank went into full production in February 1980 with an original goal of over 7,000. Weighing over 60 tons and with a speed in excess of 40 miles per hour, it was a great improvement over the M60s. Continual changes were made in the design during the 1980s, culminating in the much improved M1A1. These changes included increased armor thickness, a better automatic transmission system, and a new basic weapon. The M1 originally had a 105mm gun as its main weapon. This was replaced on the A1 by a 120mm smooth-bore gun that could fire a fin-stabilized round at increased distances and with more penetration power. Secondary armament is two 7.62mm and one .50-caliber machine guns. The M1A1 has a 1,200-horsepower gas turbine engine allowing a maximum speed of 42 miles per hour and a range of more than 300 miles. It is served by a crew of four. Six periscopes are available to the tank commander, giving a 360-degree firing capability. The Abrams is equipped with a laser range finder, solid state digital computer, thermal night sight, and a stabilization system allowing for accurate firing while the tank is moving. The army was primarily involved in the development of the M1 to reequip its armored divisions. However, the corps benefited from its production as it also adopted the Abrams to replace its M60s. During the Gulf War (q.v.), marine and army units equipped with the tank destroyed the Russian made Iraqi tanks in every armored engagement.

ALEXANDRIA. One of the largest cities in northern Egypt located in the Nile River Delta. Difficulties arose in 1880 between European bond holders and the Khedive over nonpayment of debts. In 1882 Egyptian nationalists led by the minister of war, Arabi Pasha, revolted against foreign influence, and a number of Europeans were killed. Britain sent its Mediterranean fleet to overawe the nationalists. The British admiral, exceeding his authority, bombarded Alexandria and landed British troops. The small U.S. squadron in Europe accompanied the British fleet, and on 14 July a marine landing party went ashore with the British ostensibly to protect U.S. lives and property. With more than 4,000 troops ashore, the British did not need U.S. help, and the marines were soon withdrawn. Almost 75 years later, marines were called on to play a similar role. After the seizure of the Suez Canal, Britain, France, and Israel attacked Egypt, and concern grew for the many civilians caught in the crossfire. Thus, on 31 October 1956 the 6th Fleet's battalion, the 3d Battalion, 2d Marines, was landed at Alexandria (q.v.) and provided protection for and assistance in processing 1,500 civilians caught between the armies of Israel and Egypt who were then transferred to waiting U.S. naval ships.

ANTITANK GUN (M3A1 37mm). First developed by the army in the 1930s to replace the antitank gun used in World War I, this gun was a towed weapon firing a 1.6-pound shell and had an effective range of 500 yards. When first adopted by the corps, it could destroy any tank then in service. Advancement in tank design by European military rendered the weapon obsolete there. However, Japanese tanks, less well armored, proved vulnerable to the M3 throughout the Pacific war. Marine weapons companies not only used the weapon against tanks but also against bunkers and pillboxes. Loaded with canister, it was also very effective against banzai charges. Between 1940 and 1942, 100,000 weapons were used by the corps in the early Pacific operations in wet, humid conditions. The mild steel allowed its magazines to rust easily, dirt could get into the weapon and cause jams, and the faulty safety mechanism could allow the weapon to fire while on safety.

ARMED FORCES UNIFICATION. The half-decade following the defeat of Japan in World War II (q.v.) was a period of fierce debate in Washington on the future nature of the military. One lesson of the war was that closer cooperation between the services was needed. Therefore, plans for unification were put forward immediately. This was also a period of violent reduction in the defense budget so that each service vied with the others for preference. The corps was handicapped since it was a part of the navy and received only lukewarm support from the senior navy officials. The argument against the corps was that marines at best performed functions that could be duplicated by specialized army units. The marine cause was not aided by Pres. Harry Truman's open hostility to the corps. In 1947 the National Security Act created a Department of Defense with subordinate Departments of the Army, Navy, and Air Force. The status of the corps remained questionable. In March 1948 James Forrestal, the first defense secretary, announced that a ceiling would be placed on the size of the corps in times of war. It would be restricted to only four infantry divisions. Forrestal's successor, Louis Johnson, in his sweeping cost cutting reduced the corps further. The Fleet Marine Forces (q.v.) were reduced to eight infantry battalions and 12 air squadrons. Congress had shown itself sympathetic to the corps, but by 1950 the fate of the corps had not been decided. This would wait on the performance of the corps in the Korean War (q.v.) begun by executive order in June 1950 referred to by the president as a "police action." Long before the war ended, the survival of the corps had been assured. In the spring of 1951 Congress, acting on the advice of the House Armed Services Committee, provided for three active duty divisions and three air wings. Further, the commandant was given coequal status with other members of the Joint Chiefs of Staff when matters of direct concern of the corps were under discussion.

ARMORED PERSONNEL CARRIER (APC, Model 113). The basic tracked personnel carrier designed by the Dutch and adapted by U.S. forces in the 1960s and ultimately by over 50 other nations. The design was flexible enough to allow a great number of modifications including the mounting of TOW missile launching systems. The basic M113 weighed 11 tons, carried a crew of three at a maximum speed of 45 miles per hour with a range of over 300 miles. It was armed with one .30-caliber machine gun. One equivalent of the M113 that the corps adopted was the LVTP-7 (landing vehicle, tracked personnel) (q.v.) which could carry a maximum of 25 fully equipped marines and was propelled through water by twin water jets.

"AVENGER" (TBF or TBM). Built by Grumman Aircraft Company, the Avenger was first flown in 1941. Its first action in the

Pacific was at Midway (q.v.). It had a top speed of 275 miles per hour and a service ceiling of 22,000 feet, and it could carry one short air torpedo or a total of one ton of bombs in various combinations in the enclosed bomb bay. It had a crew of three: pilot, bombardier, and radio operator. By 1943 it had almost completely replaced the older Douglas TBD as the standard torpedo bomber for the navy. Because of its specific mission, few squadrons of the corps were equipped with the Avenger. After producing 2,290 TBFs, Grumman turned over total manufacturing of the plane in December 1943 to General Motors, which then constructed an additional 2,880 TBMs. The last model was the TBM-4, which, among other improvements, had a more powerful engine.

B

BANANA WARS. A general name given to a number of policing actions in which the U.S. government intervened in the internal affairs of Caribbean and Central American states and Mexico ostensibly to prevent European states from gaining further advantage in the Western Hemisphere.

The more aggressive U.S. foreign policy of the early 20th century made it necessary to utilize the navy and marines in a wide ranging series of small-scale actions. One of the first in Central America was in Panama (q.v.) where a small detachment of marines was landed in October 1903 at Colon. Later reinforcements brought the number of marine units operating there to two battalions whose major purpose was to protect the new government established after Panama declared its independence from Colombia. One battalion of marines remained there while the canal was being built and was not withdrawn until 1914. Another troubled area was Cuba, which had received its independence from Spain following the Spanish-American War (q.v.). The Platt Amendment to an appropriation act, however, specified the U.S. special interest in Cuba (q.v.), including the possession of Guantanamo Bay (q.v.). It also stipulated that the United States reserved the right of intervention to maintain stability. Marine detachments were sent to Cuba eight times between 1906 and 1917.

A troubled area in the Caribbean was Santo Domingo (q.v.). By 1904, after an orgy of civil war, the country was bankrupt. Rumors reached Washington that European creditor nations, particularly Germany, might intervene, thus violating the Monroe Doctrine. President Theodore Roosevelt decided in December 1904 that it was a moral mandate for the United States to intervene directly in the affairs of any state whose wrongdoing might lead to European intervention. This Roosevelt Corollary (q.v.), which was followed by the president's successors, meant that the corps would be used to carry out the more aggressive policy. The problem with Santo Domingo was settled peacefully when its government agreed to a protocol whereby the United States appointed a chief fiscal officer to manage the finances and administer the customs houses in order to end the rampant corruption. This effectively ended the civil strife for over a decade.

Another troubled area was Nicaragua (q.v.),which had suffered years of misrule under the dictatorship of Juan Estrada, who was deposed and assassinated in 1909. The United States decided to support the conservative government that had replaced Estrada against the followers of the deposed dictator. In December 1909 a provisional regiment was sent to bolster the government. Ultimately over 750 marines served in Nicaragua. Once order was restored, the marines were withdrawn. Not long afterward rebel forces once again threatened the government, and in the fall of 1912 the marines were ordered to Nicaragua once again. This time the marines pursued the rebels into the countryside and in early October defeated the major rebel force. By January 1913 most of the marines had left. However, a cadre force of 100 men was left behind.

In December 1913 the Marine Advance Base Force was created to meet the new challenges posed by the more aggressive policies of the government. It was primarily a rapid deployment force made up of two regiments, one organized for defensive action and the other for offense. The latter was organized as were army regiments with four rifle companies, a machine gun company, and a headquarters company. The regiments were located in the southern United States so that they could be rapidly embarked to meet potential problems in the Caribbean and Latin America. One was sited at New Orleans (q.v.) and the other at Pensacola (q.v.).

The new organization was soon put to the test. President Woodrow Wilson, altering a century-old practice of simply recognizing a de facto government, refused to recognize the government of Gen. Victoriano Huerta in Mexico. Huerta had seized power after the assassination of Pres. Francisco Madero. A portion of the U.S. fleet under the command of Rear Adm. Henry Mayo became involved with the Mexican authorities at

Veracruz (q.v.) who had seized some sailors. Mayo refused to accept the apology of the Mexican authorities and in a high handed manner demanded a 21-gun salute, which was refused. Learning of a German ship bringing arms to Huerta, Mayo established a virtual blockade of the port. This in turn escalated to orders to seize the city. On 21 April 1914 the 2d Regiment of marines landed, later to be supported by a provisional regiment, the 1st Regiment, and a naval brigade, ultimately over 3,000 marines. The major goals of the landing force had been achieved the first day, but a series of small actions followed before the Mexican defenders surrendered on the 24th. This activity combined with continual diplomatic pressure and internal unrest forced Huerta to resign in July, to be succeeded by Gen. Venustiano Carranza, a man more acceptable to the United States.

The next troubled spot was in Haiti (q.v.) where the government had encumbered itself with heavy foreign debts. A marine detachment was landed in December 1914 at Port au Prince to remove all the funds in the treasury for safekeeping. Unrest in the island escalated, and in July 1915 there was a bloody uprising in the capital and the unpopular president was killed. Sailors and marines from the U.S. fleet were landed to restore order. These were quickly reinforced, and by the end of August over 2,000 marines were on the island. The major threat to a restoration of order were the Cacos, rebels who dominated northern Haiti in the Cap Haitien region. Marine units invaded the Cacos-held area, and in November two hard-fought engagements, Fort Capais and Grande Rivière, destroyed the rebels' military. A new government friendly to the United States was recognized, and the Haitian Constabulary was established to maintain law and order. The officers and noncommissioned officers of the constabulary were all marines. In the months that followed, more than 100 marines served in the constabulary.

Although the European war took precedence over all other areas, marines were active in their traditional roles and continued to act to defend the government's aggressive Caribbean and Latin American policy. Serious disturbances arose in Cuba early in 1917, and marines were landed to help stabilize the government and to make sure that sugar production was not interrupted. The marine contingent there was not withdrawn until August 1919.

The situation in Santo Domingo had worsened since the marines had left in 1907, threatening civil war. In response, two companies of marines were shifted from Haiti in April 1916, and these were soon reinforced by more marines and sailors. The marines occupied Santo Domingo city without resistance in May. However, serious resistance against the government developed in the northern part of the island. The 2d Marine Brigade arrived in the country after a long voyage from San Diego, bringing the marine forces available to 1,750 men. The rebel forces made a stand on a ridge line at Los Trencheros on 27 June but were forced to retreat after a two-day battle in which the marines' machine guns took a heavy toll.

The final action in 1916 was at Guyacanes, and the rebel defeat opened the way to the occupation of Santiago, the major city in the north. Later in the year Rear Adm. Harry Knapp became military governor, and the most important towns were garrisoned by the *Guarda Nacional Dominicana*, an organization patterned on the Haitian model. Most of the *Guarda's* officers were marines, although a few Dominicans eventually were commissioned. It was hoped that a small marine garrison in the country with the *Guarda* would maintain peace. However, in the following year the ex-governor and his followers took to the hills and were pursued throughout 1917 by marine and *Guarda* forces.

Two bandit leaders in different parts of the country also caused difficulty, and dozens of skirmishes were fought by marines of the 2d Brigade, which had been brought into the country and by the end of the year included over 2,000 men. There were continual patrols, firefights, and cordoned-off searches for the next three years before the bandits' activities were controlled. In 1920 Pres. Woodrow Wilson announced that he intended to remove the marines. Gradually the numbers were reduced as the numbers of the *Guarda* (now renamed the National Police) were increased. In September 1924 the last of the small marine garrison was removed as the new civilian government and police seemed able to maintain order.

Meanwhile endemic disorder continued in Haiti as a new leader of the Cacos emerged. Charlemagne Peralte had by early 1919 taken command of an estimated 5,000 guerrillas operating in the hilly country of northern Haiti. The understrength 1st Brigade, which had not taken part in the early actions against Charlemagne, became engaged when it was obvious that the *Gendarmerie* would not be able to defeat the Cacos. The brigade was reinforced with more men and also 13 aircraft. During the summer of 1919, the marines and *Gendarmerie* fought dozens of skirmishes in the countryside and even in Port au Prince. In October a three-man patrol led by Sgt. Herman Hanneken (q.v.) sneaked by a number of outposts, entered Charlemagne's camp, and killed the rebel leader. However, this did not end the Cacos threat. A new leader, Benoit Batraville, continued the war. The marines continued their systematic searches into the new year and forced the surrender of more than 3,000 rebels. Batraville and his reduced followers were finally isolated on a hilltop where marine pilots in their Jennies (JN-4) (q.v.), cooperating with ground units, killed 200 Cacos. The rebellion was finally brought to an end with the ambush and death of Batraville on 19 May 1920. Except for a brief flareup of guerrilla violence in 1929, no serious threats were made to the established government during the rest of the decade. The 1st Brigade was finally ordered from Haiti in August 1934 in response to Pres. Franklin Roosevelt's stated good neighbor policy, which was at variance with the activist policy of his predecessors.

The always volatile political situation in Nicaragua exploded in 1926. The company-sized marine legation guard had been removed 18 months before when it appeared that the U.S. supervised elections had brought peace between the Conservatives and Liberals. The ensuing coalition government had a Conservative president and a Liberal vice president. This system was anathema to many Conservatives, and in October Gen. Emiliano Chamorro Vargas staged a military coup and forced the president, vice president, and other government officials to flee the country. In January 1926 he declared himself president. His actions split the army, and a Liberal faction led by Gen. Jose Moncado led a revolt against Chamorro. A few marines were landed to protect U.S. interests in Managua, U.S. officials brought pressure on the government, and a peace conference was convened. This led to the resignation of Chamorro, and a pro-U.S. president, Adolfo Diaz, was chosen. This compromise did not settle the problem since the ousted vice president, Juan Sacasa, returned, joined forces with Moncado, and began the war anew. The United States decided to mediate once again and in January 1927 landed a battalion of the 5th Marines with orders to guard the president and establish neutral zones between the antagonists, blocking Moncado's drive toward the capital. By March the full 2d Brigade was in place, and the air service was operating with DH-4s (q.v.).

In April 1927 another agreement was reached whereby the Conservatives would remain in power until 1928 when there would be an election supervised by the United States. One Liberal leader, Augusto Sandino, refused to abide by the agreement and with a few followers established a base of operations in the hilly country bordering Honduras. In time his rebel band grew to many thousands. The United States assumed the major task of ending Sandino's threat since the national police, the *Guarda*, was too small and untrained for such a task and the army was fragmented. On 15 July 1927 Sandino's forces attacked an outnumbered marine force at Ocotal. The situation was saved only by marine pilots in their Jennies who dive-bombed and machine gunned the insurgents. The marines kept up a patrol during the summer and autumn, attempting to corner Sandino, and fought a series of small engagements. Then in November two marine columns were intercepted by the rebels, and in the ambush 30 marines were wounded and the remainder forced back to the town of Quilali where they were besieged. Once again the intervention of the air units proved crucial in allowing the marines to hold out until relieved in early January 1928. Throughout the spring and summer of 1928, marine and *Guarda* units fought a series of small-scale engagements near the Honduras border. Although these actions seriously depleted the rebel forces, Sandino managed to escape and later in the year fled to Mexico. Elections were held in November with marines acting as poll watchers. General Moncado was elected president. A period of relative peace ensued, so much so that in August 1929 one marine regiment was shipped home.

Sandino returned to the hilly areas of northern Nicaragua in early 1930 and began once again the cycle of violence. Marine and *Guarda* units pursued the rebel forces into the rebel strongholds. The *Guarda*, officered in the main by marines such as Lewis "Chesty" Puller (q.v.), Merritt Edson (q.v.), and Herman Hanneken (q.v.) had grown to over 2,000 men and by the end of the year had taken over the bulk of the search missions. In February 1931 the United States announced that the marine presence would be reduced to a single battalion stationed in the Managua area. Elections held in the fall of 1932 confirmed Sacasa as president. The day after his inaguration on 1 January 1933 the last marines left the country.

The six years of guerrilla-style war had cost various marine units 47 killed and 67 wounded, but they left behind a relatively stable state and a strong *Guarda* headed at this time by the future dictator, Anastasio Somoza. Sandino, who had once again fled the country, returned in 1934, was finally captured, and was shot on Somoza's orders. His memory, however, became a rallying cry for many liberals and radicals a half-century later who once again plunged Nicaragua into a civil war. (See also Dominican Republic and Mexican War.)

"BANSHEE" (F2H). A single seat jet fighter built by McDonnell Douglas Aircraft Company. The prototype was first flown in January 1947. It went out of production after 800 of all versions had been delivered to the U.S. Navy and Marine Corps. The most popular version was the F2H-2, which had two Westinghouse engines giving it a maximum speed of 600 miles per hour, a ceiling of 50,000 feet, and a radius of action of 600 miles. Search radar was standard on the later models. The last Banshee was delivered to the navy in October 1953.

BARBARY PIRATES. The rulers of the petty North African states of Morocco, Algiers, Tripoli, and Tunis in the latter 18th century preyed upon shipping in the Mediterranean. European leaders found it cheaper to pay tribute for the safety of their ships rather than take direct military action. The new United States, although impoverished, concluded a treaty with Morocco in 1787, but the rulers of the other states continued their attacks on U.S. ships. Ultimately treaties were also signed with the other rulers committing the United States to pay ransom. The first two U.S. presidents, however reluctantly, sanctioned the payment of hundreds of thousands of dollars to assure the safety of American ships. In May 1801 the new bey of Tripoli, after seizing the throne, decided that his payment was not enough and declared war on the United States. In 1803 the pirates seized the U.S. frigate *Philadelphia*, and Pres. Thomas Jefferson reluctantly dispatched a naval squadron to the Mediterranean. In an early action against Tripoli by sailors and marines, the *Philadelphia* was set afire in the harbor, thus depriving the bey of this handsome prize. Little was accomplished until late in 1804 when the navy blockaded the harbor of Tripoli, and a polyglot "army" mainly of Egyptians but bolstered by a few Europeans and eight marines under the command of Lt. Presley O'Bannon (q.v.) led a revolt against the bey. After marching 600 miles across the Libyan desert, the rebels led by the marines attacked and captured Derna (q.v.) on 27 April 1805. In June the bey signed a peace treaty with the United States in return for a heavy payment to secure prisoners held in Tripoli. Jefferson's embargo and subsequently the War of 1812 (q.v.) removed the U.S. naval presence from the Mediterranean for years. However, a U.S. naval squadron under Commodore Stephen Decatur ended the most recent problems with Algiers. He eliminated the bey's fleet and in June 1815 forced an end to the paying of ransom. Later similar agreements were made with the rulers of Tunis and Tripoli. (See also Tripolitanian War.)

BARNETT, GEORGE. 12th commandant, b. Lancaster, Wisc., 9 Dec. 1859, d. Washington, D.C., 27 April 1930. Went to sea as a cadet midshipman but graduated from the Naval Academy in 1881, was commissioned second lieutenant in the Marine Corps in July 1883, and later did tours of shore and sea duty. He served on board the *New Orleans* throughout the Spanish-American War (q.v.). In September 1902 he led a battalion of marines to Panama (q.v.) to protect the railroad and in the following year led it to Cavite in the Philippines.

As a lieutenant colonel, Barrett commanded the 1st Regiment in Cuba (q.v.) in November 1906 to protect the provisional government headed by William Howard Taft after the disturbances following the earlier failed election. After a brief period in command of the Marine Barracks in Washington, General Barnett was sent to China to command the marine detachment guarding the legation in Peking (q.v.). From 1911 to 1913 he was involved with marine units in Cuba. In December 1913 Barnett took command of the newly activated Marine Advance Base Force, a small brigade of two regiments—the 1st organized as a defense regiment and the 2d organized along army infantry lines.

On 25 February 1914 Barrett succeeded Gen. William Biddle (q.v.) as major general commandant. He was the first Annapolis graduate to become commandant. He supervised the expeditions to Mexico, Santo Domingo (q.v.), and Haiti (q.v.). Barnett pressed the government to include a Marine Expeditionary Force to France in World War I (q.v.) and presided over the expansion of the corps during the war to over 76,000, of whom 32,000 served in France. He was appointed commandant for a second term in February 1918 but had growing difficulties with Secretary of the Navy Josephus Daniels, who forced him to resign and accept a reduction in rank and appointment to head the newly created Department of the Pacific in June 1920.

BASILONE, JOHN "MANILA JOHN." b. Buffalo, N.Y., 4 Nov. 1916, d. Iwo Jima, 19 Feb. 1945. After parochial school Basilone enlisted in the army and was posted to the Philippines, an assignment that was responsible for his nickname. Afterward in July 1940 he enlisted in the Marine Corps and served in Cuba (q.v.), Quantico (q.v.), and Camp Lejeune (q.v.) before being sent to the South Pacific as a member of the 7th Marines. In the Lunga area of Guadalcanal (q.v.) on the night of 24 October, in charge of two machine gun sections, Basilone was attacked by a near-overwhelming Japanese force. He was mainly responsible for throwing back attack after attack and contributed largely to the destruction of an entire Japanese regiment. For this action he was awarded the Medal of Honor (q.v.). Later as a gunnery sergeant in the 27th Marines, he was part of the force that invaded Iwo Jima (q.v.). Basilone again showed his bravery by single-handedly destroying a Japanese blockhouse under heavy fire and sacrificing himself. For this action he was posthumously awarded the Navy Cross (q.v.). Following the war Basilone was buried at Arlington, and in 1949 a destroyer was named in his honor.

BATTALION. For more than a century the battalion was the largest standing organized force owing to the small size of the Marine Corps. Throughout the 19th century, the corps' size varied from 700 men in 1800, reaching a peak of 4,100 in the Civil War (q.v.); even during the Spanish-American War (q.v.), it amounted to only 3,100 men. The size of a battalion during this period varied with the objective. It could be as few as 150 men or twice that size. The marine battalions at New Orleans in 1851 and in Mexico in 1846 numbered approximately 300 men. With the increase in size of the corps came a regularization in battalion size. During World War I (q.v.), expansion created two brigades for service in France. Each brigade numbered 9,300 men and had two regiments. Each regiment was composed of four battalions. Therefore, the combat battalions had a targeted size of 1,160 men. In 1942 the two brigades then available were upgraded to divisions and were organized along a triangular rather than a square pattern. Each regiment thus had three infantry battalions as well as specialized service battalions. The size of each infantry battalion by 1944 was reduced to 881 men. In the next 50 years this size remained roughly the same. Even the reorganization of the corps into expeditionary units in the 1980s did not significantly alter the size or organization of a battalion but simply used battalions in a more flexible manner.

BELLEAU WOOD. Located between the town of Vaux and Belleau north of the Paris-Metz highway. Lying approximately six miles west of the town of Chateau-Thierry (q.v.), this land was approximately one square mile of deep woods. The 4th

Marine Brigade, a part of the 2d Army Division, after having successfully repelled a German attack at Chateau-Thierry on 6 June 1918, was ordered by the French to clear the woods of Germans. Within the woods were two battalions of German infantry and dozens of machine gun nests. The 1st Battalion, 5th Marines, captured a key hill to the west, and shortly after noon the 2d Battalion, 5th Marines, and the 2d and 3d Battalions, 6th Marines, entered the woods. Short of grenades and without heavy weapons support, they had to destroy the machine gun nests using only rifles and bayonets. By the end of the day, two-thirds of the woods had been taken at a cost of 1,087 casualties. The marines then built shallow trenches and foxholes and were able to repel a German counterattack on 8 June. They then survived a major infantry and gas attack on 13 June. On 16 June the brigade with some of its units down to only one-third strength was relieved by the army's 7th Division. However, three days later the marines were back on line replacing the battered army units. On 23 June the marines once again attacked and by the 26th had secured all of the woods. The commanding general of the French 6th Army, reflecting his gratitude for the marine performance, renamed the woods *"Bois de la Brigade de Marine."* The Germans added a new phrase to the lexicon of marine history by calling them "devil dogs."

BIDDLE, WILLIAM P. 11th commandant, b. Philadelphia, Penn., 15 Dec. 1853, d. Nice, France, 1923. Commissioned second lieutenant in June 1875, for the next 20 years Biddle served on board a number of different ships and had shore duty in New York and Philadelphia. During the Spanish-American War (q.v.) he was on board Admiral Dewey's flagship *Olympia* during the battle for Manila Bay. As a major, he commanded the 4th Battalion of the Marine Brigade, arriving at Tientsin (q.v.) on 3 August 1900 to reinforce the marines preparing to advance with the International Force against the Boxer Rebellion (q.v.) in Peking (q.v.). He succeeded to command of the brigade before its advance on the capital and later served two years in the Philippines. Promoted to colonel, he commanded the Marine Brigade in the Philippines again from 1906 to mid-1908. In that year he took command of the expeditionary brigade slated for service in Panama (q.v.).

Biddle was acting commandant in October 1910 when Cmndt. George Elliott (q.v.) retired. After some time and controversy within and outside the corps (many supported General Waller), he was named 11th commandant on 3 February 1911 as a major general. Biddle was responsible for operations of marines in Cuba (q.v.) until 1913. He set up new recruit depots and established ready companies for expeditionary service. He activated the Marine Advance Base Force in December 1913—a small brigade of two regiments, one for defensive purposes and the other for expeditionary duty. The brigade also had an aviation section of two flying boats. By the time he left as commandant, the corps had grown to over 10,000 men. Biddle was handicapped by the ongoing pro-Waller faction, the hostility of the army, and the less than positive support given the corps by Pres. Woodrow Wilson. He retired as commandant on 24 February 1914.

"BLACK WIDOW" (F2T). Built to army specifications by North American, the big twin-engined, twin-boom fighter was first flown in May 1942. It was specifically designed as a night fighter. It carried a crew of three: a pilot, gunner, and radar operator. Fitted with the most advanced radar, capable of flying 375 miles per hour, and armed with four 20mm forward-firing cannon and four .50-caliber machine guns in a dorsal turret, it was a formidable aircraft. Marine squadrons in the Pacific generally flew the later modified version in the latter stages of the war and found the plane very effective against diminished Japanese air power.

BLADENSBURG. A town in Maryland five miles east of Washington, D.C. It was the site of a sharp skirmish on 24 August 1814 between British forces commanded by Gen. Robert Ross and the largely untrained U.S. militia that blocked the way to the capital. Crossing the Anacostia River, the British regulars quickly scattered most of the militia. However, 400 seamen and a contingent of 103 marines with five naval guns held a blocking position across the main road and repulsed three charges by the British infantry. They were eventually forced to withdraw as the British flanked their position. Once the naval and marine force withdrew, the British had a clear path to Washington. Without opposition, they occupied the capital and put the main buildings to the torch.

BOEING PW-9. A single-seat, all metal pursuit biplane that was produced first in 1926. It had a 400-horsepower Curtiss radial engine, a maximum speed of 163 miles per hour, and a service ceiling of 20,000 feet. It was one of many models manufactured by Boeing during the interwar years mainly for the Air Corps and Navy. However, a few of the PW-9s were adopted by the Marine Corps but were not the mainstay of marine aviation during this period.

BOOMER, WALTER E. b. 22 Sept. 1938, Rich Square, N.C. Boomer graduated from Randolph Macon Academy in 1956 and four years later earned a B.A. degree from Duke University. In 1973 he received a M.S. degree in technology and management from American University in Washington, D.C. After completion of Basic School in 1961, he was assigned to duty with the 2d Division at Quantico (q.v.) and served in differing positions in 1964. He was promoted to captain in 1956 and in 1966 became the commanding officer of Company H, 2d Battalion, 4th Marines in Vietnam (q.v.). Returning from Vietnam in 1967, he attended the Amphibious Warfare School, and the following year as a major he was assigned as aide-de-camp to the deputy chief of staff for plans in Washington. He then attended the Armed Forces Staff College and in 1971 attended the Short Advisors Course at Fort Bragg. In August he returned to Vietnam as an advisor to a South Vietnamese marine infantry battalion.

Returning to the United States, Boomer attended American University and in January 1974 began a three-year tour at the Naval Academy, serving as department chairman of the Department of Management during his final year. From July 1977 to June 1980, he was the executive officer of the 3d Marines in Hawaii before becoming commander of the 2d Battalion, 3d Marines. From July 1980 to June 1981, he attended the Naval War College. Upon completion of this study, he became deputy director of the 4th Corps' district in Philadelphia, and in June 1983, as a colonel, he assumed the office of director. In February 1985 Boomer took command of the Marine Security Guard at Quantico. He was promoted to brigadier general in June 1986 and became director of public affairs at the Washington headquarters. In May of the following year he took command of the 4th Division, and in March 1989 he was promoted to major general. Promoted to lieutenant general in August 1990, he took command of the Marines Central Command and the 1st Expeditionary Force and led them in the Desert Shield (q.v.) operation and the very successful marine assault on Kuwait City during Desert Storm (q.v.). In April 1991 he returned to the United States and continued commanding the 1st Expeditionary Force. On 27 September 1991 he became commanding general, Corps Combat Development Command at Quantico. Promoted to general, his next assignment on 1 September 1992 was as assistant commandant in Washington, D.C. He retired from the Marine Corps on 1 September 1994.

BOUGAINVILLE. A large island in the northern Solomon Islands (q.v.), 125 miles long by 30 miles wide. It has narrow coastal plains in the west and east, and in the interior are two extensive mountain ranges running the length of the island. The decision of U.S. naval planners to seize the island was based on the necessity of providing air bases to neutralize the main Japanese base of Rabaul in New Britain (q.v.). The Cherry Blossom operation was designed to bypass the main Japanese bases in the south and instead land the 3d Marine Division at Empress Augusta Bay, one-third of the way up the west coast, on 1 November 1943. Allied air power completely neutralized the Japanese air and naval forces on Bougainville. Few Japanese troops were in the vicinity of Empress Augusta Bay; therefore, there was only minimal resistance, and the marines quickly established a firm perimeter. On 8 November the army's 37th Division landed and took up positions on the right flank. The two main trails across the island were soon blocked, and the perimeter was expanded up the Piva River despite some Japanese resistance at Piva Forks. A fighter strip was constructed almost immediately, and shortly afterward two bomber fields were begun. By the end of December, the 3d Division was relieved by the army's Americal Division. The two army divisions in March 1944 bore the brunt of three major fruitless Japanese attacks on the perimeter. Later Australian units relieved the Americans and began a long process of conquering the entirety of the island. Fighting on Bougainville continued until the end of World War II (q.v.).

BOXER REBELLION. Refers to the antiforeign violence of the "Righteous Fists of Harmony" in China in 1900. Covertly supported by the Chinese government, the rebels in Peking (q.v.) forced the Europeans and Americans back into the Legation Quarter. Elsewhere they seized the native quarter at Tientsin (q.v.), threatening to cut off communications and reinforcements for those isolated in Peking. On 24 May Capt. John Myers landed at Taku with orders to get to Peking as soon as possible. At Tientsin he was joined by more marines, making a total of 54 marines and five sailors, the latter with their high-wheeled machine gun. Along with other European troops, they arrived in Peking by the end of the month, and the marines set up their defense at the southwest corner of Legation Square. German, British, and Russian troops manned the rest of the defenses. The marines, in conjunction with British Royal Marines, drove the Boxers away from the burning Hanlin Yuan Academy on 23 June. On the 24th the Boxers attacked the British compound and three days later made a daylight attack against the marine position. They were halted, the machine gun wreaking havoc among the attackers. On 1 July, because the Germans gave way, the marines were forced to abandon their position momentarily. Counterattacking, they regained their position on the wall. The following day the Boxers moved a wooden tower to the wall, threatening the marine position. That evening a raid by the marines and their British counterparts destroyed the tower. The fighting after that became less intense and the Chinese government abandoned the Boxers, mainly because of the loss of the native quarter at Tientsin to the multinational relief column of more than 15,000 men. The U.S. contingent in that force numbered more than 3,000, including the 1st Marine Regiment. By 13 August the relief column had reached the outskirts of Peking, and the next day the Legation buildings were liberated. The relief of Peking ended the uprising. The marines in the Legation had suffered only 17 casualties during the entire defense.

BOYINGTON, GREGORY "PAPPY." b. Coeur d'Alene, Idaho, 4 Dec. 1912, d. Fresno, Calif., 11 Jan. 1988. Boyington attended the University of Washington, receiving a B.S. degree in engineering in 1934. A member of ROTC, he was commissioned second lieutenant in the Coast Artillery Reserve. In June 1936 he enlisted in the Marine Corps Reserve and received an appointment in 1937 as an aviation cadet in the reserve. After flight training at Pensacola, he was designated a navy aviator and was later given a regular commission, attended Basic School, and took part in fleet exercises aboard the *Lexington* and *Yorktown*. As a first lieutenant, he was an instructor at Pensacola before resigning his commission to join the unit formed by Claire Chennault later known as "The Flying Tigers." During his service in China, Boyington became a squadron leader and recorded six victories flying P-40s. He returned to the United States after Pearl Harbor and was assigned to the air station in San Diego briefly as a first lieutenant. In November 1942 he was promoted to major in the reserve. The following January he was sent to the Pacific and flew with Squadron 122 in Guadalcanal. Later he became commanding officer of Fighting Squadron 214 made up of casual, green pilots and replacements that came to be known as the "Black Sheep" and Boyington was called "Pappy" because of his age (31). During the squadron's first combat tour, flying a Corsair (F4U) (q.v.), Boyington shot down 14 planes in 32 days. Flying over Bougainville (q.v.), New Georgia (q.v.), and New Britain (q.v.), he added to his score, and on a sweep over Rabaul on 3 January 1944, he shot down his 26th plane, equaling the then American record. On this engagement Boyington was shot down and made a prisoner by the Japanese. He was liberated from the prison camp at Omori on 29 August 1945. While a prisoner, it was confirmed that he had destroyed three Japanese planes before being shot down, giving him a total of 28 enemy planes destroyed.

Returning to the United States by now as a lieutenant colonel, Boyington received the Medal of Honor (q.v.) for his actions in the Solomons. He retired from the corps on 1 August 1947 as a colonel. His exploits served as the basis for a best selling book and a popular television series.

BRIGADE. For the Marine Corps, a brigade is a 20th century organization. Because of the corps' small size, the battalion was the largest combat unit deployed in the 19th century. A reorganization in 1913 created the Advance Base Force, which was a small brigade composed of two regiments (q.v.). The corps utilized the army as a pattern for its reorganization, using the square division as a model. During World War I (q.v.), the 4th Brigade, which was sent to France, was very large, consisting of over 9,300 men each in two regiments. The marine brigades in France were thus equivalent in size to British and French divisions. After the war, the ground force elements of the corps were organized into two brigades, the first located at Quantico (q.v.) and the second at San Diego. Each brigade had one infantry regiment, an artillery battalion, an antiaircraft battalion, and chemical and engineering units. In early 1942 the brigades were upgraded to divisional status utilizing the triangular division organization. This became the fundamental organization for the six divisions deployed during World War II (q.v.).

The brigade organization was revitalized after the Vietnam conflict when the mission of the corps demanded smaller units and more flexibility and the Marine Expeditionary Brigade (MEB) (q.v.) was created. The MEB can be of two types—the Marine Prepositioning Force (MPF) (q.v.) and the Amphibious

MEB. The MPF is designed to project military power quickly in any part of the world. It is heavily equipped with armor. All of its larger equipment is located on ships in strategic locations in the Atlantic, Pacific, and Indian Oceans. Each of these brigades has approximately 16,000 marines. Thus, each modern brigade is roughly the size of a World War II division.

BROWNING AUTOMATIC RIFLE (BAR, M1918 and M1918A1-A2). Invented by John Browning and produced in great quantities during World War I (q.v.), this weapon weighed a comparatively light 16 pounds, fired a 30.06 cartridge, and was capable of being used semiautomatically or as fully automatic at a rate of 500 rounds per minute. It proved itself in the fighting on the Western Front in 1918. After the war, it continued as the standard automatic rifle for all the services. The marines used it very effectively in the many small scale wars in the Caribbean and Central America. Many changes were made to the original model such as a folding buttplate, a folding bipod, and a change to only fully automatic in the A1 and A2 models. These increased the weight to 20 pounds. Beginning in 1941, the older models had these changes incorporated. During combat in World War II (q.v.), some of these modifications were removed, and the corps modified most of the A2 models to allow semiautomatic fire. It was particularly appreciated by most marine units that attempted to get more than the standard issue of the weapons since the BAR could lay down a heavy volume of fire. Negative factors were the weight of the gun and the fact that the barrels overheated under sustained fire and could be replaced only in an ordnance shop. The earlier BAR model was declared obsolete in July 1945, while the A2 remained the standard automatic rifle. It was placed back in production during the Korean War (q.v.), was continued in service even after the adoption of the M-60 machine gun (q.v.), and was used during the Vietnam War (q.v.).

"BUFFALO" (F2A). A single-seat, all-metal monocoque fighter with stressed skin built by the Brewster Aeronautical Corporation, first ordered in the summer of 1938 as a naval shipboard fighter. A total of 162 F2As of various models were delivered to the navy and marines by 1941. Although believed by evaluators to be a superior fighter, it proved to be no match for Japanese Zero and Oscar fighters in the Central Pacific. Although fast at 337 miles per hour, its slow rate of climb and maneuverability made it totally inadequate. Marine pilots flying Buffalos from Midway on 4 June 1942 against the Japanese planes attacking the island lost 17 planes and pilots. Seven other planes were badly damaged. This disappointing performance and the failure of the plane in Malaya and the East Indies made the Buffalo obsolete during the first six months of the Pacific war.

BURROWS, WILLIAM WARD. 2d commandant, b. Charleston, S.C., 16 Jan. 1758, d. 1805. After the Revolutionary War, the navy was allowed to decay. Without ships, there was no more reason for a Marine Corps, and except for a few men serving in the Revenue Cutter Service, there was no organized corps. With the Naval Act of 1794 calling for building six frigates, however, the corps became necessary once again, and the House of Representatives authorized the establishment of a battalion of marines. Burrows, practicing law in Philadelphia, was appointed major commandant of the small force in July 1798. By 1799 during the quasi-war with France, the 881-man corps was serving on board 25 ships. After the war, Congress reduced the number of ships and also the size of the corps. This policy was rapidly reversed when trouble developed with the Barbary pirates (q.v.) and Burrows had to rapidly increase the size of the corps. He was also responsible for selecting the site of Marine Headquarters at Eighth and I Streets in Washington and forming the first Marine Band. He retired because of ill health in 1804 and died the following year.

BUTLER, SMEDLEY D. b. West Chester, Penn., 30 July 1881, d. Philadelphia, 21 June 1940. Butler was commissioned a second lieutenant in May 1898 at the opening of the Spanish-American War. The following year he was ordered to the Philippines and later served in China, where he was wounded at Tientsin (q.v.) in July 1900 during the Boxer Rebellion (q.v.). For the next decade he served in a number of posts in the United States, Puerto Rico, and Panama (q.v.). In 1910 he participated in various actions in Nicaragua (q.v.), and two years later he had a major role in securing the main rail line in Nicaragua from rebel forces. Butler won his first Medal of Honor (q.v.) during the action at Veracruz (q.v.) in April 1914 for his courage in leading his men of the Panama battalion in the assault of the 22d on the city. His next action was in Haiti (q.v.), where a rebellion in the spring of 1915 had caused insurgents called Cacos to hold the northern part of Haiti. Major Butler, with five companies of marines, systematically cleared the area in a series of actions, causing heavy casualties to the rebels and finally capturing the last main bastion, Fort Capois, on 17 November 1915. For these actions he was awarded a second Medal of Honor. During World War I he served with distinction and was promoted to brigadier general at age 37, the youngest in the history of the corps. At the close of the war he commanded the 5th Brigade at Brest.

Returning to the United States, he took command of the Marine Barracks at Quantico (q.v.), a position he held until January 1924 when he took a leave of absence to became director of public safety in Philadelphia. He held that post for a year before returning to the corps with his rank of major general intact, and he assumed command of the marine base at San Diego. In March 1927 he returned to China to command the 3d Brigade, a position he held until April 1931. Butler, as the senior general in the corps, expected to be named commandant in August 1930 to replace Gen. Wendell Neville (q.v.). However, Gen. Ben Fuller (q.v.) was chosen instead, perhaps because Butler was considered too controversial. Butler's final tour lasted from April to October 1931 when once again he commanded at Quantico. After 33 years of service, disappointed by being passed over for commandant, Butler requested retirement.

C

CAMP LEJEUNE. A major marine base located in eastern North Carolina. The growth of the corps and its newly defined amphibious role called for a base other than Quantico (q.v.) to serve as the East Coast expeditionary base. Tent Camp 1 was established in September 1941 in the New River area. It soon ceased to be temporary and was named after the legendary World War I leader John A. Lejeune (q.v.). Lejeune became a key base for the organization and training of marine infantry during World War II (q.v.). The last Fleet Marine Force (q.v.) unit, the 29th Marines, left Lejeune for the Pacific in 1944. A cluster of technical schools had by then also been established there. After the war, Lejeune continued in its dual role of training and as a base for regular marine units.

CAMP PENDLETON. The major Marine Corps base in the western United States. Located adjacent to the coast north of San Diego, it was initially the Santa Margarita Ranch where one of the battles of the Mexican War (q.v.) took place. The 132,000-

acre ranch was purchased in March 1942 to help train the many new recruits who volunteered after Pearl Harbor. It was commissioned by Pres. Franklin Roosevelt and named in honor of the famous marine general, "Uncle Joe" Pendleton (q.v.). During World War II (q.v.), Pendleton became the headquarters of the Training and Replacement Command, which trained thousands of U.S. marines, army divisions, as well as foreign officers and men. After the war, the 1st Division was permanently stationed at Camp Pendleton until the Korean War (q.v.). After that long, drawn-out action, the Fleet Marine Force (q.v.) was redeployed, and the 1st Division was relieved of its policing duty in Korea and returned to its home station supported by the 3d Air Wing at neighboring El Toro. This arrangement continued for decades.

CAPE GLOUCESTER. The northernmost point of western New Britain (q.v.) Island. In 1943 the Japanese had constructed an airfield complex there defended by 7,500 men, many of whom were not combat troops. General Douglas MacArthur had at first planned to capture the major fortress of Rabaul, separated from the west by hundreds of miles of heavy jungle. Allied air power and success in New Guinea changed the plan. Henceforth, MacArthur's forces were concerned with moving northward toward the Philippines. Before this he wanted to assure that the Dampier Strait was secure, which called for the capture of the Cape Gloucester airfields. On 26 December the first of the secondary landings was made by army troops brought in by marine amphibians at Cape Merkus across the Arawe Channel on the south coast. The same day a marine battalion landed on the northwest coast 6.5 miles southwest of the main landing area. The main landing with the troops struggling inland through swamps, as with the secondary attacks, was not heavily opposed. By D-day + 1, 12,000 marines were solidly emplaced in the north with an additional 1,500 on the Dampier side. These were to march northward to join the main group while preventing as many Japanese as possible from concentrating against the main effort. Japanese aircraft from Rabaul harassed the marine perimeter, but the main problems were the jungle, swamps, and weather. On the 29th a monsoon struck New Britain. More than 15 inches of rain fell in one day.

Despite all problems, the marines seized the airfield on the 30th and overran the other Japanese-held Cape Gloucester positions the next day. The Japanese commander had set up a defense line on the western side of Borgen Bay anchored by two hills. It took two weeks for the 5th and 7th Marines to regroup and advance through kunai grass and swampy jungle. At first contained, a battalion of the 7th Marines took the defenders by surprise on 14 January 1944 and forced the Japanese to retreat, pursued by marine patrols. The remnants of the Japanese force, numbering less than 1,000 men, finally reached Rabaul after month-long torturous marches. The Cape Gloucester airfields proved important in providing continuous air support for MacArthur's northern offensive. The marine casualties were more than 1,000, including 248 killed. These figures do not reflect the numbers debilitated from sickness in that "green hell," which many marines considered worse than Guadalcanal (q.v.).

CARBINE (CALIBER .30 M1). Developed by Winchester Arms Company and adopted by the services as a replacement for both submachine guns and the .45-caliber automatic pistol. The Carbine was a lightweight weapon utilizing a short-stroke gas piston action firing a .30-caliber round. After grueling tests in the fall of 1941, it was put into production by the government. Eventually 10 different companies produced the Carbine, and by the close of the war, 6.25 million guns had been produced. Tests by the corps were laudatory, and by 1943 the Table of Organization and Equipment designated 11,074 Carbines for a division. It had replaced the Reising machine gun. A further modification of the Carbine was the M1A1, a weapon specifically designed to meet the need of paratroops, having a folding stock that could be carried in a canvas scabbard strapped to a paratrooper's leg. When given a choice, marine infantry preferred the heavier M-1 Garand (q.v.) because of its heavier striking power. However, the Carbine ably filled the role for which it was designed and became one of the classic weapons of World War II (q.v.). Large stocks of Carbines were on hand after the war, and the weapon was continued in use through the Korean War (q.v.) and into the late 1950s.

CARLSON, EVANS F. b. Sidney, N.Y., 26 Feb. 1896, d. Portland, Ore., 27 May 1947. Leaving high school at age 16, Carlson joined the army in 1912 and during four years reached the rank of sergeant, serving in Hawaii and the Philippines. Discharged, he remained a civilian for a short period but reenlisted in time for the Mexican expedition. During World War I (q.v.), he served in France, sustaining wounds during the Argonne campaign. He had received a commission in May 1917 and was later promoted to captain. After service in the Army of Occupation, he again returned to civilian life. This, too, was a short span as Carlson joined the Marine Corps as a private in 1922. His previous military experience earned him a commission in 1923. For the next six years he served at Quantico (q.v.), Puerto Rico, Pensacola (q.v.), and a two-year tour at Shanghai. In 1930 he was ordered to Nicaragua (q.v.), where he won the Navy Cross (q.v.) by leading a small unit of marines against a superior force of insurgents. He was commended for his activity during the great earthquake in 1931 and also for his performance as chief of police there. Two years later he was ordered to the American Legation in Peking (q.v.), where he began his study of Chinese. After a brief stay in the United States, he returned to China again in 1937 as a military observer. During the next year, he traveled over much of inland China, made contact with the Communist forces, lived under the most primitive conditions, and was impressed with the Chinese concept of guerrilla warfare. Convinced of the Japanese threat, he resigned from the corps in 1934 in order to devote full time to lecturing and writing about the Japanese danger.

In 1941 he once again entered the corps with the rank of major. He took command of the 2d Marine Raider Battalion in 1942. The Raiders conformed to Carlson's concept of elite, specially trained troops. As a lieutenant colonel in August 1942, he led the Raiders in an attack on Makin (q.v.) Island to destroy the Japanese wireless station there. Carlson won a second Navy Cross for this action. In November and December he led his Raider Battalion in action on Guadalcanal (q.v.), first by carrying out a mission to Aola eastward from Henderson Field (q.v.) pursuing fleeing Japanese into the interior. Later the battalion was involved in the fighting along the Matanikau River on the west flank of the marine forces. In September 1943, because of his previous experience in the Gilbert Islands (q.v.), he was designated an observer of the Tarawa (q.v.) invasion. He landed on Betio Island shortly after Col. David Shoup (q.v.) and acted as liaison between the commander on the ground and Gen. Julian Smith (q.v.), the overall commander of the operation. He also was instrumental in organizing the flow of critical supplies to the front. Following this action, Carlson became the assistant operations officer of the 4th Division and helped plan for the Marshall Islands (q.v.) operation of early 1944. Later during the June invasion of Saipan (q.v.) he was wounded attempting to rescue an injured marine. Those wounds forced his retirement from the corps in July 1946. He was at that time advanced to the rank of brigadier general.

"CATALINA" (PBY-5A). The first models of the Catalina were produced by Consolidated Aircraft Company in the mid-1930s, first as a flying boat (PBY-5) and later as an amphibian (5A). It was produced in great quantities during World War II and was the standard long-range reconnaissance patrol amphibian for the navy and marines. It was slow (125 miles per hour cruising speed), but its 2,500-mile range made it invaluable during the Pacific war for long range operations. It was particularly valuable as an observation aircraft and played a crucial role in the Coral Sea and Midway (q.v.) battles. Marine use was generally for logistic functions and the transport of high level officers over ocean areas when normal transport aircraft did not have sufficient range.

CATES, CLIFTON B. 19th commandant, b. Tiptonville, Tenn., 31 Aug. 1893, d. Quantico, 6 June 1970. Cates attended the University of Tennessee, receiving his bachelor of laws degree in 1916. As a reserve second lieutenant, he reported for active duty in June 1917 and left for France in January 1918. At Belleau Wood (q.v.) on 6 June 1918 he led a platoon of 6th Marines into the village of Bouresches and held it against counterattacks during the Aisne defense. He commanded a company of the 6th during the general attack at Soissons (q.v.) that suffered very heavy casualties.

In World War I (q.v.) Cates was wounded six times and also gassed. For his actions he received the Navy Cross (q.v.), the Silver Star, the *Croix de Guerre* with two palms, and the French Legion of Honor. Electing to remain in the corps, in the 1920s he served on sea duty, became a White House aide to the commandant and aide-de-camp to the marine commander of the Pacific, and served as a member of the Battle Monuments commission. He joined the 4th Marines at Shanghai in May 1929, serving in China until 1932. After tours with the 7th Marines and duty with the War Plans section at Headquarters in Washington, he returned to China as commander of a regiment. In 1940 as a colonel he was appointed to command the Basic School in Philadelphia.

Colonel Cates commanded the 1st Marines during the Guadalcanal (q.v.) campaign. Returning to the United States in March 1943, by now a brigadier general, he assumed command of the Marine Corps station at Quantico (q.v.). In July 1944 he took over command of the 4th Marine Division from Harry Schmidt (q.v.) after Saipan (q.v.) and led the division in the conquest of Tinian (q.v.) in July 1944 and in the assault on Iwo Jima (q.v.) in February 1945. The 4th Division was on the right in this attack and later encountered the most determined resistance in the drive to clear the Japanese from the center and northern part of the island. Returning to the United States, he became commander of the Marine Barracks at Quantico.

On 1 January 1948 he became a full general and was appointed commandant, and he immediately became involved in the debate over the future of the corps. The first secretary of defense, James Forrestal, and his successor, Louis Johnson, limited the size and mission of the corps with the stipulation that no marine officer was to command higher than a corps. The commandant was not to be part of the Joint Chiefs of Staff, and funding for the corps suffered huge cuts. Cates testified before Congress on the weakness of the corps and rallied congressional support. The Korean War (q.v.) intervened in this debate, and action of marines there proved the worth of the corps. At the beginning of the action on 29 June 1950, Cates requested the chief of naval operations, Adm. Forrest Sherman, to offer MacArthur the use of the Marine Brigade. The offer was immediately accepted. The corps was expanded by calling up over 33,000 reserves, bringing it up to over 100,000 men. Cates visited the battlefront during action in North Korea, and the 3d Marine Division was activated in January 1952. Cates had retired before Congress finally acted to protect the corps and allow the commandant a role in the meetings of the Joint Chiefs. On the conclusion of his four-year term, Cates, not yet 60 years old, requested continued duty and reverted to three-star rank, becoming once again commandant at Quantico. Upon his retirement from the Marine Corps on 30 January 1954, he was reinstated at his higher rank.

CHAMBERS, JUSTICE M. b. Huntington, W. Va., 8 Feb. 1908. Chambers attended Marshall College and later George Washington and the National University, receiving his law degree. He spent two years in the naval reserve before joining the corps reserve as a private in 1930. Two years later he was commissioned, and by 1940, when the Washington, D.C.'s, 5th Battalion was activated, he was a major. He went to the South Pacific as a part of the 1st Division and was wounded in the invasion of Tulagi (q.v.). While in the battalion aid station, he took charge of its defense against a Japanese counterattack, an action that won him the Silver Star. Later he participated in the assault on Roi-Namur (q.v.) in the Marshall Islands (q.v.) as a commander of the 3d Battalion, 25th Marines of the 4th Division. He led this unit in the invasion of Saipan (q.v.) in June 1944, where he was wounded by a shell blast, although not seriously enough to preclude his continuing in command.

After Saipan was secured, Chambers led his battalion in the invasion and conquest of Tinian (q.v.). On 19 February, now a lieutenant colonel, he landed on Iwo Jima (q.v.) immediately after the assault waves of his battalion, whose position on the extreme right of the marine line was the most vulnerable. The Japanese, from the high ground and ridges ahead and on the flanks, poured a murderous fire on the marines. The 3d Battalion lost half of its personnel on D-day. With total disregard for his own safety, Chambers led his troops in an eight-hour battle to capture the high ground by the end of the day, thus neutralizing the Japanese threat to the right flank of the marine line. On D + 3 the unit was pinned down by small arms, mortar, and machine gun fire from hills in front. Chambers directed the first rocket barrage against the positions before he was hit by a machine gun bullet that tore into his chest. Upon evacuation, the doctors discovered the seriousness of the wound. He was promoted to colonel before he was medically retired and for his action on Iwo received the Medal of Honor (q.v.).

CHAPMAN, LEONARD F. JR. 24th commandant, b. Key West, Fla., 3 Nov. 1913. Chapman was commissioned in the Army Field Artillery Reserve from the University of Florida after ROTC before entering the Marine Corps in July 1935. After Basic School he attended the Artillery School at Fort Sill and served in the 10th Marines before being posted to Hawaii in June 1940. He was aboard the *Astoria* during the early Pacific naval battles. As a major, he was appointed an instructor in artillery at Quantico (q.v.) in August 1942 and later became the executive officer to the artillery section there. In June 1944, now a lieutenant colonel, Chapman joined the 1st Division, serving as commander of a battalion of the 11th Marines during the Peleliu (q.v.) operation in September 1944. He continued as commander of the 4th Battalion during the bloody fighting on Okinawa (q.v.) from April to July 1945. After brief service with Fleet Marine Force (q.v.) Pacific, he was stationed in Washington for two and one-half years in the Division of Plans. Later he served as chief of supporting arms at Quantico, and as a colonel at Camp Pendleton (q.v.), he took command of the 12th

Marines of the 3d Division in July 1952. He served with the unit in Japan and then took charge as commanding officer Marine Barracks Yokosuka.

By 1958 Chapman commanded the Force Troops for Fleet Marine Force Atlantic as a brigadier general and in 1961 he became deputy chief of staff at Marine Headquarters and was promoted to major general before becoming the assistant chief of staff. When Wallace Greene became commandant, Chapman became chief of staff and succeeded him on 1 January 1968, just days before the Tet offensive (q.v.) in Vietnam (q.v.). Chapman was responsible with the other members of the Joint Chiefs for phasing out American military activity in Vietnam. He retired on 31 December 1971 and became director of immigration and naturalization service, responsible for handling the influx of over 150,000 Vietnamese refugees.

CHAPULTEPEC. The name means Grasshopper Hill. This was the site of the last major battle of the Mexican War (q.v.). It is an isolated rocky mound 150 feet high located two miles southwest of the Belen Gate entrance to Mexico City. The height was protected by heavy walls with marshy areas in front of the fort. It had a garrison of an estimated 800 men and many pieces of artillery. It was also the site of a military academy whose students participated in its defense. General Winfield Scott's forces had taken El Molino del Rey, and on 13 September 1847 only Chapultepec barred the way to the two main entrances to the city. The Marine Battalion was attached to the 2d Brigade of Gen. John Quitman's division, which was assigned the task of attacking Chapultepec from the south. The bombardment of the fortress began early in the morning, and after two hours, 40 marines and soldiers in the storming party advanced to the walls with scaling ladders and crowbars. The attack was briefly halted by fire from a Mexican battery to the rear. Other marines captured the offending artillery pieces and later, with a few soldiers commanded by Lt. Ulysses S. Grant, took the Cosme Gate to the city. By then Quitman's forces had scaled the walls and captured most of the Mexican defenders. The following day marines cleared the few Mexican troops left behind in the city and raised the flag over the National Palace. This action at Chapultepec was later immortalized as "the Halls of Montezuma" in the Marine Hymn (q.v.).

CHATEAU-THIERRY. A town in France in the department of Aisne on the right bank of the Marne River 60 miles northeast of Paris. It was a main road and railway junction. One of the main objectives of the third German offensive of 1918 in World War I (q.v.) was Chateau-Thierry and the wooded areas to the west. On 30 May the 2d Division was thrown into the battle, taking over the defense from the exhausted French troops. The German advance was checked, and on 6 June the marines began a counterattack against entrenched positions seven miles east of the town at Belleau Wood (q.v.), which was taken despite heavy casualties. That attack became synonymous with elan and bravery shown by the corps during the war.

"CHICKASAW" (Army designation). Marine designation HRS. A 12-seat utility helicopter that could be used in a variety of ways for either cargo or personnel. The prototype was first flown in 1949, and a total of 1,278 were built for all services before production ended a decade later. The HRS version built for the Marine Corps was used for assault transport duties and had the capability of carrying eight armed soldiers besides its crew of two. It could carry one ton of either men or cargo at a top speed of 112 miles per hour and had a maximum rate of climb of 1,000 feet per minute.

CHOISEUL. An island in the central Solomon Islands (q.v.) approximately 20 miles wide and 75 miles long lying midway between Bougainville (q.v.) and Santa Isabel on the eastern side of the waterway known in 1943 as the "slot." In October 1943 the decision was made to land a battalion of marine paratroops on the northwestern coast to distract Japanese attention from the planned invasion of Bougainville. There was no question of a lengthy operation since the Japanese had at least 1,300 men in the vicinity of the landing areas and a further 3,000 elsewhere on the island. The raid, commanded by then Col. Victor Krulak (q.v.), began on 27 October and was successful in drawing the Japanese into the locality of the landing at Voza town and into a series of small-scale firefights. Whether the raid had any influence on Japanese dispositions on Bougainville is questionable. However, a chart of the minefields off Bougainville was discovered which helped the navy avoid problems in supplying the marines at Empress Augusta Bay where the invasion of Bougainville had begun on 1 November. The Choiseul force was evacuated on the 3d after conducting a brilliant operation in the face of overwhelming enemy superiority.

CHOSIN RESERVOIR. The site of a major hydroelectric plant located only a few miles south of the Yalu River. During the Korean War (q.v.), the 1st Marine Division, still a part of X Corps, was transported to Wonson on the east coast on 26 October 1950 and was assigned a zone of action roughly 300 miles long by 50 miles wide. The orders were to advance northward toward Chosin along a mountain road northwest of Hungnam. By 2 November, the 7th Marines had already made contact with a Chinese division before Funchilin Pass. However, by the 10th the marines had reached Koto-ri and three days later had arrived at Hagaru-ri (q.v.) at the southern end of the Chosin Reservoir. Elements of the 7th moved west to Yudam-ni, and on the 26th the 5th Marines arrived there also. The 1st Marines were left behind, strung out along the high ground to keep the lines of communication to Hungnam open. The overly optimistic plan called for the marines to swing westward across the spine of the highlands to form a part of a pincers to smash the remaining North Korean forces despite the weather, which had turned very cold—well below zero. This plan of X Corps was rudely changed when the Chinese struck the 8th Army units to the west, opening a great gap in the line. Then three Chinese divisions attacked the marines at Yudam-ni and at the units holding the Toktong Pass. Another division attacked Hagaru-ri and cut the road south to Koto-ri. The great advance to the Yalu was halted, and the marines were forced to fight for their lives. The locus of the Chinese attack was Hagaru-ri.

CIVIL WAR. The slavery question hung over the nation during the 1850s, and the governments of three presidents did little to halt the drift toward civil war. Chief among the critics of the Southern "peculiar institution" were the abolitionists, most of whom did not believe in violence. However, John Brown was one abolitionist with a long history of violence dating to the unrest in the Kansas Territory. On 16 October 1858 he and 18 armed men seized the federal arsenal at Harpers Ferry (q.v.), believing that this would be a signal for a massive slave uprising throughout the South. The local militia shot or captured all but six of the rebels. They then surrounded Brown's command in a brick building on the arsenal grounds and waited for federal troops. The only regular force available was a detachment of 86 marines from the Washington barracks commanded by Lt. Israel Greene. Lieutenant Colonel Robert E. Lee was placed in command; his aide was Lt. J. E. B. Stuart. At daybreak Stuart was ordered forward to ask for Brown's surrender. When this was not forthcoming, Lee ordered the marines forward. They battered down the door to the building and charged inside.

Despite two marines being wounded, Brown was captured, narrowly escaping with his life when Greene, thrusting at the old man, had his sword bent double as it struck a leather strap. Brown was subsequently tried and hanged. His exploit became a symbol for many abolitionists, and Brown became an unlikely hero in the months before the Civil War.

The election of Abraham Lincoln in 1860 brought on the secession of states in the deep South, followed early the next year by Virginia. After the firing on Fort Sumter (q.v.), war became inevitable. The corps, like the regular army, lost a significant number of officers who chose the Confederacy—over half the captains and two-thirds of the lieutenants resigned. It was necessary to rebuild the corps in the months that followed. Despite the confusion in personnel, a battalion of marines numbering 336 men, mostly recruits, took part in the 1st Battle of Bull Run, giving a good account of themselves defending a Union battery on Henry Hill. Once Gen. Irvin McDowell's army broke under the Confederate attacks, the marines also retreated back to Washington. Later in 1861 a battalion of marines landed on the eastern side of Hatteras Inlet and captured Forts Clark and Hatteras, both of which proved valuable for later operations in the Carolinas. The battalion also was used to occupy Saint Augustine, Florida, in March 1862. Another battalion of approximately 300 marines was used by Adm. David Farragut to land in New Orleans (q.v.) in April 1862 and hold the city until relieved by army units.

The corps reached a peak of approximately 4,100 officers and men during the war, although it was not used in any significant fashion. Only two major campaigns involved marine units. The first of these was action against Fort Sumter in September 1863. One of nine forts guarding the entrance to Charleston, it was targeted for capture after the army had seized Fort Wagner. The plan for a night landing proved faulty, and only 150 marines landed on the beaches where the Confederates drove them back, the marines suffering 44 casualties in the firefight. This battalion then was kept in camp until early 1864 when it was broken up. The other major use of a marine unit also proved a fiasco. In January 1865 a battalion formed from marines in Rear Adm. David Porter's squadron were to be landed on the seaward side of Fort Fisher (q.v.), which guarded Wilmington, North Carolina, the last functioning Confederate port. They were to provide covering fire for the sailors who would be sent to reinforce them. At the same time army troops would assault the fort from the landward side through the minefields. The Confederates shot the second attacking forces to pieces, but their attention was diverted from the army units which took the fort. This was the last action of the corps during the war.

COLT .45 PISTOL (M1911). Lessons from the Philippine insurrection led to the development of this large, more powerful semi-automatic sidearm for the U.S. armed forces. The first of this type was delivered to the corps in 1912 and became the standard sidearm then for officers, noncommissioned officers, and specialists from then until partially replaced by the M1 Carbine (q.v.) during World War II (q.v.). Colt Firearms Company had produced 55,000 of these weapons before the United States entered World War I (q.v.). Full scale production of the pistol from 1917 through 1926 produced an additional half-million weapons. An upgraded version of the M1911 was issued in the latter year and given the designation M1911A1. Modifications included a shorter serrated trigger, longer grip safety, and a contoured handgrip. Most of the 1911 models were upgraded to A1 standards. During World War II, further changes were made. Among these were the substitution of plastic grips instead of molded rubber and a change from the blue-black finish to a dull gray nonreflective finish. During the war, a number of firms were licensed by Colt to produce the weapon. One of these, Remington Rand, actually produced a half-million more guns than did the parent company. The official Table of Equipment for a division included 1,707 pistols. The actual number available, particularly before the advent of the Carbine, was always many more.

COMPANY. During and after World War II (q.v.), the size of an infantry company varied between 220 and 230 officers and men. Three rifle companies and a headquarters company made up an infantry battalion. Other companies such as service, engineering, and medical units had different complements of men. The exact size of each company had changed during the half-century since World War II, but the organization remained the same, and the numbers in a rifle company remained reasonably constant. Earlier in the 18th and 19th centuries, with the corps having few men, the company was very important with its commander exercising a great amount of freedom of action. Their size varied with the time and objective. For example, at the Battle of New Orleans the total number of marines involved was only slightly more than a modern day company.

CON THIEN. A village in northern Quang Tri Province, Vietnam (q.v.), which with Khe Sanh (q.v.) became one of the fixed defense positions for the 3d Division in I Corps' area of Vietnam. It was a major post along the test section for the anti-infiltration line ordered by Secretary of Defense Robert MacNamara in 1967. As such it was subjected to a series of artillery and infantry attacks during the spring and summer. The first of these in May was beaten off by the 4th Marines. A counterattack by the marines 10 days later captured the trench and bunker systems used by the North Vietnamese. Despite this, Con Thien continued to be an objective of the North Vietnamese. In July two battalions of the 9th and one from the 3d Marines fought an estimated Vietnamese regiment in the Con Thien area. This action, Operation Buffalo, shattered the North Vietnamese forces but resulted in 100 marines killed. In September another major attack on Con Thien was mounted, and once again the North Vietnamese suffered heavy casualties. The following month they abandoned any further massive attempts to capture Con Thien. Action continued in the area around Con Thien for the remainder of the war, but never again did the enemy make such concerted attempts on this marine bastion.

CONTINENTAL MARINES. Britain's wars with France during the 18th century involved the North American colonies, and the Royal Navy enlisted colonials to serve as marines. In 1740 three marine regiments were raised to serve in the navy's attacks on the French West Indies possessions. In the next 35 years thousands of Americans served as marines, taking part in the expeditions launched against Acadia, Louisburg, Quebec, Cartagena, and Portobello. The Second Continental Congress, debating the question of independence, agreed upon the necessity of raising a naval force and this action would require marines. Thus, on 10 November 1775 Congress authorized the raising of two battalions of Continental Marines. The first commander was a Philadelphian, Capt. Samuel Nicholas (q.v.).

The first significant action of the Continental Marines during the Revolutionary War was as a part of the eight-ship squadron commanded by Commodore Esek Hopkins. He decided to raid the Bahamas in hopes of gaining much needed supplies for Gen. George Washington's army. The target was old Nassau on New Providence Island, whose harbor was guarded by two forts manned by 200 men. On 2 March 1776 Nicholas led a party of 200 marines and 50 sailors in an assault on lightly held Fort Montague. Meeting little resistance, his force waited for the next day to begin an attack on the town proper. The presence of Hopkins's fleet and the position of the marines convinced the British governor to surrender, and Hopkins was able to carry back to the Continental Army valued artillery pieces and gunpowder. His ships encountered a small British fleet on the return voyage to New London, and the marines fought their first seaborne engagement, suffering 17 casualties. Later a battalion of marines was sent to reinforce the Continental Army and fought at Princeton. However, most served on board ships. Under John Paul Jones they participated in the famous battle between the *Ranger* and the *Drake* and on board the *Bonhomme Richard* in Jones's great victory over the *Serapis*. Despite such victories, the Continental Navy ultimately proved no match for the Royal Navy, and by the close of the war in 1783 only one of its ships had survived. The others had been sunk or captured. The end of the Continental Navy came when that ship was sold. Without a navy, there was no need for the Continental Marines, and it was disbanded.

CORPS. An organization utilized by the army during the Civil War (q.v.) based on Napoleonic models. It was composed of a number of divisions (q.v.). Throughout its first 100 years, the Marine Corps was unable to field even a division. The first corps was organized after Guadalcanal (q.v.) in 1943. Eventually two Amphibious Corps were in operation by the end of World War II (q.v.). The marine contribution to the Korean War (q.v.) was too slight (only one division) to need a corps. However, in the Vietnam War (q.v.), the 1st and 3d Marine Divisions were placed under a corps system called III Marine Amphibious Force (MAF). In the reorganization of the 1970s and 1980s, the activities of a corps were assumed by Marine Air Ground Task Forces (MAGTF) (q.v.) commands. The largest of these can contain up to 100,000 men as in the Gulf War (q.v.) of 1991.

"CORSAIR" (F4U). The first production model built by Chance Vought was flown in June 1942. The Corsair went through many different models and was still being produced a decade later. The F4U-4 was the model most used by the U.S. Navy and Marine Corps during World War II (q.v.). By the time it was withdrawn from production in 1947, 2,356 of this model had been built. The later models of this unique gull-winged fighter were capable of a top speed of more than 450 miles per hour, being arguably the fastest fighter of the war. Operating at altitudes over 20,000 feet, it was more than a match for even

the latest Japanese fighters. At first obtained to be a replacement for the F4F shipboard fighter, it proved difficult to land
on carriers because of its size and gull-wing configuration.
However, the Marine Corps found it to be the perfect all-
purpose aircraft, and by mid-1943 it had become the standard
fighter. Marine aces such as Gregory Boyington (q.v.) and Robert Hanson (q.v.) flying F4Us swept the sky over the Solomon
Islands (q.v.). At the same time, fitted with conventional or napalm weapons, it became a bomber. In addition to the number
of Corsairs produced by Chance Vought, Goodyear Aircraft
Corporation produced over 4,000 planes, which were given the
designation FG-1. Brewster Corporation also produced Corsairs designated F3A-1. The successful use by corps pilots in
bombing and strafing missions kept the Corsair in production
long after its contemporary aircraft were obsolete. An adaptation of the F4U-5 was developed specifically for close support
of Allied ground forces during the Korean War (q.v.).

"COUGAR" (F9F-8). The latest in the Panther-Cougar series. The
first of these, the F9F-1, a straight-wing aircraft, saw considerable action as a naval fighter in Korea and was the first jet
fighter produced by Grumman Aircraft Company. The redesigned plane, designated Cougar, had severe swept back wings
and a much more powerful jet engine. The F9F-8 version had
a Pratt and Whitney improved J48 engine, giving the plane a
maximum speed of 712 miles per hour at a service ceiling of
42,000 feet. It had a range of 1,100 miles. The Cougar had four
nose mounted .20mm cannon and underwing racks for bombs,
rockets, or Sidewinder missiles. There were other versions of
the Cougar for training purposes and for photo reconnaissance. Adopted by the corps in the late 1950s, some Cougars
were still in service 20 years later.

"CRUSADER" (F8). Built by Vought Aircraft Company in 13 separate models, the first production model flew in September
1955. The following year it set a number of speed records, and
Col. John Glenn (q.v.), flying the photo reconnaissance model,
set the coast-to-coast speed record in July 1957 at an average
speed of 723 miles per hour. The model used most by the Marine Corps was the D version, first flown in February 1960 and
powered by an upgraded Pratt and Whitney turbojet engine,
giving it a maximum speed approaching Mach 2. The plane
could operate within a radius of 600 miles. An outstanding feature of the Crusader was its two-position, variable-incidence

wing. It had improved radar and auto pilot systems, and its normal armament was four .20mm cannon in the nose. It carried four Sidewinder missiles in pairs on the side of the fuselage. In 1967 the D model was upgraded and given the H model number. A total of 1,250 Crusaders of all types were built, of which 152 were the D type and 89 were H type. By 1970, Crusaders had amassed more than two million flying hours, many of those in naval and marine missions in Vietnam.

CUBA. The largest island of the West Indies lying just below the Tropic of Cancer with its northernmost part only 90 miles from Key West, Florida. The island is 760 miles long, and its width varies from 25 to 124 miles. It was among the last of Spain's imperial possessions in the Western Hemisphere and was the focus of U.S. policy that led eventually to the Spanish-American War (q.v.). In June 1898 a battalion of marines was landed at Guantanamo (q.v.) on the southeastern coast approximately 40 miles from Santiago, the chief objective of the U.S. expedition. Guantanamo was needed for a coaling station and site for the buildup of U.S. forces. Particularly important were the water wells located there. After suffering three days of sniping attacks, two companies of marines attacked the Spanish defensive positions on 14 June and routed the defenders at a loss of 22 casualties. Army troops of VIII Corps landed and then bore the brunt of the fighting in Cuba. At the conclusion of the war, a republic was proclaimed based largely on the U.S. model. However, the United States retained the base at Guantanamo and reserved the right to intervene if necessary to restore order.

In the fall of 1906 after a disputed election, Cuba was on the verge of civil war. The Cuban president, before resigning, asked for assistance, and 130 marines and sailors from the West Indies Squadron were landed at Havana on 13 September. Later other detachments were landed, ostensibly to protect U.S. property. Two marine battalions from the East Coast were brought in to support the provisional government headed by the U.S. secretary of war, William Howard Taft. These units formed the nucleus of the 1st Regiment. On 1 October a second regiment was landed. Shortly thereafter army units began to arrive, and the Marine Brigade was disbanded. However, the 1st Regiment stayed behind under army command. There was no fighting, but the last marines did not leave Cuba until January 1909. The marines returned in May 1912 to protect American interests during a rebellion of black citizens. Two regiments formed a Provisional Brigade, and marines were stationed in

26 towns as well as guarding the railroads. The reconstituted Cuban government gained full control by summer, and most of the marines left by late July.

CUSHMAN, ROBERT E. JR. 25th commandant, b. St. Paul, Minn., 24 Dec. 1914, d. 2 Jan. 1985. Cushman graduated from the Naval Academy and was commissioned a second lieutenant on 6 June 1935. After completing Basic School, he was posted to the 4th Marines in Shanghai in February 1936. Later he served in New York, Portsmouth, Quantico (q.v.), and finally in June 1941 took command of the marine detachment on the *Pennsylvania* and was on board during the Pearl Harbor (q.v.) attack. In May 1942 as a major, he joined the 9th Marines and left with his battalion for the Pacific in January 1943. In May he was appointed commanding officer of the 2d Battalion, a position he held for two years. He led this unit in the invasion of Bougainville (q.v.) and later won the Navy Cross (q.v.) on Guam (q.v.) for his defense of the marine lines during a major banzai charge. Returning to the United States, he was stationed for three years at Quantico before becoming head of the Amphibious Warfare branch in Washington. Later he was on the staff of the commander of U.S. Naval Forces in the Atlantic and Mediterranean. After a tour as director of plans and operations at the Armed Forces Staff College, he took command in July 1956 of the 2d Marines at Camp Lejeune (q.v.). He served Vice Pres. Richard Nixon for four years as an assistant for National Security Affairs. Following this post, he became assistant commander of the 3d Division on Okinawa (q.v.). In July 1962 as a major general, he was assistant chief of staff to the commandant in Washington. As a lieutenant general, he replaced Gen. Lewis Walt (q.v.) in June 1967 as commander of III MAF in Vietnam, a position he held until March 1969. Returning to the United States, he became deputy director of the Central Intelligence Agency. General Cushman replaced Gen. Leonard Chapman (q.v.) as commandant on 1 January 1972.

D

DA NANG. The second largest city in South Vietnam located at the mouth of the Han River in the province of Quang Nam. It has an excellent protected harbor. The first large-scale ground force committed to the Vietnam War (q.v.), the Marine 9th Expeditionary Brigade, arrived at Da Nang in March 1965. The marines soon extended their perimeter to include the airfield, one of only three capable of handling jet aircraft. Later when U.S. involvement increased, Da Nang became the major base of operations for the two divisions that made up III Marine Amphibious Force (MAF) as it assumed responsibility for I Corps' area extending to the Demilitarized Zone (DMZ) (q.v.). Reduction of U.S. forces by 1970 left only a fraction of the total marine presence in Vietnam, and in March the army took over defense of the Da Nang area. Most of the remaining marine units were ordered to either Okinawa (q.v.) or Camp Pendleton (q.v.) by the end of the year.

"DAUNTLESS" (SBD, SCOUT BOMBER, and A-24 DIVE BOMBER). This low-wing, two-seat cantilevered monoplane built by Douglas Aircraft Company was one of the planes that brought victory to U.S. forces in the Pacific during World War II. It was the standard dive bomber for the navy until being largely replaced by the SB2s in mid-1943. Powered by a Wright cyclone engine of 1,200 horsepower, it had a top speed of 255 miles per hour. The Dauntless had two .50-caliber guns firing through the propeller in addition to twin .50-calibers on a flexible mount operated by the radio operator/observer in the rear cockpit. Perforated dive brakes above and below the trailing edge of the wing enabled accurate, controlled dives. For dive bombing it carried one 1,000-pound bomb under the fuselage and two 100-pound bombs in wing racks. The most memorable action for the bomber was at Midway in June 1942, where navy pilots sank four Japanese aircraft carriers. First delivered to the corps in late 1940, it was used in all marine operations from Guadalcanal (q.v.) to the Philippines.

DEL VALLE, PEDRO A. b. San Juan, Puerto Rico, 28 Aug. 1893, d. 28 April 1978. Del Valle graduated from the Naval Academy in June 1915 and was commissioned a second lieutenant in the Marine Corps. After a course in the Marine Officers School, he was assigned to the 1st Provisional Brigade in Haiti (q.v.). He was involved in the landings in Santo Domingo (q.v.) in 1916 and pacification campaigns there. He served on board the *Texas* and participated with the British Grand Fleet during the surrender of the German fleet in 1919. Later he was assigned to Quantico (q.v.), served another tour of sea duty, was aide-de-camp to Gen. Joseph Pendleton (q.v.), and served on the Federal Traffic Board. In 1926 he was ordered to Haiti once again and served in the *Gendarmerie* for a three-year tour. He completed the Field Officers Corps, was then assigned briefly to Nicaragua (q.v.), served at sea, and took part in the operations resulting from the Cuban difficulties in 1933. From October 1935 until mid-1937, he was assistant military atache in Rome. As such he was an observer in Ethiopia during the Italian conquest.

After completing study at the Army War College, Del Valle was assigned to headquarters in Washington until March 1941 when he became commander of the 11th Marines (artillery). He continued as the regiment's commander during the 1st Division's action on Tulagi (q.v.), Florida, and Guadalcanal (q.v.). He became commanding general of all marine forces left on Guadalcanal from May to July 1943. After this action, he became president of the corps' Equipment Board. In April 1944 he assumed command of corps artillery of III Amphibious Corps, and his big guns supported the invasion of Guam (q.v.). Later as a major general he was appointed commander of the 1st Division and led it in the invasion and desperate fighting on Okinawa (q.v.) from April until July 1945. After the war, Del Valle was designated inspector general and director of personnel, a position he held until his retirement as a lieutenant general in January 1948. He later had a distinguished business career as an executive with the communications giant, ITT.

DEMILITARIZED ZONE (DMZ). The first of these was established in Korea (q.v.) following the agreement between the United Nations and North Korea. It was a 2.5-mile wide strip separating North and South Korea. A second DMZ was created after the Geneva Accords in 1954 to divide North and South Vietnam along the 17th parallel. It was designed to be temporary pending elections to unite Vietnam (q.v.) and was later viewed as a permanent division by the U.S. government, which committed over one-half million men to aid in the defense of South Vietnam. The DMZ was continually violated during the war by North Vietnamese forces as they moved into I Corps' zone defended by the marines who were handicapped by the no pursuit policy established early in the war by the Joint Chiefs of Staff in Washington.

DEMOBILIZATION (Post–World War II). General demobilization of all the armed forces began immediately after the defeat of Japan in September 1945. The corps deactivated the 4th Division in November, the 3d in December, followed by the 5th in January 1946 and the 6th the next month. The 2d Division was brought from Japan in June 1946 and permanently assigned to Camp Lejeune (q.v.) along with its air support, the 2d Air Wing. The 1st Division was located at Camp Pendleton (q.v.), with the 1st Air Wing at El Toro. During the half-decade after the war, Congress and the administration cut back all military expenditures drastically, the legal size of the Marine Corps being set at 107,000 men. In actuality, the numbers of active duty marines were far less than this. At the beginning of the Korean War (q.v.), the corps had dwindled to only 74,000 men.

DERNA. A town on the north coast of Cyrenaica in modern day Libya. In early 1805 an expedition to take Derna, the largest town in the province of Barca, was mounted by William Eaton, the U.S. "naval agent" in the Mediterranean. He decided on this adventure to help end the depredations of the Barbary pirates (q.v.) directed by the bey of Tripoli, who demanded tribute from the United States and other European states. Eaton's idea was to overthrow the bey and put a rival on the throne. Derna was the first target of the expedition composed of a mixed Arab and Christian irregular force of 500 men. The core element of the "army" was the marine unit of seven men commanded by Lt. Presley O'Bannon (q.v.). After marching more than 600 miles across the desert from Egypt, Eaton, O'Bannon, the marines, and a portion of the irregulars assaulted the earth works defending the town on 27 April 1805. They routed the 800 defenders in a two-hour skirmish. O'Bannon then raised the U.S. flag over the town. Later Eaton's troops repelled a counterattack by the bey's forces. Six weeks after Derna was taken, a treaty was signed with the bey favorable to the U.S., and Derna was surrendered. This episode became the basis for "the Shores of Tripoli" in the Marine Hymn (q.v.).

DESERT CALM. The total defeat of the Iraqi army during Desert Storm (q.v.) meant that there was little reason to continue a major Marine Corps presence in Kuwait (q.v.). The retrograde movement referred to as Desert Calm began on 10 March 1991 when the 7th Expeditionary Brigade left Saudi Arabia. Soon the 5th had departed only to be diverted to Bangladesh to provide humanitarian aid to the area devastated by a typhoon. The 24th Expeditionary unit was dispatched to northern Iraq to provide aid to the Kurdish people of Dohuk Province. The quick movement of troops back home can be seen in the reduction of force strength from 84,498 on 28 February to only 19,743 on 16 April. As the 1st Division moved out of Kuwait, its place was taken by the 2d Division and remained in a blocking position south of Al Jahara. It, too, began a retrograde movement in late March, and the bulk of its troops were gone by early June. The same downsizing was done by the air wings. The last two line squadrons had departed from Sharkh Isa Airfield in Bahrain on 17 May. A notable feature of the movement from the area of operations was that it was done by units, thus maintaining their integrity.

DESERT SHIELD. The continuing tensions in the Persian Gulf area escalated into a full-scale, short-lived war between Iraq (q.v.) and Kuwait (q.v.) in August 1990. The Iraqi army had little trouble brushing aside sporadic resistance to occupy all of Kuwait. Fears of continued Iraqi operations aimed at Saudi Arabia and the smaller coastal states convinced the U.S. government in concert with Arab and European allies to intervene to contain further Iraqi expansion. The U.S. Central Command became the major military element in this proposed defensive action code-named Desert Shield. The overall commander of U.S. and later all allied forces was Gen. H. Norman Schwarzkopf, whose staff coordinated the movement to and the defense of Saudi Arabia and who later commanded the short-lived and very successful offensive operations that destroyed the Iraqi army.

The marine command was notified almost immediately after the decision to intervene and the 7th Marine Expeditionary Brigade (MEB) (q.v.) from Southern California was airlifted to the Middle East, arriving at Dhahran on 14 August. This advance element of Lt. Gen. Walter Boomer's (q.v.) I Expeditionary Force (MEF) (q.v.) was deployed north of the important port of Jubayal. Although at first chronically short of armor, the brigade was fully combat ready within two weeks. The 4th Expeditionary Brigade from the East Coast began its long journey to Saudi Arabia on 17 August, followed soon after by the 1st Brigade from Hawaii. By the end of September, the Expeditionary Force had grown to 30,000 men. The 1st and 7th Brigades were joined into the 1st Marine Division, which was the centerpiece of the 1st Expeditionary Force. The firepower of the force was augmented at first by the British 7th Armored Brigade and later the British 1st Armored Division. However, before ground operations began, this unit was reassigned. Its place was taken by the Tiger Brigade of the U.S. 1st Armored Division, which was attached to the 2d Division. The addition of the brigade's 116 Abrams (M1A1) tanks (q.v.) gave the MEF a total of 257 tanks. By mid-December, General Boomer had another Expeditionary Force, the 2d MEF built around the 2d Division. In addition, the corps began calling up selected reservists. By the end of the war, 31,000 reservists had been activated.

The air component of the 1st MEF was the 3d Air Wing and that of the 2d was the 2d Air Wing. Each of these, although only a small part of the massive air buildup, was a formidable force with F-18 Hornet (q.v.) fighter/attack planes, A6E Intruder bombers, EA-6B Prowler electronic support aircraft, and AV-8B Harriers (q.v.) in addition to its helicopter potential. Marine air was under the overall control of the air force, but there was a general understanding that the marine air wings' primary responsibility was to support the marine ground units. Anything beyond those tactical boundaries would be determined by the air force. The offensive air war began on 18 January 1991 and proceeded in four phases. During the first, marine aircraft participated directly in the strikes on strategic targets. By the time the ground war began, the marine wings had reverted primarily to tactical strikes.

The marine combat units had been given the task of protecting the vital coastal areas of Saudi Arabia, an area approximately 100 miles long. During this time, there was extensive training with the Saudi army and national guard units that would be a part of any direct advance on Kuwait City. In early January the bulk of the marine forces moved northward, with the 1st Division occupying an area closer to the southern Kuwait border approximately 60 miles west of Mishab. The 2d Division occupied a position to the northwest. The Iraqi high command had assumed that the marine units would be the spearhead of a direct attack on their fortified lines. Marine exercises were designed to continue this deception, although the decision had already been made to use the U.S. Army VII and XVIII Airborne Corps and French units on the extreme left to execute a wide flanking movement to roll up the enemy's position and cut off the Iraqi line of supply and routes of retreat. The deception continued until the land phase of the war actually began and it caused the Iraqi commanders to maintain two full corps composed of 17 divisions in southern and eastern Kuwait.

Immediately after the occupation of Kuwait, the Iraqis had constructed a strong static defense system. That portion along the southern border consisted of a double band of barriers, minefields, and primary defense fortifications. They had also constructed a coastal defense system of trenches, bunkers, and mine fields. Defending the approaches to Kuwait City were five divisions of the Iraqi III Corps inside the second defense belt. With Soviet-built T54, T55, and T62 tanks and a large number of 150mm guns, they appeared at least on paper to be a formidable force. Prior to the onset of the main air campaign, little hostile action occurred. The bulk of this concerned artillery duels, with the marine 155mm Howitzers proving much more accurate than the Iraqi gunners because of target identification by the Global Positioning Satellite. (See also Desert Storm.)

DESERT STORM. With the buildup of allied forces in Desert Shield (q.v.) almost complete and Saddam Hussein showing no inclination to withdraw from Kuwait (q.v.), Gen. H. Norman Schwarzkopf ordered Phase I of the offensive war to begin. Even before the first concentrated air strikes of 18 January 1991, occurred it was obvious that total aerial superiority would soon be achieved. The allied air armada numbered over 2,400 planes of all types. At first the priority targets were communication centers and fixed and mobile SCUD missile sites, which were struck with smart bombs and Tomahawk missiles. As the air war progressed, bridges, bunkers, and general forward-defense systems were struck. Tanks and trucks became tempting targets for the prowling air force, navy, and marine pilots. By the time the ground offensive began, much of the Iraqi defenses had been shattered, and the morale of the ordinary Iraqi soldier was very low.

The first serious ground action by the marines was in response to the Iraqi attack on the Saudi town of Khafji. On the night of 30 January advance Iraqi elements moved into the town, followed soon after by an estimated 4,000 troops supported by 80 tanks. Units of the 1st Division did not launch an immediate counterattack since for political reasons it was decided to allow the Saudi army to recapture its own town. On the 31st units of the Saudi National Guard supported by the marines began the attack on Khafji. Air units, particularly the A-10s, provided devastating fire on the Iraqi tanks, and the marine artillery blasted the all but defenseless enemy troops. The recapture of the town had portents for the future. First it helped cement the still fragile alliance with the Arab coalition. It also indicated clearly the reluctance of the Iraqi troops to fight. Large numbers surrendered at the first opportunity.

General Schwarzkopf's plan was to begin Desert Storm after there appeared to be few viable targets. His plan called for the marine units along with Joint Force Command (JFC) troops to invade Kuwait and liberate Kuwait City. The army's VII Corps in the center of the allied line would have the major responsibility of engaging the best Iraqi troops, the Republican Guard. The key element in his plan was to have the XVIII Airborne Corps, the British 1st Armoured, and the French units make a wide flanking movement far to the west of the main Iraqi forces. They would then wheel eastward and, if all went well, block the enemy who would be retreating from the army and marine direct attacks. His deception worked. The main Iraqi forces remained relatively stationary, and Saddam Hussein, the military dictator of Iraq, and his generals left their right flank unguarded.

The first blow of Desert Storm was launched by the marines in conjunction with JFC-East forces early on G-day, 24 February. The 1st Division was located adjacent to the elbow where the border with Kuwait turns north. The 16,000-man 2d Division had been surreptitiously moved to the left flank of the 1st while dummy headquarters and positions had been maintained further east—another ruse that fooled the Iraqis. The axis of advance of the marine and adjacent JFC units was northeast toward Kuwait City. There was an overwhelming pre-assault bombardment by marine artillery firing at ranges up to 32,000 meters, and the big guns of the battleships *Wisconsin* and *Missouri* pounded Iraqi defenses in the east. Between 0400 and 0530 mine breaching teams were at work clearing paths through the minefields. There was only minimal artillery fire from the Iraqis since the airstrikes of the previous weeks had destroyed gun positions and the Iraqi communications net was in shambles.

Marines of the 1st Division found that the first defense belt had been abandoned. Firepower from tanks, artillery, and the ever present tactical air force shattered the second defense belt. The two main offensive units, Task Forces Ripper and Papa Bear, drove inland, bypassing large numbers of Iraqi ground and tank crews. By the end of G-day, they had captured al-Jaber airfield and al-Burgon oil field, which had been set afire by the Iraqis. Further to the east the five brigades of the JFC made good progress against the weakening defense of an Iraqi division. Approximately 25 kilometers west of the 1st Division's assault the 2d Division, augmented by the army's Tiger Brigade, punched through the Iraqi 14th Division. Once through the second belt of defenses, the division fanned out northwest of al-Jaber air base and enveloped the Iraqi 7th Division.

During this first day of action, the marines had shattered the Iraqi 7th, 14th, and 29th Divisions. When the Iraqi's Soviet-made tanks did engage, they were systematically destroyed by either superior gunnery of the U.S. tankers or the omnipresent allied air support. The largest tank battle in Marine Corps history was joined at approximately 0430 on 25 February when two Iraqi brigades emerged from the al-Burgon oil fields and was met by the Abrams M1A1 (q.v.) and M60 tanks (q.v.) of the 1st Division. In one engagement 34 of 35 enemy tanks were either destroyed or disabled. In a series of actions lasting until midday, the Iraqis were defeated by a combination of tank main guns using depleted uranium rounds combined with antitank fire at very close ranges.

Even before the Iraqi counterattack had been dealt with the Marine Expeditionary Force (MEF) (q.v.) was being repositioned for an attack upon Kuwait City. This called for clearing al-Jaber air base and seizing a series of concrete-block buildings in front of the 2d Division named the Ice Tray by the marines. By midafternoon these objectives had been taken after the MEF received sporadic Iraqi artillery and tank fire. The main objective of the 2d Division then became the area around the main supply route intersections near al-Jahrah, 30 kilometers west of the city. The key objective for the 1st Division was the International Airport south of the city. Before these attacks planned for 0600 on the 26th could be launched, night sensors indicated a large amount of vehicle movement near the city. Fearing a large-scale counterattack, General Boomer (q.v.) ordered all available all-weather Intruders, Harriers (q.v.), and FA-18 Hornets (q.v.) to attack. There were to be no counterattacks; the Iraqis were attempting to flee the city. Flying in very bad weather, the marine flyers joined by others from Central Command relentlessly attacked the retreating Iraqis along the aptly named "Highway to Hell," which soon became choked with burning vehicles. Along the main supply route to Safwan, Iraq, were thousands of destroyed or abandoned vehicles of all types.

The 2d Division's first objective on the morning of the 26th was to seize water reservoirs and orchard areas on the left flank of the 1st Division. Then at 1200 the final attack began. The Tiger Brigade on the left raced northward into open desert area, seized much of the Mutla Ridge, and fought and won two separate tank battles. By evening it had sealed off two major highway junctions north of al-Jahrah. Meanwhile, the two regiments of the 2d, the 6th and 8th Marines had also reached their objectives and controlled the freeway south of the town. Little resistance was given by the Iraqis, who surrendered by the hundreds to the army brigade and marines. To the east the 1st Division, divided into two task forces and covered in part by the big guns of the *Missouri*, braved the smoke and fires of the oil field and moved into the southern outskirts of the city, and it was in position to assault the airport, which was occupied during the early morning hours of the 27th.

The marine victories were spectacular, but the main action of the war in VII and XVIII Corps' areas was even more so. The plan of attack with the wide-ranging tanks of XVIII Corps and the British and French units had broken Iraqi resistance totally, and what was left of the Iraqi army, including the Republican Guard, was in full retreat. Soon these units were pinned south of the Tigris River where they could have easily been totally destroyed. In the area of I MEF the decision had been made to confer the honor of capturing the city on Arab coalition forces. During the night of the 26th–27th, composite Arab units passed through 1st Division lines while at the same time Egyptian and Syrian units went through the 2d Division. By noon of the 27th, these two attacks linked up near the center of the city. A planned attack by the 2d Division to drive through to the coast proved unnecessary since all fighting within the city had ceased by midafternoon. However, one marine unit, a reconnaissance pathfinder team, on the late afternoon of the 26th found the route to the American Embassy open and entered the compound just before dark.

All plans for further forward displacement and combat became unnecessary when Pres. George Bush announced the cessation of hostilities to begin at 0800 on 28 February. This political action saved the remaining units of the Iraqi army from total destruction. All units of the coalition had performed extremely well. The Iraqi air force was never a factor, and U.S. navy, marine, and air force pilots had all but destroyed the Iraqi defense system even before the ground war began. The fears of a gas attack and losses from Iraqi SCUD missiles proved groundless. Marine units had fully justified the confidence placed in them by Central Command. Even after the armistice, Regimental Landing Group 5 and Aircraft Group 50 continued low intensity conflict tactics for 10 days in the oil fields and Al Wafrat Forest. There could be no adequate count of enemy casualties. However, the marines had taken 22,308 prisoners. For the marines this most spectacular victory in two generations was gained with minimal cost. There were 24 battle deaths and 92 wounded in action; non-battle deaths equaled those killed in action, and there were 46 nonbattle injuries. (See also Desert Shield.)

DEVEREUX, JAMES P. S. b. Cabana, Cuba, 20 Feb. 1903, d. Baltimore, Md., 5 Aug. 1988. Devereux attended the Army and Navy Preparatory School in Washington, D.C., and later a school in Switzerland before joining the corps in July 1923. He was commissioned a second lieutenant in February 1925. The next year he was in charge of a mail detachment in New York before being transferred to Nicaragua (q.v.) where he served until early 1927. After a brief tour at sea, he was posted to China (q.v.) where as a first lieutenant he commanded the Mounted Detachment of the Legation Guard at Peking (q.v.). Returning to the United States, Devereux served for a year at Quantico (q.v.) and later in 1933 was assigned to the Coast Artillery School at Fort Monroe. Throughout 1936 he instructed at the Base Defense Weapons School at Quantico and then served on board the *Utah* before being posted to the marine base at San Diego. In January 1941 he was ordered to Pearl Harbor (q.v.). Later that year he took command of the Wake Island (q.v.) Detachment, 1st Defense Battalion, consisting of 449 marines under the overall command of Rear Adm. Winfield Cunningham. His vastly outnumbered marines repulsed the first Japanese attempts to land on 11 December 1941. His gunners and the small air contingent sank two destroyers and damaged two cruisers and a destroyer. Returning with a much larger force supported by aircraft carriers, the Japanese on 23 December made a landing and despite heroic actions forced the marines to surrender. Devereux spent the remainder of the war as a prisoner of the Japanese on Hokkaido.

After the war, Devereux was promoted to colonel to date from 1 November 1942 to keep him on a par with his contemporaries. After a brief tour in Washington, he was ordered to Quantico and in September 1946 he was a student at the Senior Course in Amphibious Warfare. In 1947 he was posted to Camp Pendleton (q.v.) to serve with the 1st Division. He retired from the Marine Corps in August 1948 and was advanced to the rank of brigadier general. He later entered politics and was elected to the House of Representatives.

DH-4. A single-engine, two-man biplane bomber. Designed in 1916 by Geoffrey de Havilland for the British firm of Airco, it was manufactured in large numbers (4,846) in the United

States. It was named the "Liberty Plane" after the Liberty 400 engine that powered the U.S. version. It had a maximum speed of 140 miles per hour, a ceiling of 22,000 feet, and a range of 600 miles. Normally it was armed with two machine guns and could carry a maximum of 460 pounds of bombs. It was the basic aircraft for 13 squadrons of the American Expeditionary Force (AEF) during World War I (q.v.). It continued in service in the United States until 1932. The Marine Corps utilized the DH-4 in all the operations undertaken during the many interventions in the affairs of the Caribbean and Central American states during the 1920s.

DIAMOND, LELAND "OLD LOU." b. Bedford, Ohio, 30 May 1890, d. Great Lakes Training Center, 20 Sept. 1951. One of the legendary "Old Breed," at age 27 Diamond enlisted in the corps in July 1917 after having been a railroad worker. In January 1918 he was ordered to France and as a corporal in the 6th Marines participated in the battles of Chateau-Thierry, Belleau Wood (q.v.), Aisne-Marne, Saint-Mihiel (q.v.), and the Meuse-Argonne (q.v.). Promoted to sergeant, he was briefly in the army of occupation before returning to the United States. In August 1919 he was discharged from the corps, but two years later he reenlisted and by 1925 was once again a sergeant. He was posted to China as a part of the 4th Marines during the beginning of the Sino-Japanese conflict in Shanghai. Now a gunnery sergeant, Diamond returned briefly to the United States in June 1933 before being sent once more to China to join the 4th, where he served until February 1937. He was promoted to master gunnery sergeant that same year. He was assigned to the Philadelphia Depot of Supplies, where he helped design a new infantry pack.

Diamond, the archetypical noncommissioned marine officer, got his chance at a real war when he embarked with the 5th Marines for New Zealand in 1942. As a member of the 2d Battalion of the 1st Division, he first saw action at Tulagi (q.v.) and later on Guadalcanal (q.v.). As an expert with both the 60- and 81mm mortars, a story circulated through the corps that he had put a mortar shell down the smokestack of a Japanese cruiser. In all probability he merely harassed the cruiser into seeking deeper water.

After two months on Guadalcanal, the 52-year-old Diamond was evacuated to a hospital in the New Hebrides. Chafing at the inactivity, he somehow got orders to rejoin his unit. Arriving at Guadalcanal, he learned that the 1st Division had been moved to Australia. Never daunted, he managed to catch up with the division then located 1,500 miles away. However, he had seen his last combat and was returned to the United States in July 1943. At first he was assigned to Parris Island (q.v.) Recruit Depot and then later in June 1945 to Camp Lejeune (q.v.) as a member of the 5th Training Battalion. He retired five months later and returned to his home in Toledo, Ohio, leaving behind a host of stories about "the Honker" and "Old Lou."

DIVISION. At the outset of World War II (q.v.), a division was the largest unit in the Marine Corps. Organized with the army's triangular division as a model, the first two divisions were formed from the 1st and 2d Brigades in February 1942. The 1st participated in the Guadalcanal (q.v.) operation while the 2d was involved in the assault on Tarawa (q.v.). The demands of the Pacific war resulted ultimately in the creation of six divisions, each of which was involved in two or more major operations. By mid-1944 each division contained approximately 16,000 men. It included three infantry regiments each with a targeted size of 3,100 men, an artillery regiment, an engineering battalion, and headquarters and service companies. The committed divisions were under the overall command of the commander Fleet Marine Force (q.v.), Pacific, and after Guadalcanal were organized into corps of two or more divisions. After the war, the Marine Corps was greatly reduced to a targeted size of 107,000 men with only two active divisions each with its companion air wing. Each division was understrength in June 1950 when the Korean War (q.v.) began so that only a brigade of 6,500 men from the 1st Division could be sent at first. Later after the callup of reserves, the 1st Division was fleshed out and took part in the Inchon (q.v.) landing, the retreat from the Chosin (q.v.) Reservoir, and all major campaigns as a part of X Corps. During the Vietnam War (q.v.), two marine divisions were used and operated for five years under the operational command of the III Marine Amphibious Force in the far northern area of South Vietnam. With the reorganization in the 1890s into Marine Air Ground Task Force (MAGTF) (q.v.) units, the division remained a key element. The 1st and 2d Divisions during the Desert Storm (q.v.) operation were composited with their air elements into the 1st Marine Expeditionary Force (MEF) (q.v.).

DOMINICAN REPUBLIC (SANTO DOMINGO). The Cold War intruded in another area of the Caribbean. The Dominican Republic had been quiescent under the harsh dictatorial rule of Leonidas Trujillo, an ex–*Guardia* officer who had ruled the country since 1930. Trujillo was assassinated in May 1961. Afterward there was a contest for power between the traditional elites and leftist groups who wanted basic reforms. The United States sent naval and marine units to demonstrate offshore in 1961 and again in 1963 to show support for the presumably anti-Communist government. That had been enough then, but in the spring of 1965 a full-scale civil war began. The government forces lost most of the capital city of Santo Domingo, the president resigned, and the U.S. government, fearful of a hostile Communist government similar to Cuba's (q.v.), decided to act.

At first the main goal of the intervention was to rescue approximately 3,000 U.S. and foreign nationals. To effect this, a landing zone for helicopters west of the city was established on 27 April. Later when the rebels threatened the embassy, more marines were brought in to afford protection to both sites. The loyalist troops were concentrated near the airport and their commander asked for direct U.S. support. This request was approved, and on the 28th 500 marines reinforced the regular Dominican troops. The next day a battalion of the 6th Marines landed. Within four days there were three battalions ashore and one on board ship in reserve. On 29 April the first elements of the army's 82d Airborne began to arrive, and the command of U.S. troops passed to an army general.

This show of force overawed the rebels and spurred the loyalist troops to retake the city by 7 May. The Organization of American States (OAS) agreed to create an inter-American peace force, and the first of the Latin American troops arrived on 25 May. Marine strength, which had reached a peak of 8,000 men, now rapidly declined as the withdrawal began the day after the arrival of the OAS multinational troops. All were gone from the island by 6 June.

The operation had gone smoothly, but nine marines were killed and 30 wounded. Any combat type of experience learned in the Dominican Republic would be sorely needed in another part of the world—Vietnam (q.v.)—where the U.S. government decided to intervene to stop what was believed to be a Communist threat to Asia. (See also Santo Domingo.)

"DUKW." Called "duck" by the U.S. Army and the Marine Corps, this was a 2.5 ton, six-wheel drive amphibian vehicle built on a General Motors truck chassis designed in 1942. It was

31 feet long by eight feet wide and could carry 25 troops, 12 stretchers or 2.5 tons of cargo that could be unloaded by an integral A frame. It had a maximum land speed of 50 miles per hour and a top speed of five knots in calm water. DUKWs were difficult to maintain, and on shore the topside was six feet from the ground, while in the water they could have a free board of only 18 inches. Despite such drawbacks, they were in great demand. By 1945, 21,000 DUKWs had been built, most of which went to the army in the European theater. They were not used in the Pacific until January 1944 when 100 were used to land Howitzers and stores during the campaign in the Marshall Islands (q.v.). Even then, most DUKW companies belonged to the army. The corps had only one DUKW company at Iwo Jima (q.v.).

E

EDSON, MERRITT A. "RED MIKE." b. Rutland, Vt., 25 April 1897, d. Washington, D.C., 14 Aug. 1955. Edson left the University of Vermont for a commission in the corps at the outbreak of World War I (q.v.) and served in France from September 1918 to December 1919. During the 1920s he qualified as an aviator and became closely associated with the development of marksmanship in the corps, becoming a member of the National Match Rifle Team in 1921. He later coached the Marine National Rifle and Pistol Teams. In 1928 Captain Edson was ordered to Nicaragua (q.v.), where rebels led by Sandino had rebelled against the government. Supplied by air, he pursued the rebels 400 miles up the Coco River during July and August at the head of a strong contingent and engaged in two sharp encounters, but Sandino evaded capture.

By 1941 Edson was a lieutenant colonel commanding a battalion of the 5th Marines. Shortly afterward he became involved in the organization and training of the 1st Raider Battalion, the prototype of every Raider and Ranger unit of World War II (q.v.). He saw his first action in World War II as commander of this unit and led it in capturing Tulagi (q.v.) Island at the same time other marine units landed on Guadalcanal (q.v.). Moving to Guadalcanal, the Raiders, reinforced by what was left of a parachute battalion, held the key ridge one mile south of Henderson Field (q.v.). On the 12th and 13th of September they threw back a series of counterattacks by superior Japanese forces and thus blunted the most serious threat to the Henderson perimeter. For his actions along Bloody Ridge, Edson received the Medal of Honor (q.v.). Promoted to colonel, he later led a force of five battalions against the Japanese west of the airfield. By the fall of 1943, he had become chief of staff of the 2d Marine Division and helped plan the Tarawa (q.v.) operation. After the initial assault on Betio, he came ashore on the evening of 21 November 1943 and took command of all troops on the atoll. He was promoted to brigadier general after this action and participated in the Saipan (q.v.) operation. Following this he became chief of staff, Fleet Marine Force (q.v.), Pacific. After 44 months in the Pacific, he returned to the United States and held positions in the office of Chief of Naval Operations, Marine Corps Headquarters, in Washington. After retirement from the corps, Edson, then a major general, served as commissioner of public safety in Vermont and later as president of the National Rifle Association.

ELLIOTT, GEORGE F. 10th commandant, b. Eutaw, Ala., 30 Nov. 1846, d. Washington, D.C., 4 Nov. 1931. Elliott attended West Point for two years and in October 1870 was appointed second lieutenant in the Marine Corps. There followed years of typical shore and sea duty. Elliott served with the naval expedition to Panama (q.v.) in 1885 and in 1894 led a marine unit to guard the legation in Seoul (q.v.), Korea. During the Spanish-American War (q.v.), commanding a company, Captain Elliott landed on 10 June 1898 at Guantanamo Bay. Four days later he was ordered to take Cuzco Well, the main source of water for the Spanish defending the bay. Operating with two companies and guerrilla reinforcements, he routed approximately 500 Spanish troops with only 22 casualties. As a major, he landed with a battalion on 21 September 1899 at Cavite in the Philippines to support the battalion already there. Soon appointed a lieutenant colonel, his men in concert with army units attacked an insurgent held town south of Cavite and captured it.

Elliott became the 10th commandant as a brigadier general in October 1903, commanding a corps grown to 7,800 men. He actively took part in the Panama (q.v.) operation in January 1904, bringing two battalions to support the units already there. At the same time marines were landing in Santo Domingo (q.v.). Elliott, with a brigade, stayed on in Panama until the new Panamanian government had taken over, leaving in February. As commandant, Elliott continued to fight for more recognition for the corps. His perseverance was rewarded when presidents Roosevelt and Taft, by executive orders, clarified the expanded duties of the corps. Also Congress created the permanent rank of major general for the commandant of the corps. Elliott was appointed to that rank in May 1908. He retired at age 64 on 30 November 1910.

ELLIS, EARL H. "PETE." b. 1880, Pratt, Kans., d. 12 May 1923, Koror, Palau, Western Caroline Islands. Ellis enlisted in the Marine Corps in Chicago in 1900 and received a commission as a second lieutenant. An exemplary officer, he advanced rapidly, attended the Naval War College in 1911, and later served as an instructor. While there he delivered a number of papers illustrating the importance of naval bases. In 1914 he surveyed islands near Puerto Rico for advanced base exercises. The following year he was ordered to Guam where his ideas of the importance of amphibious tactics became fixed. Until the U.S. entry into World War I (q.v.), he served in Washington, D.C., Quantico (q.v.), and Philadelphia. He arrived in France in the spring of 1918 with the 4th Brigade and distinguished himself in the planning for and execution of the attack on Blanc Mont. For his actions in the war, he received the *Croix de Guerre* and the Navy Cross (q.v.).

Ordered to headquarters in Washington, D.C., in 1920, Ellis completed his famous, prophetic report "Advanced Base Operations in Micronesia" in which he predicted war and outlined the island bases necessary to defeat Japan. Convinced that Japan was fortifying the islands held under League of Nations mandate, he took a leave in 1921 to travel to the Pacific to ascertain the defenses of various Japanese held islands. He visited Samoa, Fiji, Australia, the Philippines, and Japan before traveling to the Marshall (q.v.) and Caroline Islands, where he made detailed notes and charts. Already hospitalized for acute alcoholism before leaving Japan, he became gravely ill at Koror and died there in 1923. His death, a major loss to the Marine Corps, led to speculation in the United States that he had been poisoned by the Japanese, which was not borne out by the evidence but nevertheless persisted through World War II (q.v.).

EMBLEM. The marine emblem was adapted from that of the British Royal Marines in November 1868. The globe with the Western Hemisphere facing outward is at the center of the device. Behind it is a fouled anchor, and surmounting the globe is an American bald eagle with a ribbon in its beak on which the motto "Semper Fidelis" is inscribed.

ENIWETOK. A circular atoll in the Marshall Islands (q.v.) located approximately 400 miles northwest of Kwajalein (q.v.). There are three major islands in the atoll: Engebi in the north, Parry in the east, and Eniwetok in the south. The plan for invading the islands during World War II (q.v.), code-named Catchpole, was for the 22d Marines, a part of the 1st Provisional Brigade, to land on Engebi, which was believed to be the most heavily defended. At the same time, the army's 106th Regiment of the 27th Division would land on Eniwetok. Parry would then be occupied. Two small islands near Engebi were seized, artillery emplaced there, and the howitzers added their plunging fire to the naval bombardment. The 22d landed on Engebi on 19 February 1944. There were few fixed defenses, naval gunnery and air strikes had neutralized the defenders, and within six hours the marines had control of the island. Only 16 prisoners were taken from a 1,200-man garrison. The army regiment met with much more resistance, and one marine battalion was sent in to help clear the island. By midday of the 21st, Eniwetok was declared secure. Parry Island, which U.S. intelligence had believed to be unoccupied, instead had a garrison of 1,300 men. However, under heavy covering fire from the navy, two marine battalions were able to secure the island by the 22d. In the next two months other small islands in the Marshalls were occupied. The airstrip on Engebi was lengthened, and another larger airstrip was constructed on Eniwetok. The United States had also gained possession of another major fleet anchorage that proved invaluable in supporting the operations in the Mariana Islands (q.v.).

ERSKINE, GRAVES B. b. Columbia, La., 28 June 1897, d. Washington, D.C., 21 May 1973. Erskine graduated from Louisiana State University in 1917 then went on active duty as a second lieutenant and sailed for France in January 1918 as a member of the 6th Marines. He was wounded during the action at Chateau-Thierry (q.v.) but returned to action to take part in the Saint-Mihiel (q.v.) offensive. He was seriously wounded in this campaign and was returned to the United States in October. After recovering, he was posted to the 1st Brigade in Santo Domingo (q.v.). Later after sea duty, he returned to Santo Domingo as a member of the 2d Brigade. He was ordered to Quantico (q.v.) in 1924 and later attended the Army Infantry School at Fort Benning, from which he returned to Quantico as an instructor in the Department of Tactics. In the spring of 1928, he was sent to Nicaragua where he served in its National Guard.

In the 1930s Erskine was an instructor at the Basic School, attended the army's Command and General Staff School, served at Quantico, was a part of the marine detachment at Peking (q.v.), and served as executive officer of the 5th Marines. At the beginning of World War II, he was chief of staff, Amphibious Force, Atlantic. From September 1942 for two years, he held successive chief of staff positions in the Amphibious Training staff, the V Amphibious Corps, and Fleet Marine Force (q.v.), Pacific. In this latter capacity he was involved in the Saipan (q.v.) campaign, after which he received command of the 3d Division and was responsible for the mopping-up campaign on Guam (q.v.). In February 1945 he led the division in the bloody campaign on Iwo Jima (q.v.). Giving up command of the division in October, Erskine returned to the United States, where he was appointed by Congress to head the Retraining and Reemployment Administration. Upon his release from that post in mid-1947, he assumed command of Camp Pendleton (q.v.) and later that of the 1st Division. He held a second command at this time, deputy commander Fleet Marine Force, Pacific. In June 1950 he was appointed chief of the military group for the Joint Defense-State Departments Survey Mission to Southeast Asia. Later that year he became commander of the Department of the Pacific. In July 1951 as a four-star general Erskine took command of Fleet Marine Force, Atlantic, where he commanded two air wings, one division, and assorted attached troops, a total of over 50,000 men. He retired in June 1953 to accept the position as assistant to the secretary of defense and director of special operations.

F

"FALCON" (A-3). Built by Curtiss Aircraft Company, this observation biplane was first flown in 1924. The early models were designated O-1B. In future years it was fitted with engines different from the original Liberty power plant. The A-3 version produced for the U.S. Army and Marine Corps had a Pratt and Whitney Wasp engine, giving it a top speed of 147 miles per hour. The A-3 was planned to be more than an observation platform. The basic Falcon had been changed so that the A-3 was a formidable ground attack aircraft. It had two .30-caliber guns firing through the propeller, two others mounted under the wings, and twin Lewis guns operated by the observer in the rear cockpit. In addition, 25-pound fragmentation bombs could be carried in racks under the wings.

FIJI. An island complex in the South Pacific composed of 255 separate islands, 80 of which are inhabited. The main islands of Viti Levu and Vanua Levu in the 19th century were main bases for whalers. Elements of the navy based at Valparaiso, Chile, acted as protectors of U.S. whalers and traders in the Fiji complex. Marines and sailors were landed in 1855 and again in 1858 because of conflicts with the native population. This ceased to be a problem after the islands were declared a British protectorate in 1874. During World War II (q.v.), Fiji became a major staging base for action in the South Pacific areas beginning with the buildup for the Guadalcanal (q.v.) invasion of August 1942.

FLEET MARINE FORCE. The new name given in 1933 for the old Marine Expeditionary Force and it became an integral part of the U.S. Fleet. The 1st Brigade of the force was based at Quantico (q.v.) while the 2d was at San Diego. During World War II (q.v.), a duality was established in the force, with one section for the Atlantic and one for the Pacific. The Pacific was the most important. The headquarters for the Pacific was at Pearl Harbor (q.v.). For each individual action in the Central Pacific, there were amphibious corps subordinate to the Commanding General Fleet Marine Force.

FORT FISHER. Located between the Cape Fear River and the Atlantic Ocean, this fort was a formidable earthwork erected by the Confederates to guard the port of Wilmington, North Carolina. It had parapets 25 feet thick and 20 feet high, mounted 44 heavy guns, and had a garrison of 1,400. In December 1864 the Union decided to capture the fort and close the port to blockade runners. The first attempt, a joint army-navy venture undertaken on 24 December, was unsuccessful largely because the naval bombardment had not neutralized the Confederate guns. A second attempt was made on 15 January 1865 under army command. The plan was for a large-scale naval bombardment lasting two days followed by a landing of 2,000 men, 400 of whom were marines from the naval squadron. Meanwhile, the army units would attack from the land side. The marines were in a supporting role; they were to land, dig in, and cover the sailors with rifle fire. The sailors were to attack directly at the earthworks with cutlasses and hand guns. They attacked

before the marines were in position, and the Confederate defenders cut them to pieces. The marines were then ordered into
the attack with the same disastrous results. By the time the
attack was called off, 309 dead and wounded marines and sailors littered the beach. The army, however, made it through
minefields and over the wall, capturing the fort before the end
of the day. Charges and countercharges were made in the
months following as the navy sought to make the marines
scapegoats for the disaster on the beach.

FORT SUMTER. A small island fortress located in a key position
to block entrance to the harbor of Charleston, South Carolina.
The bombardment and subsequent seizure of the fort in April
1861 was the catalyst for the beginnings of the Civil War (q.v.).
The Union navy decided in the fall of 1863 to either capture
or destroy the nine major works defending the city. The navy
brought the fort under direct fire of the big guns of the blockading squadron. In the last two weeks of August, all but one of
the casement guns were put out of action. For the sake of
honor, the Confederates decided to hold the fort and left over
400 infantry there. The Union commanders decided to occupy
the fort, and as a part of this plan 300 marines were sent to
cooperate with the army and navy. Their task was to seize the
fort by a night attack. By the time of the assault, the numbers
of available marines had been reduced by sickness, including
the commander, Maj. Jacob Zeilin (q.v.). The navy blasted Fort
Wagner into rubble, and it was taken by army troops on 7 September. The following night Fort Sumter was attacked by the
marines. Towed by tugs to within a half mile, their small boats
were then cut loose and soon became separated from one another in the darkness. Only 150 marines and sailors managed
to land on the narrow beach, and they came immediately
under accurate rifle and grenade fire from the parapets. Most
of the attacking force was captured, suffering four killed and
19 wounded. In all, the marines suffered 44 casualties. The un-
happy marine battalion retired to a neighboring island where
they encamped until early 1864, when it was broken up and
the men assigned to other units. Fort Sumter was continually
bombarded by the navy until the Confederates abandoned it in
February 1865.

FOSS, JOSEPH J. b. Sioux Falls, S.D., 17 April 1915. Foss graduated from the University of South Dakota in 1940 with a degree
in business. Taking private lessons over five years, he accumu-

lated 100 flying hours. He enlisted in the Marine Corps Reserve in June 1940 and two months later was called to active duty to attend flight school at Pensacola (q.v.) and was commissioned as a second lieutenant in March 1941. He became an instructor at Pensacola and was promoted to captain in August 1942. Posted to the Pacific, he arrived at Guadalcanal (q.v.) on 1 October as executive officer of Fighting Squadron 121 to relieve the first marine air group that had decimated the Japanese from Henderson Field (q.v.). Flying the Grumman Wildcat (q.v.), a plane inferior in performance to the Japanese Zero, Foss nevertheless shot down 23 planes in the period from 9 October to 19 November. Foss was forced to make three dead stick landings and was shot down once but rescued. On 15 January 1943 he shot down three more planes and thus tied World War I ace Eddie Rickenbacker's record of planes destroyed.

Foss was ordered to Washington in April 1943, received the Medal of Honor (q.v.) for his actions, and was sent on tours of naval and marine air stations. He returned to the Pacific as a major in command of Fighting Squadron 115 at Emirau but did not improve his record. Ordered back to the United States in September 1944, Foss was posted to a base in Oregon and later became operations officer at the air station in Santa Barbara, California. He was discharged from active duty in December 1945. Returning to South Dakota, he entered politics, was elected to the state legislature, in June 1954 became governor of the state, and was reelected two years later. Foss later became president of the National Rifle Association.

FRENCH WAR. An undeclared conflict mainly in the Caribbean begun by revolutionary France in 1796 and continued by Napoleon in retaliation for U.S. refusal to join in a war against Britain. French sea raiders captured hundreds of U.S. ships, and these actions led to public demands for a declaration of war on France. President John Adams resisted this but agreed with Congress's decision to speed up construction on three new 44-gun frigates and to authorize the raising of a battalion of 500 men. This unit was to be called the Marine Corps. The date of the congressional action, 11 July 1798, approving the muster is the real birthday of the Marine Corps. In May 1799 a marine detachment reported aboard the frigate *Constitution* and later sailed with this new ship to the Caribbean. Ninety marines were loaded on board a captured sloop in early 1800, and the ship was sailed into the harbor of Puerto Plata in Santo Domingo (q.v.). Without serious opposition, the marines and sailors captured a 14-gun French war ship. Then crossing to the opposite side of the harbor, they captured the main fort without incident. The guns were spiked, and the sloop was sailed out of the harbor. This success was a major victory for the corps in its first amphibious assault. Soon after this action, Napoleon ceased the harassment of American shipping, and the undeclared war came to an end.

FULLER, BEN H. 15th commandant, b. Big Rapids, Mich., 27 Feb. 1870, d. Washington, D.C., 8 June 1937. Fuller graduated from the Naval Academy in 1889 and then served the mandatory two-year cruise before being appointed a second lieutenant in the corps. Following this he spent seven years on sea duty in different ships. During the Spanish-American War (q.v.), he commanded the marine detachment on board the *Columbia* in the West Indies. Sent to the Philippines, he took part in the battle of Novaleta. During the Boxer Rebellion (q.v.) in 1900, he participated in the capture of Tientsin (q.v.). Later as a captain he commanded a battery of three-inch guns at the siege of the legations in Peking (q.v.). From China he was briefly posted to the Philippines. Returning to the United States, he served in a number of shore posts before taking command of the marine base in Honolulu in 1904. He then served in the Canal Zone and at Charleston, South Carolina. He joined the 5th Regiment as second in command in July 1914 in the West Indies. Later he attended the Naval War College and commanded the marine barracks in Philadelphia. As a brigadier general, he relieved General Pendleton (q.v.) in October 1918 as commander of the 2d Brigade in Santo Domingo (q.v.) against a variety of bandits in all sections of the country. In 1919 the marines were involved in 200 firefights.

Fuller was on the staff of the Naval War College in 1920 and two years later took command at Quantico (q.v.). He commanded the 1st Brigade in Haiti (q.v.) from January 1924 to December 1925 and in July 1925 became assistant commandant. He served in that capacity for the remainder of Generals Lejeune's (q.v.) and Neville's (q.v.) tenures. Fuller was named commandant and major general in August 1930 to replace General Neville, who had died in office. He had been selected over the much decorated and flamboyant Smedley Butler (q.v.). Because of his age, he served for only three and one-half years, retiring in March 1934. He spent much of his time as commandant coping with the problems of retrenchment caused by the Great Depression.

"FURY" (FJ-1 through FJ-4). Built by North American Aircraft Company, it was a single-engine swept-wing fighter differing from the company's F-86 Saberjet mainly in the undercarriage redesign for carrier landings. The FJ-1 was delivered to two navy squadrons in 1948. The later FJ-2, upgraded with new engines, had a top speed of 650 miles per hour with a service ceiling of 45,000 feet and a range of 1,000 miles. The early FJ-2s were basically the same as the air force Saberjet, which had such spectacular performance in the Korean War (q.v.). Armament originally consisted of four 20mm cannon mounted in the nose. Later versions could carry six Sidewinder air-to-air missiles. The FJ-3 had an even larger engine, and that prototype was flown first in July 1953. The FJ-4s had new thinner wings, slotted flaps, different landing gear, and a dorsal fin from cockpit back to the vertical fin. This version went into production in March 1955. Furies were introduced into the corps to replace the operational Grumman F9F Cougars (q.v.). Five Marine Corps squadrons were equipped with FJ-2s during the Korean conflict. The Fury remained the first line fighter for the corps throughout the 1950s until replaced by the Vought F8U Crusader (q.v.).

G

GALE, ANTHONY. 4th commandant, b. Dublin, Ireland, 17 Sept. 1782, d. Lincoln County, Ky., 1843. A man noted for his hot temper and overindulgence, as a marine lieutenant on board the *Ganges*, Gale ostensibly was insulted by a naval officer and later challenged him to a duel and killed him in 1801. After Cmndt. Franklin Wharton's (q.v.) death on 1 September 1818, the corps was without an official leader. Archibald Henderson filled the post temporarily, then in March 1819 Gale was appointed by the secretary of the navy. He was the senior officer by length of service and became lieutenant colonel commandant. He quarreled with the secretary of the navy and continued his drinking and carousing. Brought before an army court martial, Gale was accused of frequenting places of low repute and being drunk in public. His plea of temporary insanity was rejected, and he was convicted. President James Monroe dismissed him from the corps in October 1820. Nevertheless, he received a pension until his death in 1843.

GALER, ROBERT E. b. Seattle, Wash., 23 Oct. 1913. Galer received a commission on 1 July 1936 and after qualifying as a naval aviator in April of the following year, he was transferred to Quantico (q.v.). Later he attended the Basic School in Philadelphia and in mid-1938 was ordered to the Virgin Islands as a member of a scouting squadron. In July 1940 he joined the 2d Air Wing in San Diego; six months later as a captain, he was in Hawaii at Ewa Air Station when the Japanese struck on 7 December. In May 1942 he took command of Fighting Squadron 224 and in August joined the beleaguered air forces on Guadalcanal (q.v.). Operating with F4F Wildcats (q.v.), which were at a disadvantage against the Japanese Zero, Galer, now a major, shot down 11 planes in 29 days while his squadron downed another 16. For these actions he was awarded the Medal of Honor (q.v.).

Ordered back to the United States, Galer did not see further action in World War II (q.v.). He became assistant operations officer at Miramar and later chief of staff, Marine Air in Hawaii and in May 1944 operations officer of the 3d Air Wing. He served as an observer during the Peleliu (q.v.) campaign. After the war he held a variety of important positions, including operations and training officer at Cherry Point and assistant chief of staff for plans on the staff of the commander of the Air Force, Pacific. In March 1952 as a colonel he was ordered to Korea (q.v.), where he served as G-4 (Supply) of the 1st Air Wing and later commanding officer of the 12th Air Group. He was shot down and wounded in August 1952, and after a brief hospitalization he took over successively positions as assistant chief of staff (personnel) and then operations for Fleet Marine Force (q.v.), Pacific. He attended the Air College at Maxwell Field in mid-1953. Following this, he served as assistant director, guided missiles, for the Bureau of Aeronautics of the Navy Department and later as its director. On his retirement in July 1957, Galer was advanced to brigadier general.

GAMBLE, JOHN MARSHALL. The senior marine officer in 1814 on board the 32-gun frigate, *Essex*, commanded by Capt. David Porter, that operated successfully against British whalers and privateers in the South Pacific. Hampered by a shortage of naval officers, Porter turned over command of a captured privateer to Gamble. In an audacious manner, Gamble captured the 22-gun British vessel, *Seringapatam*, which he sailed to join Porter at Nuku Hiva (q.v.) Island in the Marquesas Islands. There he and his marines together with sailors briefly pacified the natives, who resented Porter's declaration that the island was now the property of the United States. Left behind by Porter with only a small crew, Gamble once again faced a native uprising. Soon afterward in May 1814, some of his crew mutinied, captured him, and with seven loyal followers he was set adrift in a longboat. Returning to the island, they seized one of the small ships left behind by Porter and set sail for the Hawaiian Islands. Arriving there, Gamble and his crew were captured by the British who decided to take their prisoners to England. Later, however, the British captain left Gamble and his men behind at Rio de Janeiro after they gave their parole. From there they made their way back to New York shortly after the war ended.

GARAND (M-1) RIFLE. Designed by John Garand, it was the result of developments at the Springfield Armory in the 1920s and 1930s in designing a replacement weapon for the 1903 Springfield (q.v.). The M-1 was adopted by the Army in January 1936. The first models of the M-1 produced between 1936 and 1940 had a gas system that was used to operate the mechanism. In 1940 this design was changed by drilling a port in the barrel to take off excess gas. This improvement increased the rifle's reliability. Considerable numbers of Garands had been produced and were in use by U.S. and British army units prior to Pearl Harbor (q.v.). During World War II (q.v.), Springfield and Winchester Arms Company produced over four million of the guns, which became the standard rifle for all service branches. It weighed a hefty 10 pounds and was extremely accurate at middle distances. The ammunition was the standard .30-caliber, loaded into an eight-round clip. The corps officially adopted the M-1 as the standard rifle in November 1941, but the rifle was in short supply until early 1943. This shortage of M-1s was filled by the older 1903 Springfield and Johnson 1941 (q.v.) rifles. Although a few die-hards swore by the '03 rifle, most infantrymen came to value the sturdiness and reliability of the newer weapon. The M-1 continued in production until 1957.

GEIGER, ROY S. b. Middleburg, Fla., 25 Jan. 1885, d. Bethesda, Md., 23 Jan. 1947. Geiger attended Florida State Normal School and received a bachelor of laws degree from Stetson University before enlisting in the Marine Corps in November 1907. He was commissioned a second lieutenant in February 1909. Service on board ships, foreign duty in Nicaragua (q.v.), the Philippines, and China followed. After shore duty, he returned to China as a part of the marine detachment in Peking (q.v.), serving there from 1913 to 1916. In March 1916 he began flight training at Pensacola (q.v.) and received his wings in June 1917. He was sent to France in July 1918 where he commanded a bombing squadron of the 1st Marine Aviation Force. For his actions against German targets he received the Navy Cross (q.v.). After the war, he held a variety of posts at Quantico (q.v.) and had two tours in Haiti. He attended the army's Command and General Staff School in 1925 and the War College in 1929. That year he assumed command of Aircraft Squadrons, East Coast Expeditionary Force. He returned to Quantico as commander of Aircraft One, Fleet Marine Force (q.v.), in 1935. In June 1939 he began a nearly two-year tour at Newport, Rhode Island where he completed the senior and advanced courses at the Naval War College. Following this he served briefly in the naval attaché's office in London as a brigadier general.

In August 1941 Geiger assumed command of the 1st Marine Air Wing, which he took to the South Pacific in the fall of 1942. He commanded the outnumbered marine air units on Guadalcanal (q.v.) from 3 September until 4 November 1942. Despite the superiority in numbers of the Japanese aircraft and naval ships, the marine aviators under his command shot down 268 Japanese planes and sank six enemy ships. More than anything, they provided the necessary air cover that enabled the marine ground forces to defeat the Japanese attacks aimed at Henderson Field (q.v.). For his service on Guadalcanal, Geiger, now a major general, received his second Navy Cross. In May 1943 he returned to the United States to become director of aviation. In November 1943 he replaced General Alexander Vandegrift (q.v.) as commander of the 1st Amphibious Corps and directed the corps until 15 December in the invasion of Empress Augusta Bay and subsequent actions on Bougainville (q.v.). He continued to command the corps, redesignated 3d Amphibious Corps in the invasion of Guam (q.v.) in July 1944. Later he assumed command of the marine and army units in the invasion of Peleliu (q.v.) and Angaur in September. During the assault on Okinawa (q.v.) he served as chief of staff to the commander of X Army, Gen. Simon Buckner. When Buckner was killed, Geiger, now a lieutenant general, briefly assumed command of the army until replaced by Gen. Joseph Stillwell. Geiger was thus the only marine general during World War II (q.v.) to command an army. In July he became commander of Fleet Marine Force, Pacific, a position he held until returning to the United States in November 1946. He was the only marine general invited by Gen. Douglas MacArthur to participate in the Japanese surrender on board the *Missouri*. After his death in 1947, he was promoted to the rank of full general.

GILBERT ISLANDS. Together with the Ellice chain of islands, the Gilberts are scattered over a distance of almost 2,000 miles from east to west. Formerly under British jurisdiction, the main islands were occupied by the Japanese in early 1942. They established a major radio relay station on Makin (q.v.), which was attacked by marine Raiders in August 1942. This assault alerted the Japanese to the weakness of their island defenses. They greatly improved these during the following year, particularly on Betio Island in the Tarawa (q.v.) Atoll. In November 1943 the 2d Division landed on Betio and in 72 hours of desperate fighting took the island. At the same time army units occupied Makin. These assaults were the first breach in the Japanese outer defense ring.

GLENN, JOHN H. JR. b. Cambridge, Ohio, 18 July 1921. Glenn enlisted in the Marine Corps Reserve in March 1942 and was later designated an aviation cadet. He completed flight training in March 1943. Promoted to first lieutenant in the fall, he was ordered to the Pacific in February 1944. As a member of Fighting Squadron 155, he flew 59 missions during the campaigns in the Marshalls and Marianas. Returning to the United States in February 1945, he was assigned to Cherry Point, the first of many stateside assignments interrupted by a two-year tour beginning in December 1946 on Guam (q.v.) and on north China patrol. Promoted to major in July 1952, he completed the jet refresher course at Quantico (q.v.). In February 1953 he was ordered to the Korean War (q.v.) with Fighting Squadron 311 and flew 63 missions with it. He then flew 27 missions with the army's 51st Fighter Wing. With the army interceptors, he shot down three MiGs. After his return from Korea, Glenn was sent to the navy's Test Pilot School, finishing in 1954. This stint led to a series of assignments at Patuxent River, Washington, and Los Alamitos. On 16 July he made the first nonstop supersonic coast-to-coast flight from Los Alamitos to New York in a F8U-1 Crusader (q.v.). For this he earned another Distinguished Flying Cross to match the four he had received during World War II (q.v.) and the Korea War.

Glenn was chosen as one of the 69 original selectees for the Mercury Project, and after screening he became one of the seven Mercury astronauts in April 1959. On 20 February 1962 Lieutenant Colonel Glenn, aboard *Friendship 7*, was launched into space by a modified Atlas missile and orbited the earth three times before splashing down in the Atlantic Ocean near Grand Turk Island. His 81,000-mile flight was a signal that the first step of the American space program was a success. He retired from the Marine Corps in 1965 to become a businessman and consultant to NASA. In 1974 he was elected to the United States Senate and became the senior senator from Ohio in 1994.

GRAY, ALFRED M. JR. 29th commandant, b. Rahway, N.J., 22 June 1928. Gray enlisted in the Marine Corps in 1950 and after basic training was assigned to the Amphibious Reconnaissance Platoon, Fleet Marine Force (q.v.), Pacific. His highest enlisted rank was sergeant, and he was commissioned a second lieutenant in April 1952. After attending Basic School at Quantico (q.v.) and the Army Field Artillery School, he was ordered to the Korean War (q.v.) as an artillery officer with the 1st Division. Gray also served a second tour as an infantry officer in the 7th Marines. He returned to the United States in December 1954 assigned to Camp Lejeune (q.v.) and attended Communications School at Quantico. From 1956 to 1961 he served in special command billets as a captain. Assigned to Washington headquarters in 1961, he later served at Guantanamo (q.v.) Bay. Gray's first tour in Vietnam (q.v.) began in October 1965 joining the 12th Marines of the 3d Division, serving at times as regimental communication officer, S-3, and aerial observer. He took command of the Composite Artillery Battalion and Free World Forces at Gio Link in 1967 before being assigned to III Amphibious Force at Da Nang (q.v.), where he commanded the 1st Radio Battalion for I Corps. In February 1968 he returned to Washington as a lieutenant colonel for duty with the Defense special projects. In November 1968 he was at Quantico helping develop sensor technology.

Gray's second tour of Vietnam began in June the following year to work on surveillance and reconnaissance in I Corps' area. After this tour, he served briefly as chief of the Intelligence Division at the Development Center and later attended the Command and General Staff School. Transferred to the 2d Division, he was given command of a battalion and the landing team that was deployed to the Mediterranean in September 1971. In April 1972 he became commander of the 2d Marines, and later as a colonel he was assistant chief of staff, G-3, of the 2d Division. For nine months beginning in August 1973, he attended the Army War College, after which he became commander of the 4th Marines and camp commander at Camp Hansen on Okinawa (q.v.). As deputy commander of the 9th Amphibious Brigade and commander of the 33d Amphibious Brigade, Gray directed the Southeast Asia evacuation in 1975. As a brigadier general in 1976, he was in charge of the 4th Amphibious Brigade and the Landing Force Training Command, Atlantic. Four years later, promoted to major general, he took over command of the 2d Division at Camp Lejeune. On further promotion in 1986, he was in charge of Fleet Marine Force, Atlantic, commanding general Fleet Marine Force, Europe, and commander of II Amphibious Force. Promoted to general, he became the 29th commandant on 1 July 1987.

GREENE, WALLACE M. JR. 23d commandant, b. Burlington, Vt., 27 Dec. 1907. Greene briefly attended the University of Vermont before entering the Naval Academy. He graduated in June 1930 and was commissioned a second lieutenant in the Marine Corps. For the next six years his service varied between schools, sea duty, and shore duty. In October 1936 he left for Guam (q.v.) where he served until June 1937 when he joined the 4th Marines at Shanghai. Returning to the United States for further education, he was posted to Guantanamo (q.v.) Bay. By 1941 he had been appointed assistant operations officer to the 1st Marine Division. He was ordered to England in November 1941 as a special naval observer and attended British amphibious warfare and demolition schools. In February 1942 Greene, now a major, was named assistant chief of staff of the 3d Marine Brigade and sailed with it to western Samoa, a position he held until November 1943. He was then posted to Hawaii as assistant chief of staff of the 5th Amphibious Corps, where he assisted in the planning for the Marshall Islands (q.v.) campaigns. In March 1944 Greene became operations officer for the 2d Division and served during the Saipan (q.v.) and Tinian (q.v.) operations. In October 1944 he became operations officer, Division of Plans, at Marine Headquarters in Washington and from there went to the Personnel Office.

During the next 10 years, Greene held various staff positions, attended the National War College, and in September 1955 as a brigadier general became assistant commandant at Camp Lejeune (q.v.). After further duty at Parris Island (q.v.) he became commandant at Lejeune in July 1957. Ordered to Washington in January 1958, Greene served for more than a year as assistant chief of staff to the commandant. Promoted to major general in August 1958, he became deputy chief of staff before becoming chief of staff to Cmndt. David Shoup (q.v.) in 1960. He was appointed commandant 1 January 1964.

Greene planned and carried out Operation Steel Spike with the Spanish Marine Corps, the largest amphibious operation since World War II (q.v.). Greene was responsible for aiding in planning for the April 1965 initial landing by the 6th Marine Expeditionary Unit (MEU) (q.v.) during the intervention in the Dominican Republic (q.v.) as well as the first large Marine Corps buildup by the 9th Marine Expeditionary Brigade (MEB) (q.v.) at Da Nang (q.v.) in March. After the arrival of the 1st and 3d Marine Divisions the marines advanced to I Corps' tactical zone adjacent to the Demilitarized Zone (DMZ) (q.v.). As a member of the Joint Chiefs of Staff, Greene was responsible for the deployment of the bulk of the Marine Corps to Vietnam (q.v.) and the conduct of operations there during the early, more successful phase of the war. He retired on 31 December 1967.

GRENADA. A small 18-mile-long island, the southernmost of the Grenadine chain in the Caribbean. There a revolution by left-wing elements closely associated with Cuba seized the government in mid-1983. Fears of Communist influence combined with concern for the safety of American students attending the medical school on the island caused Pres. Ronald Reagan to order the marines and the army's 82d Airborne to occupy the island. Elements of the 22d Marine Amphibious Unit (MAU) were redirected from Lebanon for the operation, which was hurriedly put in place. Planning for use of the 22d and elements of the army's 82d Airborne and Rangers was based upon what proved to be faulty information. It was believed that the Grenadian Peoples Revolutionary Army (PRA), bolstered by Cuban military advisers and backed by a large militia, would seriously contest any invasion. One basic problem of the hurried planning was the lack of any suitable maps. Communications between marine, navy, and army units also proved difficult.

The first landings early in the morning of 25 October 1983 were made by helicopter at Pearls in the northeast segment of the island. Cobra gunships took under attack suspected targets. By noon the men of Company E had captured the town and adjacent airfield. There had been no significant resistance, and the marines were welcomed by the population. At the same time, Company F helicoptered into the Greenville area, and as at Pearls, the marines met no organized resistance.

Meanwhile, Ranger units had landed in the vicinity of the main town, St. George's, and rescued the students at the campus of St. George's Medical College as well as the governor. They encountered the heaviest resistance presumably from the Cubans, but the gunships soon neutralized this. Company F was airlifted to Grand Mal Bay area north of St. George's at 0400 on D+1. The PRA units in the vicinity, frightened by the noises of landing, simply ran away. Later on D+1, units of Company F cooperated with the Rangers to take the second campus of the medical school at Grand Anse. St. George's was occupied without difficulty, the citizens welcoming the army and marines. In the north, Company E continued its operations in the midst of false reports of a potential enemy counterattack. Their patrolling continued through 27 October. By D+3, it was obvious that all reports of the potential of the PRA had been greatly exaggerated; the island was fully under U.S. control. On 31 October the 22d MAU reembarked, its place taken by troops of the 82d. On 1 November Companies F and G were landed on Carriacou Island north of Grenada once again without encountering any opposition. The following day the 22d left the Grenada area in order to take up its original mission in Lebanon (q.v.).

Despite bad planning, high-level fear, and fouled-up communications, the 22d had performed well. The Grenada operation proved to be an excellent training exercise showing up deficiencies in planning, communications, infrastructure, and interservice cooperation.

GUADALCANAL. An island in the Southwest Pacific, it is the largest in the group that before the war constituted the British Solomon Islands Protectorate. It lies southeast of the New Georgia group, northwest of San Cristobal, and across the Sealark Channel 20 miles to the south of Florida Island and Tulagi (q.v.). The island is 92 miles long and 35 miles wide. Most of the island was covered with dense tropical forests. With only a few trails used by the native Melanesians, it was nearly impenetrable. Only the north coast had seen any development since before the war, and there were large coconut plantations between the Tenaru and Matanikau Rivers. The weather is hot, with temperatures above 100 degrees and extremely high humidity. The island was a host to a wide variety of tropical diseases, the most debilitating being malaria. It was an incongruous place for some of the most important air, sea, and land battles of World War II (q.v.).

After the Japanese had moved leisurely to occupy the northern and central Solomon Islands (q.v.), they decided to build a naval station at Tulagi. On 28 May 1942 a local commander on Tulagi decided to begin construction of an airfield on Guadalcanal. Concerned that such a base when completed could threaten the long U.S. supply line to Australia and New Zealand, the Joint Chiefs decided to invade. The only unit large enough and not already engaged was the 1st Marine Division. Even then its commander, Maj. Gen. Alexander Vandegrift (q.v.), had only two of his regiments, the 1st and 5th, available for Operation Watchtower.

The marine landings on 7 August 1942 took the Japanese by surprise. The marines hastily established a perimeter around the airfield, which was soon repaired and renamed Henderson Field (q.v.) after a marine aviator killed at Midway (q.v.). The Japanese response came soon in incessant air attacks and the commitment of major naval forces against the outnumbered American ships. Imperial Headquarters poured thousands of troops of the 8th Area Army into Guadalcanal.

The most desperate time for the marines was in September when overwhelming numbers of Japanese threatened to capture the airfield. Combined with Japanese naval victories, the situation in the southern Solomons was nearly desperate. However, the arrival of the 7th Marines in mid-September bolstered the defenses, and the Japanese were pushed back, having sustained horrendous losses. In October the army's Americal Division landed, and the 2d Marine Division arrived in November followed by the army's 25th Division. The exhausted 1st Division was pulled out of Guadalcanal in December after suffering 2,700 battle casualties and 5,400 stricken with malaria. In January 1943 U.S. forces now under army command began a general offensive westward, further eroding the failing Japanese ground effort. Before the end of 1942, the marine and navy pilots had exacted a heavy toll on Japanese aircraft, while at the same time Allied naval forces had greatly reduced Japanese naval power in the Solomons.

After committing so many men and so much materiel to Guadalcanal, Imperial Japanese Headquarters decided to cut its losses after suffering 23,000 casualties. By the second week of February 1943, no more Japanese were on Guadalcanal, the remnants of the once proud Japanese force having been taken off at night by destroyers. The air, sea, and land battles on Guadalcanal combined with Allied victories in New Guinea were the turning points of the war. The Japanese were never able to

mount a serious offensive threat in the Pacific after Guadalcanal.

GUAM. The largest of the Mariana Islands (q.v.) measuring 32
miles long with a width between 4 and 10 miles. It is high and
precipitous on the western side with very narrow beaches,
while in the east lies a narrow flat plain. Guam was heavily
forested, particularly in the highlands of the north. It became
a possession of the United States in 1898 during the Spanish-
American War (q.v.) and was subsequently governed by naval
officers. Little attention was given to its defense, and thus on 8
December 1941 the Japanese met little resistance from the 125-
man marine garrison and 271 sailors.

The reconquest of the island, Operation Forager, an integral
part of the plan to establish B-29 bases in the Marianas, began
on 21 July 1944. III Amphibious Corps, composed of the 3rd
Division, the 1st Provisional Brigade, and the army's 77th Division, landed on two beaches, Asan and Agat, on the western
side of the island. After establishing firm beachheads, the 3d
Division and the 77th pushed inland while the 1st Brigade
initially cleared the Orote Peninsula and then secured southern
Guam. The Japanese garrison of 18,000 army and naval personnel had been shattered by 17 days of naval and air bombardment. Nevertheless, they resisted fanatically, both in the
defense as well as launching two large scale banzai attacks. The
U.S. attack northward had the 3d Division on the left and the
77th on the right as much of the fighting took place in heavy
scrub and forest growth. Joined by the 1st Brigade, the U.S.
forces reached the north end of the island and on 10 August
the island was declared secure.

Almost the entire Japanese garrison had been killed. Marine
and army casualties were 7,714. The loyal Chamorro population had been rescued from two and a half years of Japanese
oppression, and the United States had gained an important
naval base. Admiral Chester Nimitz later moved his headquarters there. More importantly, with its three bomber bases for B-
29s, Guam later played a key role in the defeat of Japan.

GUANTANAMO. A town in the province of Oriente in southeastern Cuba (q.v.) located near the most important harbor east of
Santiago. On 10 June 1898 during the Spanish-American War
(q.v.), a small force of marines landed on the eastern shore of
the bay and held a strategic hill and fought off numerous Spanish counterattacks, an action important to gaining total control

of the harbor. After the war, the Platt Amendment to the 1901 Military Appropriations Bill gave the United States special privileges in Cuba. Among these was the right to buy or lease land for a military base. Two years later land on both sides of the harbor entrance was leased, and soon the base established there became the chief American naval station in the West Indies. A large contingent of marines continued to be posted there and was greatly strengthened during World War II (q.v.). The base has been maintained on an alert status during much of the period that Fidel Castro has been in power, particularly during the Cuban Missile Crisis of October 1962.

GULF WAR. A short-lived conflict in January and February 1991 between a coalition of nations led by the United States to counter Iraq's invasion of Kuwait in August 1990 and a possible threat to Middle East oil supplies. The buildup of allied forces in Saudi Arabia, code-named Desert Shield (q.v.), began soon after the Iraqi invasion. The first marine units landed on 14 August 1990. By the end of the year, two marine divisions were located south of the Kuwait border opposite Kuwait City. In addition, there were two air wings, the 1st and 2d, with Intruder bombers (q.v.), Harrier (q.v.), and Hornet (F-18) (q.v.) fighters. The marine complement was only a small portion of the total allied force that was poised for the offensive.

The first phase of the war, code-named Desert Storm (q.v.), began on 18 January 1991 with massive airstrikes against strategic and tactical targets throughout Iraq. These continued until G Day, 24 February, when the ground action began. By then the Iraqi command and control structure was a shambles, and morale in all units, including the vaunted Republican Guard, had been shattered. The first blow of the ground war was struck by the marines on the extreme right of the allied line. Supported by massive artillery fire supplemented by the big guns of the battleships *Wisconsin* and *Missouri*, the two marine divisions quickly broached the Iraqi defenses. By the end of the first day, three Iraqi divisions had been largely destroyed. The following day in the largest tank battle in the history of the corps, the Iraqis lost 34 of 35 tanks engaged. By the close of the day of 27 February, Kuwait City had been liberated, and the enemy, having lost thousands of men with most of their equipment, was fleeing northward. However important was the marine activity, it was minor compared with the action far to the west where the Army VII and XVIII Corps, supported by French and British units, had flanked the main lines of Iraqi defenses. What was left of the broken Iraqi army, harried by allied aircraft, was in full retreat toward the Tigris River.

Before the allied forces could totally destroy the Iraqi forces, hostilities were brought to a close by Pres. George Bush's announcement that all action would cease at 0800 on 28 February. The decisive defeat of the Iraqi army was followed by severe restrictions on its despotic government, ending at least temporarily the major threat to security in the Persian Gulf.

H

HAGARU-RI. During the Korean War (q.v.), this town was the key marshaling area for the marines after the Chinese had pushed them back from the Chosin Reservoir (q.v.). The Chinese occupied the high ground to the north and also blocked the retreat route southward to Koto-ri. General Oliver P. Smith (q.v.) on 28 November 1950 ordered the 5th Marines to hold Hagaru-ri while the 7th attacked southward. One reinforced company of the 1st Marines at Koto-ri, with elements of the British marines and two tank companies, drove northward. Although most of the tanks and infantry fought their way through, the truck column was cut to pieces. On 1 December a relief column from the 7th Marines relieved the company that had held Toktong Pass. Only 82 marines of the original number were unwounded. The battalions of the 5th and 7th fought their way back to Hagaru-ri from Yudam-ni.

The breakout from Hagaru-ri began on 6 December. Despite the Chinese and the cold, the marines brought everything out. The road was jammed with vehicles and men, the rifle companies operating on the flanks, leapfrogging from one piece of high ground to another. Marine air controlled a one-mile-wide corridor, while navy and army planes ranged farther out. By midnight of 7 December, the 5th and 7th Marines were within the perimeter of Koto-ri. The next day the withdrawal continued with units of the 1st Marines clearing the vital Funchilin Pass. Four days later the marines reached Hungnam, completing one of the classic withdrawals in military history. The retreat had cost 730 men killed and over 3,600 wounded. The Chinese divisions were so battered that they did not contest the evacuation of marine and army units that were then transported to Pusan (q.v.).

HAITI. A state located in the far western part of the island of Hispaniola (Santo Domingo), the second largest island in the

West Indies. It was controlled by France in the 18th century until a major slave revolt resulted in the creation of the first black republic in the Western Hemisphere. From 1822 to 1844, the entire island was united under Haitian rule until a further revolution resulted in the present division. The republic in the 19th century was poor and its government generally unstable; 22 presidents led from 1844 until 1914. By then the country's finances had collapsed, and European states supporting their banks demanded payment. A receivership had been worked out in neighboring Santo Domingo (q.v.), but the Haitian government refused a similar arrangement. A marine detachment was landed in December 1914 to secure the last half-million dollars in the treasury.

The following March a bloody uprising in Port au Prince triggered even more violence. The newly elected president was killed. The U.S. naval commandant landed a battalion of sailors and two companies of marines who moved to the capital and restored order. Later in August the 1st and 2d Marines, comprising the 1st Brigade, were brought in. By then 2,000 marines were in Haiti. The insurgents, called Cacos, were concentrated in the north, and a full battalion of the 1st Marines moved to Cap Haitien. At Gonaives one band of the guerrillas was defeated on 18 September, and on 24 October an even larger number of Cacos were beaten after a night-long fight. The last major action was against the Cacos, who held an old French fort on top of a 4,000 foot mountain. Charging through an open drain into the fort's interior and in hand-to-hand fighting, the marines drove the defenders into the bush.

A new government friendly to the United States had been created in Haiti. The United States established a Haitian constabulary officered and trained by marines that garrisoned the major towns and kept the peace until March 1919 when a new Caco leader emerged and his rebellion threatened the shaky government. The slimmed-down 1st Brigade, 1,000 men strong, landed to support the Haitian *Gendarmerie*. They also had the support of a few flying boats and Jennies (q.v.).

During the summer, the marines fought a number of actions against the rebels, but the Cacos were strong enough to invade the capital in early October. The major threat of the Cacos was ended when its leader, Charlemagne Peralte, was killed in a daring action by two marines and a *gendarme* who invaded his camp and shot him. But another leader took his place, and the marine brigade, reinforced by the 8th Marines, systematically began active patrols of the entire countryside. In January 1920 in action at Port au Prince 66 Cacos were killed. The insurgents were harassed by aircraft in March. Converging columns of marines later trapped a large contingent and inflicted 200 casualties. The end of the rebellion came in May when the new Caco leader was killed by a marine patrol. Brigadier General John Russell (q.v.) was appointed U.S. High Commissioner, and with his oversight the country remained peaceful. The last marine units were withdrawn in 1934, and Haiti once again began to function as an independent state.

In the early 1950s Haiti fell under the control of François "Papa Doc" Duvalier, whose despotic regime lasted until 1971. His son tried to exercise the same control but was later forced into exile. An election under a new constitution in February 1991 returned Jean-Bertrand Aristide as president, who was overthrown by the military in September. The triumvirate type of military government was condemned by the Organization of American States (OAS) and the United Nations (UN). Ultimately the United States sent troops to the island in September 1994, and the military leaders capitulated. Marine units, as a part of the force that had returned Aristide to power, were involved in a minor firefight with the police at Cap Haitien. This was the only action in an otherwise peaceful occupation. (See also Banana Wars.)

HANNEKEN, HERMAN H. b. St. Louis, Mo., 23 June 1893, d. La Jolla, Calif., 23 Aug. 1986. Hanneken entered the corps in July 1914 and served as an enlisted man before receiving a commission in December 1919. Ordered to Haiti (q.v.) as a member of the *Gendarmerie,* he was involved in patrols seeking an insurgent leader, Charlemagne Peralte. Leading a daring raid into rebel territory, he penetrated the defenses of Peralte's camp, shot the outlaw, and returned to friendly territory without losing a man. For this action he was awarded the Medal of Honor (q.v.). Five months later he was instrumental in tracking down and killing another rebel leader, Osiris Joseph. He consequently received the Navy Cross (q.v.). Returning to the United States in 1920, he served in a variety of capacities: in the 6th Marines at Quantico (q.v.), on board the *USS Antares,* at Lakehurst, New Jersey, and at Philadelphia. In December 1928 he was assigned to the 2d Brigade, then serving in Nicaragua (q.v.). Hanneken won his second Navy Cross by tracking down and bringing in the rebel leader Sandino's chief of staff, General Jiron.

Following this service he returned to the United States to a series of assignments, including completing the senior course at Quantico. In June 1941, now a major, he was assigned to the 1st Division and the following year he took command of a battalion of the 7th Marines and accompanied it to Samoa (q.v.). On 11 September the 7th was ordered to Guadalcanal (q.v.) and soon after was committed to the limited offensive west of Henderson Field (q.v.). Then it stood on the defensive along the Mantanikau River. For his actions in these engagements, Hanneken was awarded the Silver Star. Almost a year after Guadalcanal, the 1st Division under General MacArthur's command invaded western New Britain (q.v.). Now a lieutenant colonel commanding the 7th Marines, Hanneken was a vital part of the securing of the Willaumez Peninsula. The next action for the 7th Marines was Peleliu (q.v.) in the Western Caroline Islands. Landing on 15 September 1944, Hanneken's command had the right wing of the attack and operated along the eastern coast until its relief the following month. This was his final campaign of the war.

Upon returning to the United States in November, Hanneken took command of the 2d Infantry Training Regiment at Camp Pendleton (q.v.). The following year he headed the Training and Replacement Command at San Diego and eventually became chief of staff for Troop Training Unit, Amphibious Forces, Pacific. He held this position at the time of his retirement in July 1948 with the rank of brigadier general.

HAN RIVER FORTS. In the 19th century a total of five forts guarded the river entrance to the Korean capital of Seoul (q.v.). The Korean government had maintained a hostile attitude toward all foreigners, which culminated in the killing of the crew of the shipwrecked American vessel, the *General Sherman.* The U.S. minister to China was ordered to Seoul to negotiate a peace settlement with the "Hermit Kingdom." He was escorted on his journey in May 1871 by five warships of the Asiatic squadron. A survey party sent by the commander of the fleet to discover the best passage up the Han River to Seoul was fired upon. Admiral John Rodgers demanded an apology, and when none was forthcoming, he decided to punish the Koreans. A force of sailors and 109 marines commanded by Capt. McLane Tilton on 10 June landed on the mud flats south of the first fort, fortunately a small one. The attacking force found itself temporarily mired in the mud. Only covering fire from the ships prevented what could have been a disaster. Extricating themselves, the attackers found the fort abandoned. Spiking the gun, they took the second small fort the following day. They then attacked the main fort, the Citadel. After advancing over steep hills and deep ravines under intermittent random fire, they attacked up a 150-foot hillside to the top. Climbing the walls, the marines and sailors engaged in brief, furious hand-to-hand combat. Conquest of the Citadel cost the Koreans 243 killed, while the marines suffered only two casualties. The minister then proceeded to Seoul where protracted negotiations did not produce a satisfactory treaty. Nevertheless, the action at the Han River Forts convinced the Koreans to cease their hostile actions toward Americans.

HANSON, ROBERT M. b. Lucknow, India, 4 Feb. 1920, d. Rabaul, New Britain, 3 Feb. 1944. A son of Methodist missionaries in India, Hanson went through typical naval flight training, receiving his wings in February 1943. He joined Fighting Squadron 215 at Munda, New Georgia (q.v.). Covering the landings on Bougainville (q.v.) on 1 November 1943 flying a Corsair, Hanson shot down three Japanese planes before his plane was damaged by enemy fire. He was rescued after six hours and rejoined his unit.

Hanson was perhaps the deadliest marine fighter pilot of the war. In one 17-day period he destroyed 20 enemy aircraft. Four of these victories came on 30 January 1944 while escorting a bomber strike on Rabaul. This brought his total to 25. Three days later, the day before his 24th birthday and a week before he was to return to the United States, he was shot down by ground fire while on a strafing mission to New Britain (q.v.). For his various actions in the Solomon Islands (q.v.), First Lieutenant Hanson was awarded the Medal of Honor (q.v.).

HARPERS FERRY. A key crossing of the Potomac River and in 1859 the site of a U.S. arsenal. John Brown, who had earlier become notorious in Kansas for his actions in support of slave emancipation, seized the arsenal on 16 October 1859 aided by 18 men. He believed this action was the necessary prelude to slave revolts throughout the South. No regular troops were present, and the local militia was not eager to attack the abolitionist, who had taken refuge in the firehouse with hostages. Upon receipt of the information in Washington, a detachment of 86 marines from the Marine Barracks was ordered to Harpers Ferry and its lieutenant, Israel Greene, was instructed to report to the senior army officer present. This was Col. Robert E. Lee, who was accompanied by his aide, Lt. J. E. B. Stuart.

Early in the morning of the 17th Lee ordered the marines to form two storming parties. Stuart went forward to try to talk Brown into surrendering. When this was refused, Greene led his men forward. The door was battered down, and the marines charged in. Only a leather collar kept Brown from being cut down by Greene's sword. The marines returned to barracks and Brown was brought to trial, convicted of treason, and hanged the following May.

"HARRIER" (AV-8A through C). The first operational fixed-wing, vertical takeoff (V/STOL) fighter manufactured by British Aviation. Delivery of the first Harriers to the Marine Corps was completed in January 1971, and soon three combat squadrons at Cherry Point were equipped with them. Subsequently the design was improved, and the 8As were converted to the more advanced standards of the 8C by McDonnell Douglas. Much of the improvement was to give the Harrier a more potent armament. There is no built-in armament; all weapons are carried on the wings. Depending on the configuration, a Harrier can carry 30mm guns, bombs, rockets, or Sidewinder missiles. Its top speed is far below that of the F-14, F-16, or F-18 at only 740 miles per hour at low altitude. The vertical takeoff capabilities combined with heavy armament offset this slower speed. It was a perfect adjunct to the corps, which since World War II had stressed tactical missions. The plane proved its worth in this role during Desert Storm (q.v.).

HARRIS, JOHN. 6th commandant, b. 1793, d. Washington, D.C., 12 May 1864. Harris entered the corps as a second lieutenant in April 1814 but did not see significant action during the War of 1812 (q.v.). For over 20 years he served on a number of ships and was stationed at various times in Erie, Philadelphia, Norfolk, New York, and Boston. During the Seminole War (q.v.), he commanded a detachment of mounted marines in 1836–37. He was breveted major for his actions in Florida. Harris was sent to Washington in May 1837 with a treaty with the Seminole leader. Following this action until the Mexican War (q.v.), he returned to routine service in a number of posts. During that war, he took a battalion of marines to Mexico but arrived too late for the fighting. After service at Alvarado, Mexico, as a part of the occupying force, he returned to routine peacetime duty and was promoted to lieutenant colonel in 1855.

Harris was named colonel commandant in January 1859 at age 66. He was commandant when marines were ordered in

October to Harpers Ferry (q.v.) to deal with John Brown's raid. During much of the Civil War (q.v.), he was considered by many officers too old and lethargic for the tasks of overseeing the expansion of the corps and its increased responsibilities. In 1862 he brought one of his critics, Major John Reynolds, before a court martial. Acquitted, Reynolds preferred charges against Harris. Disgusted with the higher command of the corps, the secretary of the navy ended the quarrel by sending a letter of reproof to both officers. Despite his problems, Harris was commandant while the corps was involved in the battle of Bull Run, served with the many ships of the blockading squadrons, and attacked Fort Sumter (q.v.) in September 1863. He died at age 71 in Washington, D.C.

"HELLCAT" (F6F). A single-seat fighter designed in the spring of 1942 incorporating details taken from a captured Japanese Zero. The F6F-3 was first flown in August 1942 and was quickly supplied to the Pacific Fleet. Its first action was in the strike on Marcus Island in September 1943. It quickly became the standard fighter for the navy, and without replacing the Corsair (q.v.) the Marine Corps equipped many of its squadrons with the Hellcat. It saw action in every marine operation in the Central Pacific as well as the Philippine campaigns. The corps also utilized the F6F-5N equipped with radar as a night fighter. Powered by a 2,000-horsepower engine, the F6F had a maximum speed of 375 miles per hour, an excellent rate of climb, a service ceiling of 36,000 feet, and an effective normal range (without drop tanks) of 1,050 miles. Armed with six .50-caliber wing guns, it also had the capability of carrying two 1,000-pound bombs. The night fighter version had 20mm cannon in the wings. The Hellcat was the only operational naval aircraft designed and built after Pearl Harbor (q.v.). It was taken out of production in December 1945 after Grumman had produced more than 10,000 F6Fs.

"HELLDIVER" (A-25; SB2C). The last in the line of famous planes built by Curtiss Aircraft Company given the name "Helldiver." It was built to replace the Douglas "Dauntless" SBD (q.v.) dive bombers, then the mainstay of the navy's dive bomber fleet. The Navy designation was SB2C. The first production model was flown in June 1942 and was introduced into Pacific Fleet operations in November 1943. Much larger than the SBD, powered by a 1,900-horsepower engine, it had internal bomb stowage and wing racks for more bombs. By 1944 it had generally replaced the older dive bombers on the carriers of the 3d and 5th fleets. The A-25 was in part a result of attempts at army-navy standardization and incorporated hundreds of design changes from the original. The Marine Corps adopted this version, and it was assigned to some bombing squadrons but never replaced the SBD completely.

"HELLDIVER" (F8C-5). A two-seat biplane fighter and light bomber built by Curtiss Aircraft Company. It was equipped with a 450 horsepower Pratt and Whitney radial engine, giving it a maximum speed of 140 miles per hour with a service ceiling of 18,000 feet. It was noted for its ability to dive vertically under full power in bombing operations. The F8C-5, which was first delivered to the corps in the late 1930s, was specifically for land operations and did not have the equipment its predecessor, the F8C-4, had for carrier landings.

HENDERSON, ARCHIBALD. 5th commandant, b. Colchester, Va., 21 Jan. 1783, d. 6 Jan. 1859. Henderson was appointed second lieutenant in the corps in June 1806 and rose rapidly until appointed captain in 1811. As a captain he was senior officer on board the frigate *Constitution* when "Old Ironsides" engaged the *Java* in December 1812 and also in February 1814 when the British frigate *Cyane* and the sloop *Levant* were captured after a four-hour battle. For this service he was breveted major. He was one of the officers who charged Commandant Wharton (q.v.) with dereliction of duty for not taking the field at the battle of Bladensburg (q.v.). An army court martial cleared Wharton in 1817. Subsequently Henderson was in command of the marines in New Orleans (q.v.) and was named commandant in October 1820, succeeding Anthony Gale (q.v.) who was found guilty by a court martial for drunkenness and dismissed from the service. By then the corps was authorized 50 officers and 942 enlisted men. Henderson established the policy that all commissioned officers had to serve time for training at headquarters in Washington. Most of the corps served on board naval ships and during the 1820s were involved in action against pirates in the Caribbean and Greece, slavers off the west coast of Africa, and the East Indies. Henderson and friends of the corps thwarted Pres. Andrew Jackson's attempt to discontinue the corps. As a result, in 1834 Congress reorganized the corps and put it directly under the secretary of the navy, not the War Department, and increased its size to over 1,200 men. The rank of the commandant was raised to colonel.

The decision by President Jackson to relocate the Seminole Indians precipitated the Seminole War (q.v.), and in May 1836 he ordered the marines to serve with the army to pacify first the Creeks and then the Seminoles. Despite being commandant, Henderson took command of the marine units. In January 1837 he was given command of a mixed brigade that pushed the Seminoles back to the Hatchee-Lustee River and secured the surrender of a portion of the Seminole nation. Believing the war to be over, he returned to Washington in May, leaving command of the marines there to a subordinate. They continued to serve in Florida until the summer of 1842. For his service Henderson was breveted a brigadier general, the first marine to hold that rank.

During the Mexican War (q.v.), Henderson stayed in Washington but was responsible for getting Pres. James Polk's approval to increase the corps to regimental size. One battalion served with General Scott, and another supported Commodore Perry in his Tabasco expedition. After the war, marines were involved in Panama (q.v.), Nicaragua (q.v.), Japan, and China. General Henderson died in office in January 1859, having been the commander for 39 crucial years and serving under 11 presidents.

HENDERSON FIELD. The main objective of the 1st Division that assaulted Guadalcanal (q.v.) on 7 August 1942. The Japanese had begun its construction earlier. From there Japanese planes could threaten the U.S. supply line to New Zealand. Once captured, the defense of the airfield (named in honor of a marine pilot, Lofton Henderson, killed during the operation on Midway [q.v.]), became the major task of the marine and later army units. Initially the strip was only 2,600 feet long and unmatted. While fighting raged around the field, it was extended and steel mats were laid down. On 20 August a squadron of Wildcat (q.v.) fighters and Dauntless (q.v.) bombers were brought in. During the next three months, marine pilots such as Robert Galer (q.v.) and Joe Foss (q.v.) destroyed Japanese planes at an unprecedented rate. Despite the inferiority of the U.S. planes and continued shelling from Japanese ships, the marine flyers managed to secure aerial superiority so necessary for the success of the ground forces. After the withdrawal of the Japanese from Guadalcanal, a much improved Henderson Field was a key to the success of offensive operations in the central and northern Solomons.

"HERCULES" (KC-130). This versatile four-engined transport was first ordered by the Air Force's Tactical Air Command from Lockheed Aircraft Company in 1952. The Hercules was later modified in addition to its primary cargo function to be a gunship, a weather reconnaissance vehicle, a craft for arctic operations and for air sea-rescue, and a tanker. The C-130A was first flown in April 1955. The initial contract finished in 1959 with 231 planes delivered. In Vietnam (q.v.) the gunship version had radar, an onboard fire computer, and 20mm multi-barrel guns. In 1963 an upgraded version, the KC-130H, was ordered that had more powerful engines, paratroop doors, with a maximum speed of 386 miles per hour and a range of 2,500 miles with a maximum pay load of 10 tons. It could carry a maximum of 92 paratroops. Earlier in 1962 the corps ordered 46 Hercules with the designation KC-130F, which were modified versions of the KC-130B. These planes were equipped for in-flight fueling, having a capacity of 3,000 gallons. More advanced versions such as the HC-130P were modified for refueling helicopters in flight and for midair retrieval of parachute-borne payloads. Twenty of these were ordered. Another version was designated KC-130R, with larger engines and an increased payload, and was adopted by the Marine Corps as its standard tanker aircraft.

HEYWOOD, CHARLES. 9th commandant, b. Maine, 3 Oct. 1839, d. Washington, D.C., 26 Dec. 1915. Heywood was commissioned in April 1858 and spent duty time aboard a number of naval ships. During the Civil War (q.v.) in 1861, he participated in the capture of Forts Clark and Hatteras. Later he commanded a gun battery on board the *Cumberland* in its losing fight with the *Merrimac* and was on board the *Hartford* during the battle of Mobile Bay. After the war he served on various ships before becoming commander of the Marine Barracks in Washington in 1876. He participated in putting down serious labor riots the following year. The canal schemes of Ferdinand de Lesseps in Panama (q.v.) had failed, and in 1885 antigovernment rebels seized the American owned Panama railway. Lieutenant Colonel Heywood, commanding a battalion of marines, left Brooklyn Navy Yard, and arrived in Panama 11 April, and took command of all marines there. His brigade moved across the Isthmus from the Atlantic side, and by the time Colombian troops arrived at the end of the month, the railway was secure. Heywood became colonel commandant on 30 January 1891, instituted fitness reports and promotion examinations, and in May authorized the School of Application in Washington for new marine officers. He changed the uniform of marines to add a broad-brimmed field hat and canvas leggings for field operations and also put into use the new Lee bolt-action .236-caliber rifle using smokeless powder. In May 1898 Congress raised the commandant's rank once more to brigadier general and brought wartime strength to 3,300. Heywood ordered a battalion to Key West only a week after war was declared on Spain on 19 April 1898 and it was involved in action at Guantanamo (q.v.) Bay. Other units were involved in the capture of Guam (q.v.) and also in the Philippines. Marines were also involved in Samoa (q.v.) (1899), Nicaragua (q.v.) (1899), and Panama (1901). He was promoted to major general in July 1902, the first to hold such rank in the Marine Corps. When he retired at age 64 in October 1903, the corps had grown to over 7,600 men.

HOCHMUTH, BRUNO. b. Houston, Tex., 10 May 1911, d. Vietnam, 11 Nov. 1967. Hochmuth attended Texas A & M, receiving a B.S. degree in 1935. He was commissioned in the corps shortly afterward and held a number of field-grade assignments before World War II (q.v.). He attended the corps' Staff and Command College in 1943 before assignment to the Pacific theater. Hochmuth participated as a staff officer of the 2d Division during the invasions of Saipan (q.v.) and Tinian (q.v.) in mid-1944. On Okinawa (q.v.) he commanded a battalion. After the war he attended specialists schools and in 1947 began a four-year tour as a staff officer at Marine Corps Headquarters in Washington, D.C. As a colonel he assumed command of the 2d Marines in 1951, a position he held until he attended the Canadian Army Staff College in 1953. After completion of that course in 1955, he became chief of staff of the 3d Division and two years later was appointed chief of staff of the recruit depot in San Diego. In 1960 he was placed in charge of the Research and Development Office in Washington and three years later returned to San Diego as commanding general of the recruit depot.

On 20 March 1967 as a major general, Hochmuth assumed command of the 3d Division in Vietnam (q.v.) at a crucial period in the defense of I Corps' positions in the north. The 3d Division successfully beat back concerted North Vietnamese attacks on Con Thien (q.v.), Cam Lo, and Khe Sanh (q.v.). On 11

November during a routine inspection flight, General Hochmuth's helicopter exploded. He was the highest-ranking officer killed in Vietnam.

HOLCOMB, THOMAS. 17th commandant, b. New Castle, Del., 5 Aug. 1879, d. Washington, D.C., May 1965. Holcomb was appointed a second lieutenant 13 April 1900 and served with North Atlantic Fleet, in the Philippines, and for five years as a part of the Legation Guard and attaché on the staff of the U.S. minister in Peking (q.v.). An excellent marksman, he was on the marine world champion team of 1902. He became the inspector of target practice for the corps from October 1914 to August 1917. He was promoted to major in 1916 and subsequently commanded the 2d Battalion of the 6th Regiment at Quantico (q.v.). He retained this position until appointed second in command of the regiment in August 1918.

Holcomb was involved in all the major actions of the corps during World War I (q.v.): Chateau-Thierry (q.v.), Soissons (q.v.), Saint-Mihiel (q.v.), and the Meuse-Argonne (q.v.). For his actions he received the Navy Cross (q.v.), the Silver Star, the Purple Heart (q.v.), the *Croix de Guerre*, and the Cross of the Legion of Honor. He was promoted to lieutenant colonel in 1920. Later he commanded the marine base at Guantanamo (q.v.) Bay, attended the Command and General Staff School, and commanded the marine detachment at Peking (q.v.). After attending the Naval and Army War Colleges from 1930 to 1932, Holcomb served in the office of Naval Operations. Promoted to brigadier general in February 1935, he commanded the marine station at Quantico (q.v.) before becoming commandant in December 1936. President Franklin Roosevelt agreed to his promotion to major general and his appointment over other senior generals. On 1 December 1940 the president appointed him to a further four-year term as commandant.

During Holcomb's tenure, the corps expanded from 15,000 to 305,000 men, including five combat divisions then active in the Central Pacific area during World War II (q.v.). In January 1942 Holcomb was advanced to the rank of lieutenant general, the highest rank ever achieved by a marine officer. With the tide turned in the war, General Holcomb retired in April 1944. Promoted to full general before his retirement, he left almost immediately to take up the post of ambassador to South Africa where he served for four years.

"HORNET" (F-18A and A-18). Built by McDonnell Douglas, this plane was basically a redesign of Northrop's YF-17 lightweight fighter. The plane was under development from 1976 until it was fully accepted by the navy in 1982. The A-18 version was identical to the F-18 except for laser trackers for new rocketry pods to take the place of fuselage-mounted Sparrow rockets. The earlier F-18 was combined with the features of the A-18 before full production began and the new aircraft was designated as the FA-18A; these joined the navy and marine squadrons after 1983 replacing the F-4 Phantom (q.v.). This first-line fighter continued to be modified and updated through the 1980s.

The FA-18 had a speed of Mach 1.8 (1,370 miles per hour) and a combat ceiling of over 50,000 feet. It had the latest radar and a head up display on the windscreen, which did away with much traditional instrumentation. It had nine external weapons stations with mixed ordnance. Two wingtip stations were for Sidewinder air-to-air missiles; inboard of these were stations for Sparrow missiles and two nacelle stations for Sparrows. Mounted in the nose was a 20mm six-barrel gun with 570 rounds directed by a laser gunsight. A few TF-18As—a two-seat combat capable training aircraft—were also built.

HORSE MARINES. They were organized from the Legation Guard at Peking during the late 1920s. Initially only 20 men were in this group, trained and equipped like their army counterparts in the cavalry. By the mid-1930s the size of the unit had grown to 50 men. Although organized to help protect American lives and property, their main function proved to be climaxing Marine Corps parades by staging wild charges.

HOWARD, JIMMIE E. b. Burlington, Ia., 27 July 1929. During the Vietnam War (q.v.), a decision was made in 1966 to place six teams from the 1st Reconnaissance Battalion on hills overlooking the Que Son Valley to track Viet Cong (q.v.) movements and report on its strength before sending large-scale allied forces into the valley. The most important of these was Nui Vu, a 1,500 foot hill, and 18 men from C Company were helicoptered in on 13 June. The observation team was commanded by Staff Sergeant Howard who already had three Purple Hearts (q.v.) and a Silver Star for action in the Korean War (q.v.). Their observation of the valley in the next two days resulted in disrupting the Viet Cong units there, but it also brought them to the attention of the enemy. Late in the evening of 15 June an enemy infantry battalion began to climb the slopes. Howard moved his men back to a defensive position 20 yards in diameter on a rocky knoll and began to repulse the many Viet Cong attacks, which lasted for 12 hours. They were supported by gunships and helicopters, bringing the valley under direct attack. The helicopters fired within 25 yards of the entrenched marines.

By early morning most of Howard's command were either dead or wounded including the sergeant, so seriously wounded in the back that he could not move his legs. Nevertheless, he stayed on the radio directing all attacks and later relief efforts. A relief column from the 5th Marines fought its way to Howard's perimeter by early morning of the 16th, and medical evacuation helicopters braved the heavy sniper fire to take off Howard and his men. Of the 18 men in Howard's platoon, six had been killed and the others wounded, but they had taken a heavy toll of the attacking Viet Cong. Fifteen of his men were nominated for the Silver Star, two for the Navy Cross (q.v.), and Howard was later awarded the Medal of Honor (q.v.).

HOWITZER. See Pack Howitzer.

HUE. An important city in central Vietnam located on the Perfume River. It was the capital of Vietnam from 1802 to 1945. Reflecting its imperial past, the city contained many historic buildings, including the old Imperial Palace and the Thien Mu Pagoda. The city became one of the major targets of the North Vietnamese and Viet Cong (q.v.) forces during the Tet offensive (q.v.) of 1968 during the Vietnam War (q.v.). After announcing a truce during the religious holiday, the North Vietnamese infiltrated its forces into most of the cities of the south. By the evening of 30 January they had established control over most of Hue. The 1st Battalion, 1st Marines, fought its way into the city and established contact with South Vietnamese Army (ARVN) forces there. Joined by the 5th Battalion, 5th Marines, they began the arduous task of clearing the enemy from the area south of the Perfume River in fierce house-to-house combat. By 9 February the southern area had been retaken. On the 12th ARVN units and the 1st Battalion, 5th Marines, attacked the main area of the city from the north. Ten more days of heavy fighting was necessary before all of the city was recaptured. A major tactical defeat for the North Vietnamese, their Tet offensive nevertheless destroyed a large portion of the old city, and the U.S. public erroneously believed that Tet represented a defeat.

HWACHON RESERVOIR. The base area for the 1st Division in Korea in April 1951. The Chinese began their spring offensive on 21 April and during the first few hours of fighting had broken through a Republic of Korea division on the marines' right flank, opening a 10-mile gap in the allied line. The 1st Marines' battalions were fed into action one by one on the 22d. With support from the 7th Marines and the British Commonwealth Brigade, the gap was sealed off and the situation normalized. After a brief period under X Corps in the defense of Hongchon, on the right of the 8th Army where the division once again stopped a Chinese breakthrough, it was returned to the Hwachon Reservoir area. By June all three regiments were on line and advancing against the North Koreans toward a ridge line dominating a circular valley that came to be called the "Punchbowl." On 5 September the division moved into the valley and was involved in 18 days of inconclusive fighting.

I

ICELAND. A large strategically located island in the North Atlantic that in 1941 was ruled by the Danish government in exile. The British had posted 25,000 troops there to prevent its possible occupation by the Germans. In May 1941 Prime Minister Winston Churchill asked Pres. Franklin Roosevelt if the United States would take over this responsibility, thus freeing up the British troops for use elsewhere. As a result, the 6th Marines, which was on its way from the West Coast to join the 1st Division, was directed northward and with support troops became the 1st Provisional Brigade. Over 4,000 strong, the marines reached Reykjavik, the Icelandic capital, on 7 July. They moved into camps vacated by the British and began what was fundamentally guard duty. The first units of an army brigade began arriving in August 1941, gradually replacing the 6th Marines. The last marine units left Iceland in March 1942, three months after the United States entered the war.

INCHON. Located on the western coast of Korea, Inchon is the main port for the capital of Seoul (q.v.) and the site of a crucial operation during the Korean War (q.v.). In 1950 the North Koreans pushed the U.S. and South Korean forces to the far southeast corner of Korea in a small defensible enclave surrounding the port of Pusan (q.v.). General Douglas MacArthur conceived the strategy of landing two divisions behind the enemy lines and, in conjunction with a breakout of his 8th Army, catch the enemy in a vise. For this task he created X Corps, composed of the 1st Marine Division and the army's 7th Division. The marines led the attack first on the island of Wolmi-do, which guarded the entrance to the main port area. The Pentagon at first opposed the plan largely because of the narrow inlet to the port and the tides, which were among the world's highest. Finally approved, Operation Chromite called for continuous bombardment of the target area for three days by seven destroyers and four cruisers combined with marine air attacks from two aircraft carriers.

At 0630 on 15 September a battalion of the 5th Marines landed on Green Beach on Wolmi-do. Supported by tanks, the marines secured the island within two hours and set up blocking positions at the beginning of the causeway to the mainland. At 1730 the other battalions of the 5th Marines landed at Red Beach on the western side of the city. Despite problems with the landing and considerable enemy fire from the hills, most of the objectives were taken before dark. The assault by the 1st Marines supported by 18 gun-equipped army amtracs (LVT-As [q.v.]) on Blue Beach south of the city went even better than that on Red Beach. During the night reinforcements, particularly the artillery of the 11th Marines, were brought in to Wolmi-do. United Nations forces including South Korean army, and marine units were also landed to aid in clearing Seoul of the enemy.

Early on the morning of the 16th, the 1st and 5th Marines linked up east of Inchon. The North Koreans had believed Inchon secure and thus had few troops available to counter the marine landings. Their counterattack on the 17th was easily contained, and the marines began the advance on Seoul. Elements of the army's 7th Division were landed on the 18th, taking up positions on the right flank of the 1st Division. Two days earlier the UN forces began the breakout from the Pusan perimeter. MacArthur's gamble had paid off. In the first seven days of the operation, the joint task force had suffered only 70 killed and 470 wounded. The battle for Seoul cost much more.

INTEGRATION. During World War II (q.v.), all branches of the armed forces followed a segregationist policy. However, under pressure from the president, the commandant in mid-1941 appointed a commission to recommend how black soldiers could best be used. The conclusion was that they be used in a composite defense battalion. Soon after Pearl Harbor (q.v.) the corps was ordered to accept black enlistments. A training camp was established near Camp Lejeune (q.v.), and the first recruits arrived in August 1942 to fill out the 51st Defense Battalion. All officers were white, as initially were the drill instructors. As soon as possible, the white instructors were replaced with qualified blacks. Intermingling of white and black troops was discouraged. The 51st, comprised of over 1,400 men, was sent to Funafuti in the Ellis Islands and ultimately was posted to the Marshall Islands (q.v.), where the men remained until the war's end. Another defense battalion, the 52d, was organized in December 1943 and sent to Roi-Namur (q.v.) and later to the Mariana Islands (q.v.). A stewards branch was also established in early 1943, as were pioneer infantry units that were used almost exclusively as labor troops. In all, 51 depot companies and 12 ammunition companies were organized during the war. Only 19,000 black troops served in the corps in World War II, most of these having been drafted.

The corps was reluctant to commission black officers. The first black officer in the corps was not commissioned until November 1945 and then only in the reserve. Not until May 1948 was a black man given a regular commission.

After the war, the commandant set a 10 percent limit on the number of blacks in the still segregated corps. However, segregation came to an end in mid-1949 when the secretary of the navy ordered complete integration of the U.S. Navy and Marine Corps. From this date forward, black marines have played an important distinguished part in all phases of the corps' activities.

"INTRUDER" (A-6A and EA-6). Built by Grumman Aircraft Company, it was basically a carrier-based attack bomber first flown in 1960; the 6A was adopted by the navy in February 1963. A total of 463 of this basic model were built by the time of the last delivery in 1969. Both navy and marine A-6As saw considerable duty in the Vietnam War (q.v.). One modified version of the 6A was the EA-6A, which was supplied with the latest electronic equipment to gain tactical electronic intelligence and to jam enemy radiation. Twenty-seven of these planes were provided to the corps. This version was later updated with different electronic components and given the title of "Prowler" (EA-6B). An advanced conversion of the A-6A was the A-6E, which had the multimode radar and computer system proven on the EA-6B. The first of these planes was deployed in 1972, and 119 had been delivered by 1976. The A-6E was powered by two turbojet engines, enabling a maximum speed of 650 miles per hour with a service ceiling of 47,500 feet and a combat range of 2,700 miles. The Intruder had five weapons attack points, allowing for a variety of bombs totaling nine tons.

IRAN. A key Middle Eastern state in U.S. containment policy until the overthrow of the shah and subsequent takeover of the government by religious extremists in February 1979. Plans to evacuate 7,800 U.S. citizens were delayed after the U.S. embassy in Teheran was stormed by guerrillas. The embassy guard of 19 marines fought off attackers by using tear gas and birdshot but was forced to surrender. All Americans in the embassy were soon released, but two injured marines were hospitalized. One was taken by guerrillas and held captive for a week. Following this episode in February, the embassy staff was greatly reduced, the marine security guards numbering only 13 men. Excited by the U.S.decision to allow the deposed shah to enter the United States for medical treatment, an angry mob stormed the embassy on 4 November. They forced the gates, climbed the walls, and forced the marines to retreat to the main building. The marine corporal in charge prudently ordered the marines not to fire on the attackers. A total of 61 Americans were taken prisoner, for many the beginning of 444 days of captivity. In January 1980 five secretaries and five marines were released.

Despite the most active diplomatic attempts by Pres. Jimmy Carter's administration, negotiations could not secure the release of the hostages. Finally, on 11 April the president approved a plan to free them by military means. From the beginning the plan was flawed. Instead of one branch being responsible for the relief effort, all services were represented. The plan called for eight navy helicopters flown by marines to take off on 24 April from an aircraft carrier and land at a checkpoint in Iran, where they would be joined by army troops flown in on board C-130s. These would be helicoptered to a point nearer Teheran and thence trucked into the city. The plan went awry because of the mechanical failure of the helicopters. One had rotor trouble, another had instrument failure, and a third had hydraulic problems. Needing a minimum of six helicopters and with no backup, the army commander called off the operation. The ill-fated operation became tragic when one of the helicopters on takeoff crashed into a transport plane, killing eight people, including five marines. The captives in Teheran remained prisoners until the Iranian government had secured every item of propaganda from them before releasing them on 20 January 1981.

IRAQ. A large state occupying much of ancient Mesopotamia, the land between the Tigris and Euphrates Rivers. It borders Turkey on the north, Iran (q.v.) and the Persian Gulf on the east, and Kuwait (q.v.) to the south. It was ruled by the Ottoman Turks until after World War I (q.v.) when the peace treaties recognized its independence. A constitutional monarchy until 1958, it subsequently was controlled by the military. General Saddam Hussein succeeded to power in 1979 and led the country into a long debilitating war with Iran. Iraq was one of the world's largest suppliers of petroleum, and the government used much income derived from its sale to rebuild and modernize its army.

In 1990, reviving a border claim to oil-producing areas of neighboring Kuwait, Hussein sent his army into Kuwait despite warnings from European states, the United States, and other Arab countries. With the largest army in the region, Iraq thus posed a threat to the stability of the area and to the continued unfettered supply of petroleum from the Middle East. After the Iraqi government ignored diplomatic pressure to withdraw from Kuwait, the United States orchestrated a military coalition to drive the Iraqi military from Kuwait. During the last months of 1990, there was a rapid buildup of allied forces in neighboring Saudi Arabia code-named Desert Shield (q.v.). The 1st and 2d Marine Divisions were among the first to arrive and were given the critical position directly south of Kuwait City. Marine air participated in the air war begun on 18 January 1991, and then when the ground war began, they supported the marine drive into Kuwait City. The wide flanking movement of the allied armies combined with aerial superiority crushed Iraq's army in a lightning campaign.

After the war was over, a Marine Expeditionary Unit (q.v.) was sent to northern Iraq to help the Kurdish population there. Although Hussein remained in power, the allies established no-fly zones in the north and south patrolled by allied planes and the sale of Iraqi oil was boycotted. (See also Gulf War.)

IWO JIMA. A small lamb-chop-shaped volcanic island only four miles long by two and a half miles wide in the Bonin group. Its most significant landmark is Mount Suribachi, an inactive volcano 550 feet high in the southwest. The only good beaches available for landing, consisting of deep black sand, are adjacent to the mountain. In 1944 two airfields were on the northern plateau, which were the main reasons for U.S. interest in the island during World War II (q.v.). Possession of these would allow U.S. fighters to accompany the B-29s to Japan, and they would also enable crippled bombers to land.

The Japanese had over 20,000 men on the island and had spent months constructing pillboxes, blockhouses, and bunkers and enlarging the many natural caves. They also had many large-caliber guns as well as medium range artillery. The U.S. invasion, code-named Detachment, was scheduled for 19 February 1945 and was the responsibility of V Amphibious Corps consisting of the 3d, 4th, and 5th Divisions. Prior to the landings, the army and navy air forces and the full weight of the battleship bombardment team delivered the heaviest pre-invasion bombardment of the war. Nevertheless, when men of the 4th and 5th Divisions landed, they were met with a hail of combined arms fire that pinned them down on the beaches with heavy casualties until midmorning. However, by the afternoon riflemen of the 5th had reached the western coast, cutting off the Japanese on Suribachi from the rest of the garrison. The 4th Division had established a lodgement three-fourths of a mile long and over 700 yards deep in the center while taking 2,400 casualties.

The fighting henceforth was in two distinct operations. One was in the southwest, with the objective of Mount Suribachi (q.v.). Under cover of heavy bombardment, the 28th Marines on the 21st had breached the Japanese defenses. The next morning one battalion reached the crater's rim and raised a small flag. Later a larger flag more visible to marines below was raised. The photograph of this second flag raising became the most popular photograph of the Pacific war and became an unofficial symbol of the Marine Corps.

The major part of the battle occurred on the flat lands to the northeast where the Japanese had built three defense belts. By the 22d one regiment of the 3d Division was committed, and units from all divisions made only slow progress against the thousands of bunkers, caves, mortar pits, and machine gun nests. By the close of the day on 24 February, the marines controlled only half of the island. Combat efficiency was down to 60 percent, another regiment of the 3d was committed, and the slow reduction of the Japanese defenders continued. By 3 March the 4th Division captured two strong points, the Amphitheater and the Turkey Knob, and five days later, it survived a massive banzai attack. The 3d Division fought for three weeks before the Japanese were cleared from the area in and around a pocket of fanatical defenders on 16 March. Meanwhile, the 5th had almost reached the northernmost tip of the island. Senior U.S. commanders prematurely had a flag-raising ceremony on 13 March, but fighting continued for another two weeks. The Japanese commander committed suicide on the 26th, an indication that the island was really secure.

This small speck of an island, however necessary for strategic purposes, cost the marines heavily. V Amphibious Corps suffered 6,821 killed and 19,207 wounded. Almost the entire Japanese garrison was destroyed.

J

JAPANESE DISARMAMENT. The immediate postwar task was to aid in the disarmament of the huge Japanese military. Marine units from the 3d Fleet were combined in provisional units and were among the first to land in Japan. Two battalions of the 4th Marines went ashore at Yokosuka on 30 August 1945, and soon Marine Air Group 31 was brought in from Okinawa (q.v.). Elements of V Corps occupied Kyushu, the 5th Division landing at Sasebo on 22 November, and the following day the 23d moved into ruined Nagasaki. As elsewhere in Japan there was no trouble; the Japanese armed forces, obedient to the emperor, assisted the occupying force in all ways. Meanwhile, III Corps had been given the dual responsibility of disarming the Japanese in northern China and also keeping the coal mines and railways operating there. The 1st Division from Okinawa landed at Taku on 30 September and disarmed 50,000 troops at Tientsin (q.v.) on 6 October. A further 50,000 surrendered at Peking. The 6th Division had landed at Tsingtao and on 25 October disarmed the Japanese garrison there. In the meantime, marines were guarding the rail lines. Later Chinese Nationalist troops were brought into the marine-occupied areas in an attempt to block the Communists from seizing control of the territory.

"JENNY" (JN-4). A biplane, first designed by an Englishman as a tandem trainer, it was produced by the thousands before World War I (q.v.) ended. There was a series of models; the main version was the JN-4D built by Curtiss Aircraft Company and a number of other firms. A later version was used as a bombing and gunnery trainer. The Jenny was very slow—75

miles per hour top speed. It was a sturdy, fabric-covered plane
that could be repaired easily. The corps used it extensively as
a trainer and in various actions in the Caribbean and Central
America in the early 1920s.

JOHNSON LIGHT MACHINE GUN (M1941). Though designed
as a replacement for the venerable Browning automatic rifle
(BAR) (q.v.), this weapon was not adopted by the Army. The
corps, however, could not get enough BARs for its needs and
therefore procured a quantity of the M1941s. They were primarily intended for specialized units such as the Raiders or
parachute battalions. The 1942 Table of Organization and
Equipment called for 87 Johnsons for each division. Weighing
only 12.3 pounds, much less than the BAR, its rate of fire of
the standard 30.06 cartridge could be adjusted from 300 to 900
rounds per minute. The gun was very popular with marines
although it never replaced the BAR.

JOHNSON M1941 RIFLE. A .30-caliber weapon with a unique
rotary side-feed mechanism and a detachable barrel. It
weighed only eight and a half pounds, and its accuracy was
excellent. As such, it competed with the Garand M-1 (q.v.) for
adoption as the standard rifle for all services. Designed by a
marine officer, the prototype was built in 1937. The following
year it was tested against the Garand by the Army Ordnance
Department and was found to be satisfactory but no better than
the M-1. Further tests were made in 1939 and 1940 with similar
results. The M-1 continued as the standard rifle for the army,
and the Marine Corps also rejected the Johnson in 1941. However, later the rifle was adopted for issue to airborne units. The
Marine First Parachute Battalion was equipped with Johnsons
prior to the action in the Solomon Islands (q.v.). Some Raiders
used the Johnson, but problems with the barrel and the side-
feed mechanism showed the M-1 to be a more dependable
weapon.

K

KELLEY, PAUL X. 28th commandant, b. Boston, Mass., 11 Nov.
1928. Kelley graduated from Villanova and was commissioned
a second lieutenant in June 1950. During the 1950s, he served
at Camp Lejeune (q.v.), Camp Pendleton (q.v.), and for 20
months of sea duty with the 6th Fleet before being ordered to

Japan for a year. During this period he also served as aide-de-camp to the deputy commander of Fleet Marine Force (q.v.), Pacific, and after duty in Washington he completed the Airborne Pathfinder School at Fort Benning. From September 1960 to May 1961 as a captain, he was an exchange officer to the British Royal Marines and served in Aden and later commanded a troop of the Royal Marines in Singapore, Malaya, and Borneo. On returning to the United States, Kelley was assigned to the schools at Quantico before becoming commanding officer of the Marine Barracks at Newport, Rhode Island.

Kelley was ordered to Vietnam in June 1964 first as an intelligence officer to the 3d Amphibious Force and later as commander of a battalion of the 4th Marines. Promoted to lieutenant colonel, he returned to the United States in 1966 to take the position of senior Marine Corps representative at Fort Benning. Afterward he attended the Air War College and in June 1969 was a military assistant to the commandant. Promoted to colonel, he returned to Vietnam in June 1970 as the commander of the 1st Marines. In May 1971 he redeployed the regiment, the last marine combat unit to leave Vietnam, to Camp Pendleton.

Kelley was ordered to Washington in July 1971 in the Plans and Policy area and as an assistant to the director of the Joint Staff. As a brigadier general in August 1974, he was assigned to command the 4th Division, a post he held until the following year when he became the director of the Development Center at Quantico (q.v.). In 1978 he was appointed deputy chief of staff at Marine Corps Headquarters.

The most prestigious command Kelley held before his appointment as assistant commandant on 1 July 1981 was the command of the Rapid Deployment Joint Task Force, a four-service force headquartered at MacDill Air Force Base. Promoted to four-star rank, he served as assistant commandant from July 1981 until his appointment to commandant by Pres. Ronald Reagan two years later. During his tenure, marines were dispatched to Lebanon (q.v.) on a peacekeeping mission that ended tragically. He served as commandant until 30 June 1987.

KHE SANH. A small village located in Quang Tri Province, Vietnam, only a few miles south of the Demilitarized Zone (DMZ) (q.v.). At first in 1967 it was simply one of a number of strong points from which marines could attempt to control North Vietnamese Army (NVA) military movements in the south. Defended by the 26th Marines, it became a hub for the projected infiltration barrier envisioned by the Defense Department to stretch across Vietnam.

During the failed NVA offensive of the spring of 1967, Khe Sanh was attacked along with Con Thien (q.v.). Counterattacking units of the 3d and 9th Marines drove the North Vietnamese back and seized a number of key hills. This first battle for Khe Sanh was over by 12 May.

In February 1968 the North Vietnamese decided to contest the marines' control of the main defense bastion and the hills surrounding Khe Sanh. For this offensive, they committed two divisions. The NVA had soon established control of the land routes to Khe Sanh and began their artillery bombardment against the entrenched marines. In addition, there were continual infantry attacks on the marine perimeter.

Khe Sanh soon became more important politically than for its military value. Both sides believed it necessary to win a victory there. In defense of Khe Sanh, the United States launched massive air strikes against the North Vietnamese. In all, over 110,000 tons of bombs were dropped, and U.S. tactical air controlled the skies over Khe Sanh. On 1 April a relief force of 24 marine and 28 army battalions began the counteroffensive. The 1st Marines and South Vietnamese Army (ARVN) units cleared the enemy from vital Route 9. The army's 1st Air Cavalry and ARVN airborne were flown forward as the marines in Khe Sanh attacked southwest. On 4 April contact was made with the airborne units. The 77-day siege of Khe Sanh had ended.

The NVA, for all the expenditure of men and equipment, had failed. However, Khe Sanh was soon abandoned as a major U.S. base. The area around Khe Sanh continued to be important, but never again did it assume such a central role in the marine defenses in the northern I Corps area.

KOREAN WAR. On 25 June 1950 the Russian-trained North Korean army invaded the southern part of the peninsula governed by the U.S.-supported Republic of Korea. Very quickly the South Korean forces were overrun, and Pres. Harry Truman authorized the use of American air power first and later, under the banner of the United Nations, the army divisions available in Japan and the Central Pacific. Fighting at times a desperate delaying action, the UN forces were confined to the extreme southeastern part of Korea centered on the port of Pusan (q.v.) by the end of July. At the beginning of the conflict, there were no plans for the use of marine forces. However, all marine reserves were immediately called to active duty, and the commandant offered the use of available marine units to Gen. Douglas MacArthur, who welcomed the possibility of using marines in an amphibious operation he hoped would reverse the fortunes of the United Nations.

On 7 July the 1st Provisional Brigade was formed from the understrength 1st Division and left Camp Pendleton (q.v.) on 12 July. Marine Air Group 33, built around three squadrons of Corsairs (q.v.), also was sent to Korea. MacArthur had hoped to keep the 6,500-man brigade in reserve for use specifically for the Inchon (q.v.), operation but the situation at Pusan was so desperate that on 2 August he committed it to act as a fire brigade. On the extreme left of the allied line, the 5th Marines halted the North Korean push toward Masan and drove them back to Sachon. Transferred 70 miles north to the Naktong Bulge near Obong-ni, they tore up the attacking Koreans supported by T-34 tanks and forced the enemy to retreat across the river. On 3 September they were shifted to a sector where the army's 2d Division had been badly mauled. In three days the North Koreans had been driven back more than five miles after sustaining heavy losses. The brigade was pulled back into reserve on 5 September to prepare for Inchon.

By this time the 1st Marines had arrived at Kobe, but the 7th was still in transit. A Korean regiment was added to bring the 1st Division up to approximate strength. MacArthur's audacious plan was for the navy to bring the 1st Division to Inchon through the narrow Flying Fish Channel, where the tides reached over 30 feet, among the highest in the world. MacArthur had chosen Inchon against the advice of his superiors in Washington for this very reason. The operation was under the overall command of the army's X Corps, and the army's 7th Division would act as a reserve. Air and naval strikes at the Inchon area began on 10 September. Five days later at 0630 a battalion of the 5th Marines landed on Wolmi-do, a small island separated from Inchon by a 600-yard causeway. The main landings could not be made for over 12 hours when the tide was again in. Then the remainder of the 5th would land to the north and the 1st Marines to the south. Clambering up the sea walls, the marines soon had a secure lodgement and were moving inland, and on the 17th the 5th took the Kimpo airport and seized the high ground north of Seoul. The 1st Marines had a more difficult time and did not finish with Korean opposition west of the Han River until the 21st.

The 1st Marines crossed the Han on the 24th and the following day both regiments were within Seoul. The Korean defenders, numbering more than 10,000 men, put up a fierce resistance. Artillery and air strikes were used sparingly because of the large number of civilians caught in the fighting. Thus, the capture of Seoul (q.v.) was achieved as an infantry battle in which enemy strong points had to be reduced with rifles and grenades. Despite infantry and tank counterattacks, Seoul was secured by the 27th, and two days later MacArthur and President Syngman Rhee entered the battered capital. The army's 7th Division had landed on the 18th and had advanced on the marines' right, fought in the southern parts of the city, and then advanced south toward Osan while the two marine regiments expanded the perimeter by pushing east from Seoul. Meanwhile, the 8th Army within the perimeter, now grown to over 140,000 men, double the size of the North Korean forces, began the breakout on the 22d. The 1st Cavalry Division began its rapid advance up the central corridor toward X Corps' perimeter. The linkup was made on 31 September when a special cavalry detachment met units of the 7th Division. By then the pursuit of the North Koreans was fully under way. Fewer than 25,000 of their troops reached the 38th parallel, with UN forces in close pursuit. The United Nations then authorized MacArthur to begin a new phase by crossing the parallel.

The decision had been made to use X Corps in the eastern flank of the UN forces, and the marines thus were moved from Inchon and disembarked at Wonson harbor on the east coast. MacArthur decided to control the operations of X Corps separately from the overall 8th Army command. The 1st Division was assigned a zone of action 300 miles from north to south and 50 miles wide. The 5th and 7th Marines moved north to Hamhung and prepared for an advancement to the Yalu River, the northern border of Korea. The 1st Marines operated out of Wonson in a mopping up operation. This proved to be a difficult problem, with two of its battalions at Kojo and Majon-ni taking heavy casualties from intact North Korean units. Afterward the division was ordered northwest of the port city of Hungnam astride a mountain road to the Chosin Reservoir (q.v.) and from there to the Yalu River.

Despite various warnings of Chinese intervention, MacArthur's staff and most field commanders were caught by surprise when large numbers of Chinese troops crossed the Yalu River. The 5th and 7th Marines were involved in three weeks of fighting against North Korean and, as was soon discovered, Chinese volunteers. By 13 November the marines had reached the southern part of the reservoir. The plan was developed to have the two marine regiments attack to the west and become a part of a giant pincers, with the 8th Army 80 miles to the west forming the southern part, thus trapping thousands of Koreans and presumably ending the war. However, on 25 November the Chinese launched a major attack against the 8th Army and broke the UN line. The 8th Army advance was stopped, but the marines continued to attack westward until struck by three Chinese divisions. Other Chinese elements cut a part of the retreat route to Hagaru-ri (q.v.), while another division attacked Hagaru-ri defended by only a partial marine battalion. The desperate fighting that occurred in the marine and army withdrawals was made worse by the weather. Snow had fallen by mid-November, and the temperature dropped to 20 degrees below zero. The key positions for the marines were Hagaru-ri and Toktong Pass, through which the retreating column had to pass. General Oliver P. Smith (q.v.), the divisional commander, ordered a relief column from the 1st Marines and a company of British Royal Marines to Hagaru-ri. On 3 December the marines holding the pass were relieved by a battalion of the 7th. The route southward to Hagaru-ri had been cleared, and the bulk of both regiments was in the environs of the town by 5 December. The next day the breakout toward Koto-ri, 11 miles away, began.

With the 7th Marines leading, followed by the 5th and elements of the 1st and the British, Koto-ri had been reached by midnight of the 7th. This movement was made possible by marine air units that had cleared a corridor one mile wide along the road. Army and navy planes struck the Chinese farther away. The following day the march to Hungnam continued. The 1st Marines cleared the Funchilin Pass which had been seized by the Chinese on 8 December. Four days later the cold and hungry marines reached Hungnam. They had suffered 4,400 battle casualties, with 730 dead and thousands more with frostbite and pneumonia. The better part of six Chinese divisions had been destroyed, losing perhaps as many as 25,000 killed. They did not interfere with the evacuation of X Corps personnel from the port. The marines loaded on transports could watch the engineers destroy Hungnam as the ships pulled away toward Pusan. Finally, they were taken by road to Masan where the survivors spent Christmas.

The retreat southward of both 8th Army and X Corps was halted south of the 38th parallel, and a new commander, Gen. Matthew Ridgeway, planned to retake the lost territory, but mainly he wanted to destroy the Chinese army. The 1st Division as a part of IX Corps was moved to the center of the line and took part in the forward advance in Operation Killer (q.v.) of late February 1951 and of the succeeding Operation Ripper (q.v.) of early March. By the end of March, the Chinese forces were in full retreat almost everywhere, Seoul was recaptured, and the UN line was once again generally north of the parallel. The division was in the Hwachon Reservoir (q.v.) area when the Chinese launched their spring offensive on 21 April and broached the UN line. The division joined by the British Commonwealth Brigade restored the line. Once again in mid-May the division acted as a stopper when the army's 2d Division was in danger of being flanked. In June all three regiments were involved in X Corps' offensive in the Hwachon Reservoir sector and took the heights overlooking a broad valley called the "Punchbowl." By then peace talks had begun and much to the chagrin of the military commanders, the UN forces adopted a primarily defensive stance.

Much of the fighting during the remainder of the war was to attack and seize strategic strong points to deny the enemy their use. Thus, after a relatively quiet summer, the division was ordered to take the rest of the Punchbowl and in three weeks of hard fighting had secured most of the valley. By the beginning of a new cold winter, the division was holding 11 miles of front north of the Punchbowl. On 23 March 1952 the marines were pulled out of that sector and moved almost 200 miles west to the extreme left of the UN line and assigned 35 miles of front overlooking Panmunjom, the site of the peace talks. There were no major offensives during the rest of the war as the discussions regarding peace dragged on. The cessation of the U.S. offensive had allowed a buildup of Chinese and North Korean forces. Combined with the terrain, this development meant that even if the discussions had ended without an agreement, it would have been difficult to dislodge the enemy from its prepared defenses. This was clearly shown by the marine-localized actions at "Bunker Hill" in August 1952 and in October at the "Hook." Vying for strong points named "Berlin," "East Berlin," "Reno," "Carson," and "Vegas" in early 1953, the marines held their positions despite considerable losses.

An agreement was finally reached after Pres. Dwight Eisenhower threatened to use maximum force to end the war. On 27 July 1953 the truce went into effect after two years of obstruction by the Communists. The border remained generally as it was on that date, with a wide demilitarized zone separating North and South Korea. This "police action" fought basically with World War II equipment restored the status quo that had existed before it was begun three years before. This UN operation had cost 33,629 American lives, of which 4,267 were marines. In addition, the marines suffered 23,744 wounded. The 1st Marine Air Wing in close support of ground operations had flown more than 127,000 combat missions and lost 436 planes. Although the fighting had been ended by the truce, the 1st Division was kept in Korea until 1955 when it returned to Camp Pendleton, and the 3d Division, which had been activated in early 1952, was stationed first in Japan and then Okinawa. (See also Pyongyang-Seoul Corridor.)

KRAG-JORGENSEN. A .30-caliber rifle adopted by the U.S. Army and Marine Corps and first issued to troops in 1894. It was a modification of a Danish bolt-action rifle. The unique feature of the Krag was a side-mounted magazine gate holding five cartridges normally of 40 grains of smokeless powder. This gave an initial velocity to the bullet of 2,000 feet per second, far better than that of the black powder cartridges used in the Trapdoor Springfields still in use during the Spanish-American War (q.v.). The Krag was the standard arm of the marines defending the Legation at Peking (q.v.) during the Boxer Rebellion (q.v.) and during the long, drawn-out Philippine Insurrection (q.v.). During that latter conflict, soldiers and marines referred to their mission as civilizing the Filipinos with a Krag. However well the Krag had performed during the Spanish-American War, it was clearly inferior to the stripper clip Mauser rifle used by the Spanish. By 1903 a Mauser-type weapon had been designed and accepted as a replacement for the Krag. This was the famous 1903 Springfield (q.v.).

KRULAK, CHARLES C. 31st commandant, b. Quantico, Va., 4 March 1942. Krulak attended Philips Exeter Academy and graduated from the U.S. Naval Academy in 1964. In 1973 he received a master's degree from George Washington University and graduated from the Amphibious Warfare School (1968), the Army Command and General Staff College (1976), and the National War College (1982). He served two tours in Vietnam commanding first a platoon and then two rifle companies. From 1966 to 1968 he served as commanding officer Special Training Branch at San Diego and later as commanding officer Counter Guerrilla Warfare School on Okinawa (q.v.) in 1970. General Krulak was company officer at the Naval Academy, and from 1973 to 1976 he commanded the Marine Barracks at the air station at North Island, California. From 1983 to 1985 he was commanding officer of the 3d Battalion, 3d Marines. His staff assignments were as S-3 of 2d Battalion, 9th Marines, chief of Combat Arms Monitor Section at Washington, D.C., and from 1978 to 1981 was executive assistant to director of Personnel Management. In 1982–83 he was plans officer to Fleet Marine Force (q.v.), Pacific. He became deputy director to the White House Military Office in 1987, was promoted to brigadier general in June 1989, and became commanding general 10th Marine Expeditionary Brigade (MEB) (q.v.) and assistant divisional commander, 2d Division, the following month.

The next year Krulak became commander of the 6th Marine Expeditionary Brigade before being assigned to duty as assistant deputy chief of staff for manpower on August 1991. In March 1992 he was promoted to major general. He was assigned as commander of Combat Development Command at Quantico in August and the following month was promoted to lieutenant general. In July 1994 he assumed command of Fleet Marine Force, Pacific. He was promoted to general on 29 June 1995 and became commandant the following day.

KRULAK, VICTOR H. b. Denver, Colo., 7 Jan. 1913. He graduated from the Naval Academy and was commissioned a second lieutenant in May 1934. After Basic School, he was assigned to sea duty and then for a brief period at the Naval Academy, and finally in July 1936 he joined the 6th Marines at San Diego. The following year he was in Shanghai, where he served for two years with the 4th Marines. Returning to the United States, he attended the junior course at Quantico (q.v.), after which he was assigned to the 1st Brigade. In April 1941 he was appointed to the staff of the Amphibious Corps, Atlantic, as a captain. He continued on the staff of Maj. Gen. Holland M. Smith (q.v.) when the corps moved to San Diego in September 1942. He volunteered for parachute training and qualified in February 1943. The next month he was transferred to New Caledonia, where he took command of the 2d Parachute Battalion of the corps. Promoted to lieutenant colonel, he led the battalion in action at Vella Lavella in September and in late October led the successful diversionary raid on Choiseul (q.v.) Island to draw attention away from the projected invasion of Bougainville (q.v.). For this action he received the Navy Cross (q.v.). Wounded, he returned to the United States in November and for a year served in the Division of Plans at Headquarters in Washington, D.C. In October 1944 he joined the new 6th Division as assistant chief of staff for operations and was directly involved in the planning for and execution of the invasion of Okinawa (q.v.) after 1 April 1945, for which he received the Legion of Merit. At the conclusion of the war, he was instrumental in negotiating the surrender of Japanese forces at Tsingtao.

After the war Krulak was in charge of the Research Section and assistant director of the Senior School at Quantico. In June 1949 he took command of the 5th Marines at Camp Pendleton (q.v.). One year later as a colonel he became assistant chief of staff for Operations of Fleet Marine Force (q.v.), Pacific, a position he held until mid-1951 when he became chief of staff, Fleet Marine Corps, Pacific. After his promotion to brigadier general in July 1956, he became assistant division commander of the 3d Division on Okinawa. His next assignment was as director of the Educational Center at Quantico, and he was promoted to major general in November 1959. Soon thereafter he assumed command of the recruiting depot in San Diego. In February 1962 he was appointed special assistant to the director for Counter Insurgency under the Joint Chiefs of Staff.

Krulak was chief of the Joint Staff Mission to Vietnam in January 1963 and was a key figure in Washington in the early stages of U.S. involvement in Vietnam. Appointed commander of Fleet Marine Force, Pacific, Krulak was in charge of logistical and strategic support for the growing number of marines in III Amphibious Force. By 1965 he had favored a strategy of pacification rather than total confrontation, which was the plan of the overall army command. Considered seriously for the post of commandant, he retired soon after the Vietnam War (q.v.) and became a successful businessman and civic leader in San Diego.

KUWAIT. A small Persian Gulf state bounded on the north by Iraq (q.v.) and on the south by Saudi Arabia. The population of approximately two million are mainly Sunni Muslims. Until 1961 the state was a British protectorate. In that year the emir and his council began ruling an independent state with close diplomatic and economic ties to Saudi Arabia. Because of its petroleum resources Kuwait was one of the wealthiest countries in the Middle East. The northern border was in dispute, and Iraq's government claimed that many of the oil-producing areas had traditionally belonged to Iraq. Acting on this in the fall of 1990, Iraqi forces invaded Kuwait and quickly overcame all resistance. This action spurred a coalition of powers concerned with stability in the area. After diplomacy failed, the United States and its allies began to build up a military force to liberate Kuwait. Eventually in February 1991 in a lightning war code-named Desert Storm (q.v.), the Iraqi army was driven out and almost completely destroyed. Marine air units participated in all phases of the air war, and the 1st and 2d Marine Divisions played a key role in the capture of Kuwait City. (See also Gulf War.)

KWAJALEIN. The world's largest atoll located in the Marshall Islands (q.v.), composed of more than 90 islands. The most important were the 70-mile-long Kwajalein Island and 40 miles to the north the twin islands of Roi-Namur (q.v.). During World War II (q.v.), two regiments of the 4th Division landed on Roi-Namur on 1 February 1944. The former island was secured within hours, but the Japanese on Namur put up heavier resistance, and that island was not cleared until the following day. Meanwhile, men of the army's 7th Division had occupied a number of smaller islands before attacking Kwajalein, which was captured in three days. The possession of Kwajalein Atoll gave the navy an excellent harbor for staging further attacks into the Mariana Islands (q.v.) as well as a good bomber field on Roi.

L

LANDING CRAFT, PERSONNEL (LCP). At first it was an adaptation of a boat constructed by the Eureka Tugboat Company of New Orleans. In conjunction with the Marine Corps, its owner redesigned the craft, and these LCP(L)s were available for landing exercises in 1940. These 36-foot boats were able to carry a maximum of 36 armed troops. Some were powered by gas engines and others with diesel, giving a maximum speed of eight knots. All LCPs were made of wood with planked bottoms and plywood sides. This construction was adequate under normal circumstances, but they were easily holed by obstacles or wrecks, which resulted in a high loss rate even in unopposed beach landings such as Guadalcanal (q.v.). The major fault of this design was the high prow that forced troops to leap down four feet to the shore. Before a superior craft was introduced in mid-1942, 2,200 of the LCP(L)s were built. This new vehicle was the LCP(R), which had a forward ramp allowing for easier and quicker unloading of assault troops. This model was replaced by early 1943 with the landing craft, vehicle personnel (LCVP) (q.v.). Also by that time many of the troops in the first waves were being carried by LVTs (q.v.).

LANDING CRAFT, TANK (LCT). The first models of this ship were designed and built in England and used extensively in various amphibious operations including the Dieppe raid. The U.S. version (LCT, Mk5) entered service in late 1942. A total of 470 Mk5s were built. Normally constructed in three sections for transportation as deck cargo, they were then reassembled at the destination. The assembled broad-beamed craft was 112 feet long, weighted 286 tons, and could carry five 25-ton or four 40-ton tanks. They were slow, with a top speed of only seven knots. An Mk6 version with mostly internal design changes was available for action in the Pacific in 1944. A total of 965 of these were built before the end of World War II (q.v.). Because of the slowness, they were generally towed for long passages in Pacific operations or on board landing ship tanks (LSTs) (q.v.). The LCT was ramped, and the normal procedure for landing was to beach the craft, lower the ramp, and allow the tanks or other vehicles to proceed directly up the beach area toward the front. LCTs were modified to perform a variety of tasks such as hospital ships, dredgers, and salvage operations. Plans for a larger, better-designed LCT, the Mk7, became the landing ship medium (LSM), a 203-foot- long, 513-ton armed craft that was faster and could carry five Sherman tanks or six LVTs (q.v.). Both LCTs and LSMs were used in the Iwo Jima (q.v.) and Okinawa (q.v.) operations.

LANDING CRAFT, VEHICLE PERSONNEL (LCVP). By mid-1942 there was a recognized need for a new type of craft that could take troops from the transport to the slow-moving amphibians (LVTs [q.v.]) for the final run to the beach. The first design of such a craft was the LCV, which was a redesigned LCP(R) (q.v.) with a larger armored ramp. Over 2,000 of this type were built. The major problem with the LCV was that it took in water from the front unless it was securely beached. A further improved design was the LCVP, which began to reach the war front in mid-1942. This was a 36-foot-long wooden craft with increased armor and a 225-horsepower engine that could move it at a maximum of nine knots per hour. It could carry 36 troops and a crew of three.

Besides its primary role, the LCVP was utilized for a great variety of tasks, ranging from ambulance transport to a cargo carrier. This latter function became even more important as the war progressed. For the first time at Peleliu (q.v.), bulk cargoes were loaded on pallets and coded for easier and quicker unloading onto the amphibians at the reef. They were initially carried on deck or in three-tiered davits on the transports and launched when loaded. Eventually LCVPs were launched directly from LSTs (q.v.). Between 1942 and 1945 there were 23,358 LCVPs built, and they were used not only for army and marine operations but also in all the amphibious assaults in Europe.

LANDING OPERATIONS DOCTRINE (FTP-167). A publication by the Navy in 1938 that was a revised version of a Marine Corps text, *Tentative Manual for Landing Operations* issued four years previous. These contained the results of the corps investigations of the problems of amphibious warfare. Later the army in its own field manual, *Landing Operations on Hostile Shores* (FM31-5), adopted the tactics and techniques recommended by the corps. The work of the members of the Equipment Board and the Marine Corps schools responsible for the earlier manual thus had far reaching effects as their ideas were proved in dozens of amphibious assaults in World War II (q.v.).

LANDING SHIP, TANK (LST). Designed by the Department of Naval Construction, the original contract was let in February 1942 for an ocean-going tank-landing craft. The Mk1. The LST was 327 feet long with a beam of 50 feet. The main feature of the ship was the 288 foot by 30 foot tank deck located under the top deck. It could carry over 2,000 tons of supplies and equipment at a speed of over nine knots. Its range fully loaded was 6,000 miles. The LST normally had a crew of 163 officers and men. It could carry a wide variety of cargo that was offloaded through a front ramp. One example of its capacity was that it could carry 32 trucks, a 5-ton crane, two antiaircraft guns, 40 tons of ammunition, 115 tons of rations, and 200 tons of fuel in drums. First used in the invasion of Bougainville (q.v.), the LST's ideal was to preload trucks, trailers, and general cargo in certain sequences to allow for quick unloading. By 1945 most of the general cargo was placed on pallets with identification signs for even faster unloading. LST construction in 1943 was given priority even over destroyer construction. By then it was recognized that the LST was to be an important key to ultimate victory. Its role in supporting marines in the many amphibious operations was crucial. At Tarawa (q.v.), in addition to its regular cargo, LSTs carried multipontoon jetties for floating jetties; at Iwo Jima (q.v.) they carried eight and a half miles of steel matting as well as trucks, trailers, tractors, guns, food, and units of fire.

LANDING VEHICLE TRACKED (LVT AND LVT[A]). The first series was designed by Donald Roebling and delivered to the corps in 1940. It was an amphibian designed to be carried by larger ships (LSTs [q.v.]) and, after launching, power its way through the surf, over reefs, and on to land where its tracks would then carry it forward. The LVT-1, better known as the amtrac, was designed primarily for logistical support. It was used first in the Guadalcanal (q.v.) campaigns.

Over the next three years 1,225 LVT-1s were built. The much improved LVT-2 (Water Buffalo) entered production in June 1942. It had greater power than its predecessor, a redesigned suspension system, W-shaped treads, and rubber-tired road wheels. It was larger and could carry 1,500 pounds more cargo than the LVT-1. The first use of the LVT-2 was at Tarawa (q.v.) in November 1943 where the corps utilized 50 of them, only half as many as was requested from the navy. Hastily modified with a boiler plate to give the driver more protection, they were invaluable during the Tarawa operation even though 30 of them were lost to Japanese fire. The need for more protection led to the LVT(A)-2, which had factory-installed armored plating and was used by the corps during the Cape Gloucester (q.v.) campaign. Although most of the LVTs used by the corps throughout the war were the unarmored version, the LVT(A)s wherever possible were used as assault weapons in the first waves of a landing.

The only major deficiency in the vehicle was that it lacked a ramp. Troops and equipment had to be off-loaded over the sides, which could make landing of troops extremely hazardous. Nevertheless, the LVTs became invaluable in all landing operations and were particularly valuable in crossing reefs. After a beachhead was secured, the LVTs became the primary vehicles for delivering supplies to front line troops. More than 3,000 LVT-2s and LVT(A)-2s were manufactured during the war.

LANDING VEHICLE TRACKED PERSONNEL (LVTP). Also named assault amphibious vehicle (AAV), it is the later generation of armored personnel carriers (APCs) developed after the Korean War (q.v.) and built by Food Machinery Corporation

(FMC). The LVTP-5 was ready for use during the Vietnam War (q.v.). It was a huge, 40-ton vehicle with a bow ramp capable of carrying 37 armed men. Although used throughout the conflict, it had certain major disadvantages. It was gasoline powered with the tanks directly underneath the vehicle, which proved very dangerous to crews operating in mined areas. Before the end of the war the corps had requested FMC to design and build a smaller, less costly amtrac with better cross-country performance. The result was the LVTP-7, a smaller improved version of the LVTP-5. Between 1971 and 1975 the corps took delivery of 996 of these vehicles. In 1982 a modernization of the LVTP-7 was ordered and this conversion amounted to a thorough redesign. All but two of the corps' LVTP-7 were rebuilt. The designation was changed from LVTP to AAV at this time and the newly refitted crafts were designated AAV7A1.

The following details of the personnel carrier are those of the A1. It is a large boxlike vehicle made of welded aluminum alloy, 26 feet long, 10 feet wide, and 10 feet from ground to deck. The craft weighs slightly over 23 tons unloaded. It is powered by a 400-horsepower diesel engine that on land gives it a cruising speed of 20 miles per hour and a range of 300 miles. It can operate in the water for a maximum of seven hours cruising at six miles per hour and in plunging surf up to 10 feet. The A1 is armed with one .50-caliber machine gun and three 40mm guns. It can carry 21 combat-equipped troops or five tons of cargo.

LEATHERNECK. A nickname for a marine. In September 1776 the Navy established a standard uniform for the Continental Marines (q.v.). Part of the uniform was a leather collar that was meant to ward off sword cuts to the throat. However questionable the purpose and however much enlisted marines detested it, the leather stock continued to be a part of the marines' uniform until after the Civil War (q.v.). The uncomfortable appendage was distinctive enough for the marines to be called "leathernecks," a title that continued long after that part of a marine's uniform had become obsolete.

LEBANON. A small Middle Eastern country bordering on Syria and Israel. Once a model of peace and prosperity, its government became increasingly involved in the wars designed to crush Israel instigated by other Muslim states. Lebanon thus became a pawn and its political parties even more polarized. The legal government in the late spring of 1958 was threatened by a revolution aided by support from Syria. President Dwight Eisenhower, in response to a request by the Lebanese president, ordered three battalions of marines into the country in mid-July 1958. They seized control of key dockside areas and a few bridges in Beirut and were later reinforced by the army's 24th Airborne Brigade. Cooperation with the Lebanese army secured a relatively peaceful election on 31 July. As the crisis ended the marine units were pulled out of the country; all were gone by 18 October.

During the next 20 years, the Lebanese situation worsened as two more wars against Israel failed to destroy the Jewish state. The Palestine Liberation Organization (PLO) was very active in southern Lebanon and in cooperation with local Muslims escalated its guerrilla attacks on Israel. Israel finally invaded Lebanon and drove to the outskirts of Beirut. This action prompted Syria also to send in troops. The weak Lebanese government was powerless against the two antagonistic states and appealed to the United States for support. Diplomatic pressure forced Israel to retreat to southern Lebanon, but the Syrian army and local Muslim militia still held parts of Beirut and western Lebanon. It was in this confused situation that the Reagan administration decided to cooperate with the United Nations and in August 1982 committed 800 marines of the 32nd Marine Amphibious Unit (MAU) to act with French and Italian troops as peacekeepers. From its base near the Beirut airport the marine presence continued until February 1984.

The 32d was relieved by the 24th on 30 October 1982 and extended its zone of peacekeeping into east Beirut, patrolling along the so-called Green Line separating the warring factions. Artillery and some armor were brought in by late fall, and the marines began to train elements of the Lebanese army. The relative peace that marked the first months of the marine presence was shattered in early March when five marines were wounded in an attack by Islamic fundamentalists. The violence escalated in April when a car bomb exploded at the U.S. embassy and killed 61, including 17 Americans. The withdrawal of Israeli troops to southern Lebanon in May did not bring a halt to the fighting. The Syrians still held a large segment of Lebanon, and antigovernment forces were entrenched in the hills east of Beirut. The Lebanese government and its army were not strong enough to restore order. By the summer of 1983 the peacekeeping forces had become prime targets of the rebels, who shelled the airport intermittently. The 24th MAU, relieved briefly by the 22d which had been involved in the Grenada (q.v.) operation, had returned to Lebanon by 30 May and began almost immediately to take casualties. Three marines were wounded in July, and in August two were killed by sniper fire and 14 were wounded. On 6 September two more marines were killed. The U.S. government ordered more ships of the Mediterranean Fleet to the Lebanese coast, and these, including the battleship *New Jersey*, took the rebel areas in the hills under fire. The 31st MAU was ordered to the Mediterranean to support the marine forces on the ground.

By October 1983 it was obvious that the marines had become major targets for the rebels as the artillery and sniper fire increased. By this time the marines had suffered six men killed and 52 wounded. On October the 22d MAU lost one more killed and nine more wounded from sniper fire. This was but a prelude to the major disaster for the peacekeepers. On 23 October a truck driven by a fundamentalist on a suicide mission crashed through the defense network surrounding the headquarters building of the 1st Battalion, 8th Marines, at the airport. Triggering the 12,000 pounds of explosives, the bomber destroyed the building, killing 241 marines and wounding 70 others. At the same time another suicide bomber attacked a building occupied by French paratroops, killing 58. Such a totally unexpected loss of life caused a furor in Washington. A commission headed by a retired admiral was charged with investigating the tragedy. However, the marine presence continued, and the U.S. role was even expanded. For the next three months U.S. ships and planes continued the bombardment of fundamentalists' strongholds in the hills, and marines were caught up in firefights with snipers.

The U.S. policy toward maintaining the facade of peacekeeping changed only after the rebel forces had seized the largest part of the capital and forced the resignation of the president. On 7 February 1984 Pres. Ronald Reagan announced the withdrawal of the bulk of the marine force. Except for a small contingent left behind to guard the embassy, the last element of the 22d MAU was withdrawn by the 26th. The commission on the airport bombing had made its report the previous December and had concluded that the marines had not been properly trained to deal with the political complexities of the Lebanese situation. It faulted the chain of command and by implication the misuse of combat troops. This report confirmed to a large degree what the commandant had earlier stated: that the Lebanese affair was not a military but a diplomatic and political exercise.

LEGATION GUARDS. One of the key ongoing duties of the corps dating from the 19th century is to provide security for the many embassies throughout the world. Normally the duty is ceremonial. However there were a number of instances during the 20th century when marine guards were involved in dangerous conflict situations. The first and most serious was during the Boxer Rebellion (q.v.) in May 1900 when Chinese rebels threatened all the foreign legations in Peking (q.v.). Although few in number, marines played a key role in holding off a number of attacks by the Boxers until a multinational force arrived. A second very volatile situation occurred in November 1979 after the overthrow of the shah in Iran (q.v.). Irate anti-Western mobs stormed the embassy. In all probability the decision to resist prevented a blood bath. Some of the marine guards remained with other embassy staff as hostages to the revolutionary government for 444 days. Another situation fraught with danger was during the latter stage of the Vietnam War (q.v.) when the marines were key members helping evacuate U.S. and foreign personnel from Saigon.

LEJEUNE, JOHN A. 13th commandant, b. Pointe Coupee Parish, La., 10 Jan. 1867, d. Baltimore, Md., 20 Nov. 1942. A Cajun, Lejeune attended Louisiana State University receiving a B.A. degree, and later the Naval Academy, graduating in 1888. After a two-year cruise as a midshipman, he entered the Marine Corps as a second lieutenant. Lejeune was posted to command the marines on *U.S.S. Cincinnati* during the Spanish-American War (q.v.). As a major commanding a battalion ordered from Jamaica, he landed at Colon in Panama (q.v.) 5 November 1903 to protect the newly formed Panamanian government from the Colombian troops stationed there. There was no fighting, and the Colombian troops left just before Pres. Theodore Roosevelt recognized the new government.

As a colonel, Lejeune commanded the 3,000-man Marine Brigade that was ordered by Pres. Woodrow Wilson to occupy Veracruz (q.v.) in April 1914 to avenge an imagined slight to the American flag and to oppose the Huerta regime in Mexico. This action forced General Huerta to leave Mexico, and the civilian government of President Carranza took power. At the start of World War I (q.v.) Lejeune was in command of the marine base at Quantico (q.v.). He arrived in France in early July 1918 in advance of the 4th Marine Brigade. When General Harbord was appointed to control supply for the American Expeditionary Force (AEF), Lejeune became commander as a major general of the 2d Division just before its action at Saint-Mihiel (q.v.). Later the division, under the French Fourth Army, took part in the Meuse-Argonne (q.v.) campaign. The 5th and 6th Marine Regiments took Blanc Mont and by 6 October Saint-Etienne. The action cost over 2,500 casualties. Shifted back to U.S. 1st Army, the division, spearheaded by the Marine Brigade, was involved in the final assault of the war. Lejeune remained in command of the 2d Division until August 1919. Once again he served briefly as commandant at Quantico. He was appointed commandant in January 1920 and was then reappointed in succession by Pres. Warren Harding and Pres. Calvin Coolidge. He served for a total of nine years.

During his tenure, reinforcements were sent to Shanghai during the civil war to help protect the International Settlement, and later a regiment was sent to Tientsin (q.v.) in north China. Marine Corps actions continued in Haiti (q.v.) and Santo Domingo (q.v.) and a major commitment was made in Nicaragua (q.v.) in attempts to restore order and undermine the influence of the followers of Augusto Sandino. Lejeune was responsible for consolidating the Marine Corps schools (basic course, company officers course, and field officers course). Advanced Base Force Headquarters was moved in 1922 to Quantico and named the East Coast Expeditionary Force. At the age of 62, Lejeune retired in 1929 and soon became superintendent of the Virginia Military Academy. In February 1942 he was advanced to the rank of lieutenant general on the retired list.

LIVERSEDGE, HARRY B. "HARRY THE HORSE." b. Volcano, Calif., 21 Sept. 1894, d. Bethesda, Md., 25 Nov. 1951. Liversedge attended the University of California–Berkeley, majoring in agriculture. He was a distinguished athlete, becoming the first West Coast selectee to Walter Camp's All-American football team. He also excelled at the hammer throw, javelin, and discus. Liversedge left the university in May 1917 to enlist as a private in the Marine Corps. He was commissioned in September 1918 and the following July was promoted to first lieutenant while serving in France with the 5th Brigade. Returning to Quantico (q.v.), he was shortly transferred to Santo Domingo (q.v.), but was released from line duty in 1920 to participate in the 1920 Olympics. Four years later he was again a participant in the games. Until 1927 he served mainly at Quantico until ordered to China and served at Tientsin (q.v.) and Shanghai. During the 1930s, he served in a variety of stations: Quantico, San Diego, Philadelphia, and aboard ship. He also completed the Senior Course at the Marine Corps School and acted on the staff of the Basic School at Philadelphia. By 1940 as a lieutenant colonel he was assigned to the 8th Marines. In January he took the 2d Battalion to Samoa (q.v.) and in August he assumed command of the 3d Raider Battalion. The following February the battalion made an unopposed landing on Pavuvu in the Russell Islands.

In March 1943 Liversedge, now a colonel, was given command of all the Raider battalions, now formed into a regiment. On 4 July he led two raider and two army battalions in landings on the northwest coast of New Georgia (q.v.), hoping to block the Japanese escape route through Bairoko. After a series of firefights, the force reached the outskirts of the town only to be halted by overwhelming Japanese resistance. In January 1944 he assumed command of the 28th Marines, a part of the 5th Division, and later led them ashore on Iwo Jima (q.v.) on 19 February 1945. The 28th had the responsibility of securing Mount Suribachi, and on the 23d Liversedge's marines raised the flag, an action captured by a news photographer and destined to become a lasting symbol for marine sacrifice. For his actions on Iwo, Liversedge was awarded his second Navy Cross (q.v.).

After the war he served briefly in Japan before returning to the United States to serve as director of the 12th Reserve District. In February 1948 he was named assistant commander of the 1st Division. Promoted to brigadier general, he took command of Fleet Marine Force (q.v.), Guam, and in 1950 returned to become deputy commander at Camp Pendleton (q.v.). His final posting was as director of the Marine Corps Reserve.

M

MACHINE GUN (Browning M1917A1). A .30-caliber water-cooled heavy weapon. The gun and its tripod weighed 93 pounds. Throughout most of its usage it was fed by a 250-round fabric belt, but later in World War II (q.v.) a disintegrating link belt was introduced. The rate of fire was between 450 and 600 rounds per minute. The weight of the gun restricted its use to primarily a defensive weapon since it was difficult to deploy it forward in a moving infantry assault. In various actions in the Pacific the gun did yeoman service halting Japanese mass infantry attacks. The weapon was one of the primary reasons that the marines deployed on Edson Ridge on Guadalcanal (q.v.) repelled the major Japanese effort to take Henderson Field (q.v.). However, the restricted use of the gun caused a drastic cutback in the number of weapons authorized per division. In 1942 there were 544 assigned, the following year 108, and the number was raised only slightly in 1944 to 162. It was continued in production after the war and was used during the Korean War (q.v.).

MACHINE GUN (Browning M1919A4). A .30-caliber air-cooled weapon designed during World War I (q.v.) but not fully tested until after the war. It weighed only 31 pounds, and its tripod was an additional 14, making a total weight half that of the M1917A1 (q.v.). It had a high rate of fire, and its weight made it an ideal weapon for troops on the offensive, particularly in the early phase of an action. The weapon had a low profile and thus could be easily dug in. It was reliable, suffering very few stoppages if properly maintained. The gun was highly favored by the Marine Corps. In 1942 a division was equipped with 682 of these weapons. Even in 1945 after other automatic weapons had become available, each division was authorized 356 guns. The 1919A4 was placed back into production after the war and it was widely used in the Korean War (q.v.). It continued as an important weapon in the corps' arsenal until replaced by the M-60 (q.v.).

MACHINE GUN (Browning M1919A6). Manufactured by Saginaw, it resulted from requests by the army's Ordnance Department for a lighter-weight, air-cooled machine gun. A 1943 evaluation of the .30-caliber A4 model pointed to some of the negatives of that weapon; for example, it took too much time to get that weapon into action, and the crew was too vulnerable. It suggested a new mount and a butt rest similar to the BAR. The army's Infantry Board eventually approved the new design in February 1943, and this model began to be issued in the fall. The weapon had a detachable shoulder stock, a folding bipod, and a different barrel than the A4. It weighed only 32.5 pounds, and since it did not need a tripod, its weight was 12.5 pounds less than the A4 gun. Its firing characteristic was the same as the other. A total of over 43,000 of the A6s were manufactured during World War II (q.v.), and a large number of A4s were converted to the A6 configuration. The weapon was used in Korea and some were still in operation during the early stages of the Vietnam War (q.v.).

MACHINE GUN (Browning M2-HB). The standard air-cooled heavy machine gun (.50 caliber) for all services. It could be used as a ground-mounted weapon or on almost every type of vehicle. The most devastating mounting was the four-gun configuration (the quad 50), which could wreak havoc on light-skinned vehicles or trucks. Although the M2-HB's weight of 125 pounds with tripod restricted its use in any rapid moving offensive, and thus its antipersonnel use was generally restricted to defensive actions. When used against infantry the shock of the .50-caliber slugs simply tore apart troops taking direct hits. It had an effective range of over 1,000 yards, and in many cases gunners could destroy targets that the enemy believed far beyond small-arms range. The authorized allocation of ammunition was 600 rounds per gun, but whenever possible supplies were kept above this level. The authorized allowance of the M2-HB for marine divisions in 1942 was 360 guns. Reflecting the use of other lighter automatic weapons, this allocation had fallen to 162 guns by 1945.

MACHINE GUN (M-60). A 7.62 general-purpose, air-cooled weapon whose design was partially based on German machine guns used during World War II (q.v.). The first design was bulky and tempermental and was generally unpopular. Later modifications improved the gun, and it has become the standard heavy weapon squad support firearm for both the U.S. Army and the Marine Corps. It is gas operated with a bipod, and it is designed to fire at a rate of 550 rounds per minute on full automatic but is slow enough for an infantryman to fire off single shots.

MAKIN. A large atoll in the Gilbert Islands (q.v.). The Japanese earlier in World War II (q.v.) had built a radio station on the main island, Butaritari. On 17 October 1942 Col. Evans Carlson (q.v.) led the 2d Raider Battalion in an attack on the island. It was successful; the radio station and support installations were destroyed, and the small Japanese garrison was almost wiped out. However, the raid alerted the Japanese as to the vulnerability of the islands in their outer defense ring, and they began seriously to fortify them. Thus, when the decision was made to capture bases in the Gilberts the following year, the marines and army troops found the islands much better fortified. This was particularly true of Tarawa (q.v.). The capture of Makin was one part of the operation begun on 20 November of which Tarawa was the most important. A regiment of the army's 27th

Division in a three-day campaign captured Butaritari. Colonel James Roosevelt and a few other marines who had been involved in the previous raid on Makin were also involved.

MAMELUK SWORD. It was reputedly given in 1805 to Lt. Presley O'Bannon (q.v.) by the deposed bey of Tripoli, Yiusef Hamet, in recognition of the marines' action at Derna (q.v.) in North Africa. In 1826 O'Bannon's scimitar became the model for marine officers' dress swords. In 1859 it was supplanted by the heavier army dress sabre. However, the scimitar-style sword was readopted in 1876 and remains the dress sword for marine officers.

MARIANA ISLANDS. Also called the Ladrones, they are composed of 14 islands extending over an area 380 miles from north to south, 1,500 miles east of the Philippines. The 10 northernmost are small, volcanic, and generally unoccupied. After the Spanish-American War (q.v.), three of the largest islands— Saipan (q.v.), Tinian (q.v.), and Rota—were ceded to Germany, which after World War I (q.v.) became a part of the League of Nations Mandate administered by Japan. The largest of the islands, Guam (q.v.), had by then become a possession of the United States. On 8 December 1941 the Japanese captured Guam against only token opposition. Saipan, located only 1,500 miles from Tokyo, was the main base, but by mid-1944 its garrison had been isolated by U.S. naval attacks. On 15 June the 2d and 4th Marines and 27th Army Division landed on Saipan and by 9 July had secured the island. Following this, the 3d Division and 1st Brigade assaulted Guam on 21 July. Aided by the army's 77th Division, the liberation of the U.S. possession was complete by 10 August. The last island targeted was Tinian, which fell to the 2d and 4th Divisions by 1 August. The possession of these islands enabled squadrons of B-29 superbombers to relentlessly attack the Japanese home islands.

MARINE AIR GROUND TASK FORCE (MAGTF). Designed to improve the integration of marine forces of varying sizes, the center of each force is an infantry unit backed by fixed-wing and rotary aircraft of appropriate numbers. The largest MAGTF is the Marine Expeditionary Force (MEF) (q.v.), which contains at a minimum a division and an air wing. Its size can vary between 40,000 and 100,000 men. The midrange MAGTF is the Marine Expeditionary Brigade (MEB) (q.v.). There are four general types of MEB: Maritime Prepositioning Force,

Amphibious MEB, Norway air-landed MEB, and Air Contingency Force. The size of the MEB can vary from 12,500 to 16,500 men, with its centerpiece an infantry battalion. The air contingent is an air group. The smallest MAGTF is the Marine Expeditionary Unit (MEU) (q.v.), which can vary in size from 1,000 to 4,000 men. It normally has a reinforced infantry battalion, a reinforced helicopter squadron, and support troops. The MEU concept is flexible enough to allow for quick response to a variety of threats.

MARINE EXPEDITIONARY BRIGADE (MEB). Organized to give the corps more flexibility in response to changing challenges in the post-Vietnam era, it is designed to be the forward element of a Marine Expeditionary Force (MEF) (q.v.). The ground element is normally composed of an infantry regiment of three battalions, an artillery battalion, a tank company, light-armored infantry company, and an anti-tank platoon. The air element is an Air Group with fixed-wing aircraft and helicopters along with its service detachments. The size of an MEB is normally 16,000 men and is commanded by a colonel or in some cases a brigadier general. Typically there are four types of MEBs. One is the Maritime Prepositioned Force (MPF). There are three squadrons of ships operating, one each for the Atlantic, Pacific, and Indian Ocean areas. These ships contain the armor and heavy equipment. In a crisis situation marines of the MEB would be transported to the crucial area and "marry up" with their equipment. The second type of MEB is the Amphibious MEB. Its organization is much the same as the Prepositioned Force. It can operate from shore bases or from supporting ships, and its task is to assault enemy positions in a ship to shore assault requiring a mid-sized force. A third type of MEB is the Air Contingency Force (ACF), which was developed for a short-notice, airlifted light MEB that can be deployed rapidly to act on its own or in conjunction with other marine units.

A special MEB was created in 1981 as a result of an agreement with Norway to support NATO's northern flank. It was designed for rapid air deployment of its 12,500 marines. Most equipment needed for an operation was prepositioned at Norwegian bases. With an infantry regiment, artillery, and tank support, this MEB would add significantly to Norway's defense in case of a war.

MARINE EXPEDITIONARY FORCE (MEF). The largest of the Marine Air Ground Task Forces (MAGTFs) (q.v.), it is normally composed of at least one division, although in Desert Storm (q.v.), the MEF contained two divisions. Generally an MEF commanded by a lieutenant general has approximately 50,000 men. The air component is a Marine Air Wing made up of Air Groups with both fixed-wing aircraft and helicopters. The smallest MEF would have one division composed of one artillery and three infantry regiments, a tank battalion, an assault amphibious battalion, an engineer battalion, and service units. The MEF would be deployed with 60 days' supply and could conduct major amphibious operations and long-term shore operations.

MARINE EXPEDITIONARY UNIT (MEU). The result of the reorganization of the Marine Corps in the post-Vietnam era to make it more flexibile. It is a Marine Air Ground Task Force (MAGTF) (q.v.) that can vary in size from 1,000 to 4,000 men. It is normally made up of a reinforced infantry battalion, a helicopter squadron, a service support group, an armored unit, and an artillery battery. MEUs are regularly deployed in the Mediterranean and the Pacific and periodically in the Atlantic, Caribbean, and Indian Oceans. A MEU is task oriented, trained, and equipped to carry out a variety of missions including peacekeeping activities. It has a response time of only six hours. For sustained operations ashore a MEU can act as the point unit for a more complex operation by a Marine Expeditionary Brigade (MEB) (q.v.).

MARINE HYMN. Without question the Marine Hymn is the most recognizable of any song associated with a branch of the U.S. military. The melody is almost the same as the marching song from Jacques Offenbach's *Geneviève de Brabant*. The author of the poem is unknown, but he obviously penned the words shortly after the Civil War (q.v.). Despite the inversion of the time sequence, the first stanza beginning "From the halls of Montezuma, to the shores of Tripoli" fully expresses the pride and devotion to the corps held by marines for more than two centuries.

MARITIME PREPOSITIONING SQUADRONS (MPSs). Substitutes for large, expensive assault fleets necessary to meet threats to U.S. and allied security during the latter stages of the Cold War. Initially there was a Near Team Prepositioning Force (NTPF) that concentrated 30 days' supplies for a division in the Indian Ocean and Western Pacific. This was replaced by three permanent Prepositioning Squadrons, which by 1986 had grown to 13 ships. One squadron was placed in the Eastern Atlantic, a second at Diego Garcia in the Indian Ocean, and a third off the Mariana Islands (q.v.) in the Central Pacific. With basic supplies on board, all that was needed in case of a crisis was to fly in the necessary complement of marines.

MARSHALL ISLANDS. A series of atolls located 1,500 miles southeast of Saipan (q.v.). They stretch from Jaluit and Mili Islands in the south to Eniwetok (q.v.) over 600 miles to the northwest. The main atolls of Jaluit, Mili, Maloelop, Majuro, Wotje, Kwajalein (q.v.), and Eniwetok had fallen under Japanese jurisdiction following World War I (q.v.). Even before World War II (q.v.), the Japanese had built airfields and begun major defensive works on some of the main islands. By 1944 Adm. Chester Nimitz's planners decided in furtherance of the Orange Plan to strike at Kwajalein, the very heart of the Marshalls. On 1 February two regiments of the 4th Division landed on Roi-Namur (q.v.) Islands at the same time the army was clearing a number of small islands and then Kwajalein Island. Majuro was occupied, but the Japanese on the rest of the southern islands were simply bypassed. On 19 February islands in the Eniwetok atoll 360 miles from Kwajelein were assaulted. A regiment of the 1st Brigade landed on Engebi Island and quickly captured it. Three days later they secured Parry Island. Meanwhile, an army regiment seized Eniwetok Island. Possession of Kwajalein and Eniwetok atolls gave the navy two excellent harbors and forward staging grounds for the assault on the Mariana Islands (q.v.).

MAYAGUEZ. An American container ship enroute from Hong Kong to Thailand that was stopped by a Cambodian gunboat on 12 May 1975. The ship was ordered to proceed to anchor off Koh Tang, a small heavily jungled island approximately 30 miles from the main Cambodian port of Kampong Som. The 39 crew members were taken to Kompong Som. Upon receipt of this information, Pres. Gerald Ford ordered U.S. forces to recapture the vessel and free the crew. The entire combined arms operation was under the control of the senior air force officer in Thailand who planned a double strike at the Cambodians. Already air force planes had sunk five of the Cambodian gunboats. Fortunately, the prisoners' boat was not hit. The 2d Battalion (reinforced), 9th Marines, was flown to Thailand from Okinawa (q.v.). Backed by naval aircraft and a guided missile destroyer, the first strike force on the 15th from a destroyer escort boarded the abandoned *Mayaguez* without incident. The destroyer escort *Wilson* intercepted the boats bringing the prisoners back to Koh Tang and freed them. The second group of marines, Company G, 2d Battalion, landed from helicopters at Koh Tang under cover of fighter bomber fire and immediately encountered very heavy ground fire. Returning fire and supported by heavy air strikes, the marines who had been pinned down were evacuated on the night of the 16th. The incident was very costly. Three air force helicopters were shot down and 11 others damaged. Eleven marines, 2 sailors, and 2 air force men were killed, and 41 marines, 2 sailors, and 7 airmen were wounded.

McCAWLEY, CHARLES G. 8th commandant, b. Philadelphia, 29 Jan. 1827, d. Rosemont, Pa., 13 Oct. 1891. The son of a marine captain, McCawley was commissioned in 1847 and left almost immediately to join the Veracruz (q.v.) detachment. He was breveted first lieutenant after Chapultepec (q.v.). As a captain in the Civil War (q.v.), he commanded a detachment that helped take Port Royal, Carolina. He also commanded a battalion in the attempts in 1863 to take the forts defending Charleston. In a poorly planned attack on Fort Sumter (q.v.) on 8 September, the marines and sailors were beaten back, suffering one-third casualties. Retiring to camp, the battalion saw its effectiveness reduced by sickness, and it was broken up in early 1864.

McCawley was breveted major after the Fort Sumter affair. Brought to Washington by General Zeilin (q.v.) in 1871, he became commandant in November 1876, but Congress had specified that commandants now should hold only the rank of colonel. He was responsible for raising standards for enlistment and establishing uniform regulations and tables of organization. His most lasting contribution was to secure a quota of Annapolis graduates to become corps officers in 1882. Until the Spanish-American War (q.v.), this was the only source of marine officers. During his tenure, the corps adopted a new rifle, the 45–70 single-shot breech loader. In 1880 he assigned John Philip Sousa (q.v.) to be leader of the Marine Band.

During McCawley's tenure, a small detachment of marines landed in Egypt at the same time in 1882 when the British landed at Alexandria (q.v.). In April 1885 he ordered a brigade to land in Panama (q.v.) to protect the American owned railway from rebels against Colombian rule. Marines were also used to protect property and lives in Haiti (q.v.), Samoa (q.v.), Korea (q.v.), and Argentina, and were active in Alaskan waters to help eliminate seal poaching. Colonel McCawley retired on 29 January 1891.

McNAMARA LINE. Conceived by Secretary of Defense Robert McNamara as a way to halt massive North Vietnamese movement across the Demilitarized Zone (DMZ) (q.v.) in Vietnam. Although marine commanders were openly opposed to the concept because of its expense and impracticality, because of their location in I Corps they were chosen to implement it in the spring of 1967. Originally given the code name Practice Nine, the line was planned to eventually stretch from Con Thien (q.v.) in the west, eastward across Vietnam. It was to be a swath of bulldozed land strewn with mines, complete with obstacles, and saturated with sensors. This was to be backed by a system of strong points. Its construction was given the highest priority. Much of the energy of the 3d Division was taken up during the spring and summer in the construction of the line. This preoccupation with the line precluded any large-scale offensive action. Con Thien, one of the proposed strong points, became the scene of major fighting during the summer and early fall as the North Vietnamese attempted to neutralize that position, and the marines were under siege there until the end of October. The first test section of the barrier was completed by August, and all North Vietnamese attempts to knock out the suppport bases were foiled by aggressive defenses. The project to build the line was a costly experiment. It was never completed across Vietnam, and McNamara's idea of extending it to Laos later was also abandoned. Renamed Project Dye Marker, the plan became redundant with the loss of the western portion of Highway 9 and the decision the following year to abandon Khe Sanh (q.v.).

MEDAL OF HONOR. The highest award given for valor. It was first authorized by Congress in July 1862 as a medal to be given to enlisted men for gallantry in action. The following year officers were made eligible. Initially there was but one medal for all branches of the service. Later the medal was redesigned— the ribbon from which the medal was suspended was changed to bright blue containing a cluster of 13 stars. Each service branch now has a medal of a different design, although the breast ribbon for all are the same. The U.S. Navy and Marine Corps medal is a five-pointed bronze star tipped with trefoils, each ray containing laurel and oak leaves. In the center is a portrait of Minerva, representing the United States, repulsing Discord, represented by snakes. The medal itself is always worn suspended from the neck.

MEGEE, VERNON E. b. Tulsa, Okla., 5 June 1900, d. Albuquerque, N.M., 16 Jan. 1992. Megee enlisted in the corps in March 1919 and was commissioned in May 1922. After the Basic Course, he was posted to Haiti (q.v.) in October 1923 and served for two years with the 1st Brigade. Returning to the United States, he was assigned to the 10th Marines at Quantico (q.v.) until being ordered to China in 1927. After this duty he was assigned to the Naval Air Station in San Diego for preliminary aviation training. Before entering flight training at Pensacola in January 1931, he served with the aircraft squadrons in Haiti. After winning his wings, he was assigned to Quantico as a student and later instructor, then executive officer of a fighter squadron. As a captain in 1936 he attended the Air Corps Tactical Training School, after which he returned to Quantico as an instructor in aviation tactics. In July 1939 Major Megee took command of Fighter Squadron 2 of the 2d Air Group. In October 1942 he was a member of the Naval Air Mission to Peru acting as an adviser to the Ministry of Aviation. By the fall of 1943, now a colonel, he became chief of staff to the 3d Air Wing at Cherry Point. He was sent to the Pacific with this wing in May 1944. Later that year he was appointed commander of the Provisional Air Support Command. He led a control unit during the Iwo Jima (q.v.) operation, giving close support to the ground troops. He returned to the United States in September 1945 to become a member of the Joint Amphibious Operations and Doctrines Committee and later served as an instructor at the National War College.

Promoted to brigadier general, Megee became chief of staff to the Fleet Marine Force (q.v.), Atlantic, in January 1947. Following this service, he was appointed assistant director of aviation and served until he joined the joint staff of the Defense Department in January 1950. Leaving Washington as a major general in August 1951, he briefly took command of the air station at Cherry Point before becoming commander of Aircraft, Fleet Marine Force, Pacific. In January 1953 he took command of the 1st Air Wing in Korea and served there for a year. His next assignment was as deputy commander, fleet Marine Force, Pacific, which he held only briefly before taking over command of Aircraft Fleet Marine Force, Atlantic, in June 1955.

Promoted to lieutenant general in January 1956, he was appointed assistant commandant and chief of staff, Headquarters Marine Corps, the first aviator to serve at this high level. He ended his career as commander Fleet Marine Force, Pacific. He retired from the corps in November 1959.

MEUSE-ARGONNE. The final campaign of World War I (q.v.). The 4th Brigade, an integral part of the army's 2d Division, after action at Saint-Mihiel (q.v.) and Soissons (q.v.), took up positions adjacent to the French Fourth Army in Champagne in late September 1918. On 2 October the brigade launched a direct frontal attack on a key position called Blanc Mont and then survived a number of fierce German counterattacks. Resuming the forward motion, the brigade drove ahead and reached the village of Saint-Etienne, three miles beyond the initial starting point. This action cost the brigade 2,500 casualties. It was the final action of the 2d Division as the Armistice was declared on 11 November.

MEXICAN WAR. Aside from the futility of continuing the drawn out Seminole War (q.v.), a more pressing issue was facing the nation. Since the Texans had won their independence from Mexico, the question of annexation of that vast area had been the subject of debate between southern congressmen who favored it and their northern counterparts who generally opposed it because of the fear of adding another slave state. However, the forward policy of Pres. James Polk was finally approved, and Texas was added to the Union by Joint Resolution of Congress in January and February 1845 despite warnings from Mexico that this would mean war. General Zachary Taylor, already at Corpus Christi, was ordered to the Rio Grande to protect U.S. claims to southern Texas and was later confronted by substantial Mexican forces. The U.S. army was victorious in the first two engagements of the war on 8 and 9 May 1846. The navy's Gulf Squadron, with complements of marines on each ship, supported Taylor's early moves into Mexico and later Gen. Winfield Scott's operations against Mexico City. A marine battalion was created from all the detachments on board ships, later raided Frontera and Tampico, and was involved in the capture of the latter in November 1846.

The centrum of the war shifted in the early months of 1847 to General Scott's operations. On 9 March he landed 12,000 troops on an undefended beach south of Veracruz (q.v.). With naval support Veracruz was taken two weeks later. Commodore Matthew Perry created a landing force brigade composed of the marine battalion augmented by sailors. He used these to secure the gulf ports remaining under Mexican control.

The advance battalion of a newly formed marine regiment reached Scott at Puebla in early August as he prepared for the final assault on Mexico City. While Scott's army of 11,000 men fought its way to the gates of the city, the marines were consigned to guarding the baggage trains. However, the marines were brought up when the assault of Chapultepec (q.v.) Castle, the key to the two main gates of the city, was set. On 13 September after a heavy bombardment, the assault began. A marine unit supported by a few soldiers and artillery took the San Cosme Gate. Later that day the other gate was secured, and inexplicably the Mexican general, Santa Ana, decided to evacuate the city. Marines were called on to secure the *Palacio Nacional* and a marine cut down the Mexican flag and ran up the Stars and Stripes.

Meanwhile, in California in April 1846, marine Lt. Archibald Gillespie had delivered despatches from the president to the American consul in Monterrey and later to John Fremont who would be instrumental in the Bear Flag revolt. Gillespie became the adjutant of the newly formed California Battalion, which was transported by ship to San Diego and helped secure the city on 29 July. Left with 50 men to defend San Diego, he was soon besieged and elected to march out with honors, thus avoiding a battle. Later the marines participated in the battle of San Pascual, the relief of Gen. Stephen Kearny at San Bernardino, and the occupation of Los Angeles in January 1847. Following the conquest of California, the Pacific Squadron began its attacks on Mexico's west coast ports. Amphibious forces very quickly occupied Guaymas, San Blas, and San Jose. Covered by the guns of the squadron, a force of over 700 sailors and marines landed at Mazatlan on 10 November 1847 and took the town without difficulty. Captain Jacob Zeilin (q.v.) was left behind as governor with a small force where he remained until after the Treaty of Guadalupe Hidalgo ended the war. (See also Banana Wars.)

MIDWAY. A coral atoll located 1,100 miles northwest of Hawaii that had been a U.S. possession since 1867. The two main islets, Sand and Eastern, were garrisoned by the 6th Defense Battalion and two air squadrons in 1941. One fighter squadron, (VMF) 221, initially had 21 outclassed Brewster Buffalos (q.v.), while the Scout Bomber Squadron (VMSB 241) had 17 nearly useless old single-engined bombers. On 26 May the squadrons were reinforced with 26 newer F4Fs and SBDs. Admiral Yamamoto's complex plan for the capture of Midway and the negation of Pearl Harbor began for the marines on 4 June 1942. Pilots of VMF 221 engaged a Japanese force of over 100 planes headed for the islands, and 13 Buffalos and two F4Fs were shot down by the Japanese Zero fighters. Pilots of VMSB 24 without escort attacked two Japanese carriers but did not inflict any damage and lost eight of the bombers. At the close of the day only two fighters and 11 bombers were still operational. By then the three U.S. carriers were in position, and on the 6th the pivotal air battle began. With great skill and considerable good fortune, the navy bombers were able to sink four Japanese carriers. Never again would Midway or Hawaii be threatened.

"MITCHELL" (PBJ). A twin-engined bomber built by North American Aviation Company. The prototype was first flown in August 1940. The air force versions (B-25s) of this medium bomber were used extensively in both the Pacific and European theaters during World War II (q.v.). The B model was used on the Tokyo raid in April 1942. The PBJ was the standard aircraft in seven marine bomber squadrons during the war. They were used first against the Japanese at Rabaul, New Britain (q.v.). North American built a number of versions of the plane, including one armed with a 75mm cannon. The Mitchell normally carried a crew of five at a maximum speed of 300 miles per hour with a service ceiling of 24,000 feet. Depending on the model, the PBJ could carry up to 3,000 pounds of bombs internally and, with later modification, 2,400 pounds of bombs mounted on external wing racks. One modification of the Mitchell (PBJ-15) utilized radar in night rocket attacks in the Mariana Islands (q.v.).

MODRZEJEWSKI, ROBERT. b. Milwaukee, Wis., 3 July 1934. Early in the morning of 15 July 1966 as a captain commanding K Company, 3d Battalion, 4th Marines, Modrzejewski and his men were landed a mile south of the Demilitarized Zone (DMZ) (q.v.) as a part of a major four-battalion operation seeking to destroy a North Vietnamese division. The 3d Battalion was to establish a block to prevent the North Vietnamese from escaping and were to be joined by the 2d Battalion moving in from the east. K Company moved south to its blocking position along an infiltration trail and attempted to cross the Song Nang River but was prevented by enemy machine gun fire. Other attempts failed, and Captain Modrzejewski ordered the company to set up a night position on a small knoll where they were surrounded. The company survived a series of night attacks, which continued throughout 16 July. During the night of the 16th, K Company in a four-hour firefight beat off a series of frontal attacks all around the company perimeter. Captain Modrzejewski received a number of wounds during the fighting but continued to direct supporting artillery fire as well as provide much needed ammunition to the forward elements of the company. On the 17th a search of the area revealed 79 North Vietnamese bodies; the company had only one killed but 45 wounded, mostly by grenade fragments.

A linkup with the 2d Battalion was made on the 17th, and the decision was made to move eastward along the river, clearing the enemy as they went. K Company brought up the rear, and its 1st Platoon sustained a battering by the enemy before fire superiority was established and the wounded could be evacuated. On 19 July what was left of K Company moved to rear areas. For his outstanding command presence during this entire action, Captain Modrzejewski received the Medal of Honor (q.v.).

"MOJAVE" (army designation). Known in the Marine Corps as the CH-37, this helicopter was built by Sikorsky Aircraft Company. The CH-37C was first flown in October 1955. Powered by two 2,100-horsepower engines in outboard nacelles built on wing stubs, the helicopter could fly 130 miles per hour with a range of 145 miles. The C model could carry 20 passengers or 24 litter patients in addition to the crew of two. Its cargo capacity was equal to that of a R-4D. Cargo could be loaded from the nose clamshell door or from a rear door.

MUNDAY, CARL E. JR. 30th commandant, b. Atlanta, Ga., 16 July 1935. Munday graduated from Auburn and was commissioned a second lieutenant in June 1957. Early assignments were sea duty, service in the 2d Division, and instructor at the Basic School. Ordered to Vietnam (q.v.), he served in 1966–67 as an operations officer and executive officer with the 3d Battalion, 26th Marines, and later as intelligence officer in III Amphibious Force. After Vietnam he held successively more important positions: aide-de-camp to the assistant commandant, commander of the 2d Battalion, 4th Marines, assistant chief of staff 2d Division, chief of staff 6th Amphibious Brigade, then commanding officer of the 2d Marines. Promoted to brigadier general in 1982, he became director of personnel at Marine Headquarters and eventually commanded the 4th Amphibious Brigade. From there he became director of operations for the corps. He was advanced to major general in 1986 and lieutenant general two years later. Munday had attended the Naval War College and the corps' Command and Staff College. After a brief period of being the deputy chief of staff and deputy to the Joint Chiefs, he assumed command of Fleet Marine Force (q.v.), Atlantic, and was designated to command all marine forces that might be used in Europe. On 1 July 1991 he was promoted to general and replaced Gen. Alfred Gray (q.v.) as commandant.

N

NAVY CROSS. The second highest award given to marine and naval personnel for heroism against an armed enemy. Until World War I (q.v.), only the Medal of Honor (q.v.) was consistently available for all branches of the service, although Congress could authorize special medals as was the case in the Spanish-American War (q.v.). In 1918 the army authorized the award of the Distinguished Service Cross and the Distinguished Service Medal. The following year the Navy Department approved the issuance of the Navy Cross.

NEVILLE, WENDELL C. "WHISPERING BUCK." 14th commandant, b. Portsmouth, Va., 12 May 1870, d. Washington, D.C., 8 July 1930. Neville graduated from the Naval Academy in 1890 and after a two year cruise as a midshipman he was commissioned a second lieutenant in the corps. During the Spanish-American War (q.v.) as a member of the 1st Battalion, he landed at Guantanamo (q.v.) Bay. For his heroic actions there he received the Brevet Medal, the highest marine decoration at that time. Transferred to China, he took part in four battles during the Boxer Rebellion (q.v.) in 1900. Later he served in the Philippines, Cuba (q.v.), Nicaragua (q.v.), Panama (q.v.), and Hawaii.

On orders from Pres. Woodrow Wilson, as a lieutenant colonel Neville led the 2d Marines ashore at Veracruz (q.v.) on 21 April 1914 to punish General Huerta for imprisonment of a boat crew at Tampico when he refused an apology. After some house-to-house fighting the 2d, later reinforced by other units, seized Veracruz. For his gallant actions Neville was awarded the Medal of Honor (q.v.). As a colonel during World War I (q.v.), he commanded the 5th Marines, a part of the large mixed U.S. 2d Division at Belleau Wood (q.v.), beginning on 6 June 1918, helping blunt an attack by the German IV Corps. Counterattacking against German machine guns, fortified positions, and mustard gas, the division cleared the area of Germans by 30 June. Neville was promoted to brigadier general and placed in command of the brigade.

General Ludendorf launched the last great German offensive in July. The brigade at Soissons (q.v.) was used to counterattack against an entire German corps and suffered 1,972 casualties during two days of fighting. Neville returned with his brigade in August 1919 and was promoted to major general the following year.

Neville served as assistant commandant and later commanded the Department of the Pacific before becoming commandant in 1929. He died in office in 1930.

NEW BRITAIN. A large crescent-shaped island 330 miles long in the Bismarck chain located across the Solomon Sea from New Guinea. The eastern areas adjacent to Rabaul were occupied by the Japanese early in World War II (q.v.), and Rabaul with its five airfields and excellent harbor became their main base of operations in the South Pacific. For the next two years much of the strategy of the Allies was concentrated on destroying Rabaul. Marine contributions to the war in the area under General MacArthur's control were in the western area of New Britain. Moving steadily up the north coast, army and Australian troops in late 1943 were poised for the final assaults on Japanese positions in Dutch New Guinea. MacArthur wanted to be certain that the area around Cape Gloucester (q.v.) on New Britain was secure. Therefore, the 1st Division on the day after Christmas 1943 was landed on two beaches at the cape with the primary objective of capturing the airfield. Fighting through the monsoon, it captured the airfield and drove the Japanese from the highlands and into a long torturous retreat along the coast in the direction of Rabaul. The Cape Gloucester campaign was remembered by marines as one of the most difficult operations not only for Japanese resistance but for the terrain and weather.

NEW GEORGIA. An island northwest of Guadalcanal (q.v.) in the central Solomon Islands (q.v.). Like most Pacific islands, New Georgia was covered by jungle growth except along the coasts and had few usable trails. The key position to be secured by the invasion was Munda airfield. The main landing in June 1944 was made on the south coast by the army's 43d Division. However, on 21 June the marine 4th Raider Battalion landed on the northern part of the island and quickly secured Viru Harbor. It then moved out southwest to secure the harbor at Bairoko hoping to cut off the Japanese retreat from Munda. Miserable terrain and stubborn Japanese resistance kept the Raiders from reaching Bairoko. Elsewhere the 43d Division had been halted short of Munda, and it became necessary to commit two other army divisions before the airfield was captured on 5 August. Four days later army units made contact with the marines. However, most of the surviving Japanese had escaped to Kolombangara. The airfield at Munda became a major base for the later invasion of Bougainville (q.v.) and the negation of the Japanese base at Rabaul, New Britain.

NEW ORLEANS. The largest and most important port city on the lower Mississippi River that had been acquired from France in 1803 as part of the Louisiana Purchase. The following year a marine force of 122 men was dispatched there to help maintain law and order and later in futile attempts to destroy the pirate, Jean Lafitte. General Andrew Jackson took over the defense of the city during the War of 1812 (q.v.). Later in 1814 the city was alerted that Gen. Edward Packenham with a large force of veterans of the Peninsular War had left Jamaica with orders to capture the city. The marine force led by Maj. Daniel Carmick, now numbering 400 men, became a key part of Jackson's defense plan. Some of the marines helped man the five gunboats that challenged the British landing. Later the bulk of the marine unit was deployed in the center of Jackson's defense line. He had chosen the ground well so that the British could not flank his position. On 28 December the British attempted a probing attack aimed at the marine area, which was contained. Eleven days later Packenham ordered his main attack with 3,500 men marching directly against the American lines in formal parade ground formation. The result was a disaster, with the British suffering 2,300 casualties, including Packenham. The city was saved as the British were allowed to withdraw quietly. The marine units under Carmick, numbering three-fifths of the entire corps, acquitted themselves so well that even Jackson was impressed. The tragedy of the battle was that it was needless since the Treaty of Ghent ending the war had already been signed.

NICARAGUA. The largest state in Central America with two large coastal plains, one adjacent to the Pacific and the other to the Caribbean. The interior, particularly in the north abutting Honduras, is heavily wooded highlands. The history of Nicaragua, like that of so many states in Central America, after independence from Spain was a series of wars, revolutionary movements, and unstable governments. The marines made three landings in the Bluefields area in the southeast between 1852 and 1854 to protect American lives and property. Following an abortive attempt to control the state by an American adventurer, William Walker, a general agreement was reached between Conservatives and Liberals to abide by a republican constitution. The Conservatives provided 30 years of peace and prosperity until 1893, when a Liberal leader, Jose Zelaya, seized power and maintained dictatorial control until 1909. The state, however, was deeply in debt to U.S. and European interests, and the Conservatives, denied a stake in the government, rebelled against Zelaya. The U.S. government decided to support the Conservatives, and a provisional regiment of 750 marines from Philadelphia and Panama (q.v.) was landed. The situation appeared to have stabilized with the Conservatives in power, and the marines were withdrawn in September 1910. But the Liberals were not finished, and by 1912 the Conservatives had lost control of the southeastern areas. A battalion of 350 men from Panama landed in May, which was later reinforced by 780 more marines. They took the offensive, defeating the rebel units twice and opening the vital railroad. Once again the situation seemed stable, and all the marines were withdrawn except 100 Legation Guards (q.v.).

The enmity between Conservatives and Liberals continued, although there was a decade of relative peace. Then after an abortive Liberal revolt in 1922, a coalition government was formed in 1924. Prospects for peace seemed well enough advanced that the Legation Guard was removed. This was a signal for a further confused rebellion, which resulted in the Liberal leaders fleeing the country. Further fighting in the Bluefields area brought marines and sailors once again to Nicaragua in the summer of 1926. A brokered truce soon fell apart, and fighting resumed with the rebels in control of the Mosquito Coast. A further battalion of marines was landed at Bluefields in January 1927 followed by a contingent of six airplanes. The Nicaraguan regular army received new arms from the United States, and with the arrival of the 5th Marines, the 2d Brigade was reconstituted. By May a further truce was arranged by the

United States. The Conservatives were to stay in power until new elections were held in 1928. However, one Liberal leader, Augusto Sandino, did not comply, and the war continued. Men of the newly formed *Guardia Nacional* along with 38 marines were attacked at Ocotal in the north on 5 July. With the aid of marine aircraft, the attack was beaten off. Taking the offensive, the marines and their allies fought a series of battles with the Sandanistas. One segment of the marine attackers was besieged by a large rebel force but held on until relieved on 10 January 1928. With marine aircraft bombing ahead of them, the ground troops took El Chipote, Sandino's headquarters. Sandino had escaped to Honduras only to return the following month to attack a marine pack train. During the summer the marines moved inland along the Coco River, fighting a number of skirmishes with the rebels, but he once again escaped.

The elections of November 1928 returning a one-time rebel general to the presidency did not stop the fighting. The marine and *Guardia* forces continued to operate in northern Nicaragua even after Pres. Herbert Hoover in 1931 announced the withdrawal of the marines. The last element of the brigade left Nicaragua on 2 January 1933. In the last campaign in Nicaragua the marines lost 47 men killed and 67 wounded. Sandino, once again in Nicaragua, was finally captured and hung by the orders of a new strongman, Anastasio Somoza, the head of the *Guardia*. (See also Banana Wars.)

NICHOLAS, SAMUEL. 1st commandant, b. Philadelphia, Pa., 1744, d. Philadelphia, 27 Aug. 1790. Considered by marines to be the first Marine Corps commandant, although never officially designated commandant, Nicholas was appointed a captain by the Continental Congress on 28 November 1775. In the spring of 1776 he led the first marine amphibious attack. Nicholas sailed on board the newly refurbished ship, the *Black Prince*, leading a small naval squadron against New Providence in the Bahamas. Landing with a force of 200 marines and 50 naval personnel, he captured the town and its forts and took away valuable supplies. In December 1776 with three companies (80 men), Nicholas was ordered to join General Washington and took part in the capture of Trenton, and the company stayed with Washington at Morristown until February 1777. Nicholas returned to Philadelphia, and his shore-based marines were used for defensive duty in Delaware. During that summer an additional 20 marines were recruited to accompany John Paul Jones in the *Ranger* to France. From there he raided the English coast in 1778, and a few were with him on the *Bonhomme Richard* in August 1779. In July 1779 marines provided the striking force in the thwarted attack on Fort George in the Penobscot River. In September 1781 Nicholas, by then a major, and a force of marines escorted the oxcarts carrying a million silver crowns loaned by France from Boston to Philadelphia. At the close of the war all naval ships were sold and the Marine Corps disbanded. Nicholas then returned to civilian life in Philadelphia.

NUKU HIVA. An island in the Marquesas Islands in the Pacific. During the War of 1812 (q.v.), David Porter, captain of the frigate *Essex*, was very successful in his attacks on British ships in the South Pacific. He turned over command of one of these to his senior marine officer, Lt. John Gamble (q.v.), who used the privateer to capture a much larger British vessel, the *Seringapatam*. Porter had retired to Nuku Hiva where he formally took possession of the island for the United States. Many of the natives who had not been consulted on the takeover rebelled, and the marines and sailors were ordered to burn a number of villages. Later Porter left Gamble behind with only a few men to face continued native turmoil combined with a mutiny of his own men in May 1814. After considerable difficulty, Gamble and those still loyal made their way to Hawaii, where they were made prisoners by the British. The United States never acted on Porter's annexation of the island.

O

O'BANNON, PRESLEY N. b. Faquier County, Va., 1776, d. Logan County, Ky., Sept. 1850. O'Bannon was appointed second lieutenant in the corps in January 1801 and was promoted to first lieutenant in October the following year. In 1804 he commanded a small contingent of marines in Commodore Barron's fleet sent to restore American prestige in the Mediterranean and end the threat of the Barbary pirates. With Pres. Thomas Jefferson's knowledge, William Eaton, an Arabic scholar, persuaded the brother of the bey of Tunis to take part in an expedition designed to overthrow the bey. A very mixed force of Arabs and European mercenaries was formed in Alexandria (q.v.). O'Bannon and seven marine enlisted men were designated to accompany this force in the long march across the coastal reaches of the Libyan Desert. After a 600-mile march, the "army" reached the fortified town of Derna (q.v.) on 27 April 1805. Supported by the guns from three American ships, O'Bannon's marines broke through the weak defenses, allowing the Arab elements to drive the bey's troops into the desert. O'Bannon raised the American flag over the fort for the first time on foreign soil. On 3 June a peace treaty was concluded with Tripoli. O'Bannon's exploits were later the basis of the phrase "to the shores of Tripoli" in the Marine Hymn (q.v.). O'Bannon was also responsible for another marine tradition. The jeweled Mameluk sword (q.v.) given to him by the pasha became the model for the officers' dress sword. O'Bannon retired from the corps in May 1807 and spent the remainder of his life in Kentucky.

OKINAWA. The largest of the Ryukyu Islands, approximately 60 miles long on a southwest to northeast axis and 18 miles across at its widest. The northern two-thirds is mountainous and generally heavily wooded. The south was mostly open but with a number of low-lying hills and ridges. The bulk of the population during World War II (q.v.) estimated at one-half million lived in the south, with the largest cities being Naha and Shuri. It was in the south that the Japanese commander made his stand. With Okinawan conscripts added to his regular forces, he had over 100,000 men, many large- and small-caliber guns, and complex defenses located in three broad belts.

Possession of Okinawa would move U.S. planes within 650 miles of Tokyo and provide an excellent forward staging for the proposed invasion of Japan. The plan for the invasion, code-named Iceberg, called for X Army divided into two corps to land on the west coast opposite the two airfields. The marine contingent, the 1st and 6th Divisions, comprised III Amphibious Corps, while the army's XXIV Corps at first contained the army's 7th and 96th Divisions, with the 27th and 77th in reserve. The landings were made on Easter Sunday, 1 April 1945, against little opposition. The 6th Division was routed to the north to secure that portion of the island.

Organized resistance in the north had ended by 21 April. The 1st Division met little resistance in its drive across the island. The bulk of the fighting had been in XXIV Corps' sector as the army divisions began their drive southward. The 27th Division was landed on 9 April and took up positions on the extreme right flank, and in conjunction with the 96th, it moved against the Shuri defenses. Despite the heaviest artillery and naval concentration of the war, this attack was halted. The relative stalemate was broken by a major offensive in XXIV Corps' area begun on 19 April, which within 10 days drove the Japanese back to another defense line. On 1 May the 1st Division was brought on line, replacing the army's 27th Division, and immediately helped contain a major Japanese counteroffensive. On 11 May the 6th Division was inserted to the right of the 1st, giving X Army two corps abreast. The 6th fought a bitter four-day battle for a major hill position before being halted by fire from the Shuri heights. In this 10-day period the division suffered 2,600 casualties. The 1st Division fighting in the draws and for ridges before Shuri had advanced to Wana Ridge by 14 May. It took two more weeks before the ridge was cleared.

Elsewhere the army divisions were making slow but substantial gains against a series of strong points based on the many hills of central and eastern Okinawa. Monsoon rains in late May brought most action to a near standstill. When the offensive resumed, the 6th Division crossed the Asato River and captured Naha. After two months of fighting, X Army had still not taken the most important defenses on the island. III Corps had suffered 11,000 casualties, while XXIV had sustained 15,000. However, on 30 May elements of the 1st Division took Shuri Ridge and in conjunction with the army's 77th Division captured Shuri. The Japanese commander, having lost three-fourths of his force, now retreated to the far south. Operating in foul weather, the 6th Division cleared the vital Oroku Peninsula in the first week of June. The army's 7th and 96th Divisions in the center broke through the Japanese main defenses along a line defending a major escarpment, while the 1st Division was battling to overrun the heavy defenses along Kunishi Ridge.

An estimated 9,000 Japanese troops were killed between 19 and 21 June, and the way was finally open to extend U.S. control over the entire southern area. The bulk of the reduction of the scattered defenses in the south was left to the marine 2d Division, which had been landed in early June. Final clearance of the Japanese resulted in an additional 8,900 Japanese killed.

The conquest of Okinawa had taken longer than planned and cost X Army and naval casualties in the fight against the kamikazes a total of 12,500 dead. The Japanese losses were estimated at 110,000 killed and a surprising 7,400 of their troops surrendered. In addition, all of Okinawa's cities were leveled, and an estimated 80,000 civilians had lost their lives. The marine casualties in this long, desperate fight were 2,938 killed. The possession of Okinawa increased the direct pressure on

Japan by providing heavy bomber bases, excellent harbors, and bases for X Army, which was designated as a part of the projected invasion of Japan.

OPERATION KILLER. The plan of the new 8th Army commander during the Korean War (q.v.) to regain the initiative from the Chinese and North Koreans in early 1951. As the name suggests, the main purpose of these operations was to kill the enemy; retaking territory was secondary. For this operation the 1st Division was attached to IX Corps in the center of the 8th Army line at Wonju. On 21 February the 1st and 5th Marines in the assault took their objective, Hoengsong, nine miles to the north.

OPERATION RIPPER. The second of the 8th Army's offensives during the Korean War (q.v.) in early 1951. Still operating under IX Corps' command, the 1st and 7th Marines in conjunction with Republic of Korea (ROK) and U.S. Army forces punched their way through the enemy lines. By April the 8th Army's line was generally north of the 38th parallel. The 1st Division was located near the Hwachon Reservoir a few miles to the north of the parallel.

OPERATION STARLIGHT. The first major operation against the Viet Cong (q.v.) undertaken by the 7th Marines. The 1st Viet Cong Regiment held a number of hamlets 15 miles south of Chu Lai on the Van Tuong Peninsula. The plan for the marine attack was for one company to move overland to take up a blocking position along the Tra Bong River on 17 August 1965. The following day a battalion of the 3d Marines would be landed by helicopter, while a battalion of the 4th was landed by tracked amphibians on the opposite side. Thus, the Viet Cong would be trapped between the two marine battalions. The Seaborne landings would be covered by A4 Skyraiders (q.v.) and by naval gunfire, and the helicopter landings would be defended by army gunships. The entire operation went according to plan despite the oppressive heat, heavy opposition for hill positions, and the stubborn defense of the strongly defended hamlets. Heavy firepower from M48 tanks and amtracs helped neutralize the Viet Cong positions. By 19 August the Viet Cong had been pushed back toward the ocean as the marines cleared the last pockets of resistance. This first significant encounter with the Viet Cong was a resounding success. A full enemy regiment had been destroyed, and the marines' flexible combined-arms approach had been proved in combat.

P

PACK HOWITZER 1923-E2 (75mm). In 1930 the corps began replacing the French 75mm guns that had been the staple light-artillery pieces since World War I (q.v.). The Howitzer had been designed in 1923 for use as mountain artillery and could be broken down into sections. In amphibious operations it could be brought ashore in six sections and quickly reassembled. Crewed by five, the Howitzer fired a 16-pound shell to a maximum 10,000-yard range. During World War II (q.v.), there were three pack Howitzer battalions for each artillery regiment. The gun could even be mounted on half-tracks for greater mobility. The Howitzer was used extensively in every campaign in the Pacific because of its mobility and firepower.

PAIGE, MITCHELL. b. Charleroi, Pa., 31 Aug. 1918. At age 18, Paige enlisted in the Marine Corps and after boot camp was stationed at Quantico (q.v.). Later he was ordered to sea duty and served at Mare Island. In early May 1937 he was posted to Cavite in the Philippines and the following year was posted to North China. Returning to the United States, he participated in maneuvers in the Caribbean and finally was posted to the new base at Camp Lejeune (q.v.). Paige was ordered to Samoa (q.v.) in mid-1942 as a member of the 7th Marines and in September to Guadalcanal (q.v.). On 26 October while commanding a machine gun section, Platoon Sergeant Paige alone stopped the Japanese advance through his company's position. Reinforced, he led a bayonet charge against the enemy. For that action he was awarded the Medal of Honor (q.v.) and was commissioned.

Paige left Guadalcanal in January 1943 with the 1st Division. Later that year he participated in the difficult operation at Cape Gloucester (q.v.), New Britain (q.v.). In July 1944 he was ordered back to Camp Lejeune, and the following year as a captain he became tactical training officer at Camp Matthews, California. He was placed on inactive duty in May 1946, returning to active status in July 1950. During the Korean War (q.v.), he served as a training officer in San Diego and then attended the Junior Course at Quantico. During the 1950s, he served in a variety of positions, including commanding a battalion of the

7th Marines before taking charge of the Marine Corps Recruiting Station in San Francisco, then serving as an instructor at San Bruno, California, and finally as executive officer of the marine base at the Naval Station in San Diego. He was placed on the disabled retired list in November 1959 and promoted to colonel.

PANAMA. A republic whose territory is coterminous with the isthmus that joins North and South America. It was a part of Colombia until disagreements between the Panamanians and that government led to a declaration of independence in early November 1903. The heart of the differences concerned a proposed lease of a zone to the United States to build a canal. Panamanian independence was preserved by the action of the U.S. navy, which prevented the landing of Colombian troops. Earlier in January 1885 a small detachment of marines landed to protect the American-owned Panama Railroad from anti-Colombian forces. Within a few months the railroad was secured. Soon after the agreement had been signed with the new Panamanian government, a battalion of marines landed at Colon. The Colombian troops were persuaded to leave peacefully. Three more battalions were soon in Panama, constituting a brigade. Digging on the canal began in May 1904, and this miracle of 20th-century engineering was completed in 1913. At least one battalion of marines remained in the Canal Zone, and it later became a major staging base for expeditions against Nicaragua (q.v.), Haiti (q.v.), and Honduras.

Good relations were maintained with a succession of elected Panamanian governments, and this rapport continued even after Gen. Omar Torrijos overthrew the civilian government in 1968. Panamanian pressure on the United States resulted in an agreement to turn the canal over to Panama in 1999. At first Gen. Manuel Noriega, Torrijos's successor as military strongman, was at pains to court U.S. economic and political support, and in return the United States used Panama as a base to combat the drug trade and Communist activities in Central America. By 1987 the relationship had changed. Noriega was recognized as being one of the major players in the drug trade. Further, it became obvious that the majority of Panamanians wanted to be free of Noriega. As a result of this changed climate, the U.S. government suspended all military and economic aid in July 1987. In the following months Noriega actively courted radical elements in Latin America, further straining his relations with Washington. The Panama elections of 1989 were openly fradulent, and a coup in October failed to oust the dictator. Noriega then declared a virtual state of war with the United States. He was indicted and later convicted in a U.S. court on drug charges. Using the excuse of a danger to the canal, Pres. George Bush decided to use force to oust the unpopular and potentially dangerous dictator.

The large scale operation code-named Just Cause was primarily an army show. The force included 3,000 Special Forces personnel regularly stationed in the Canal Zone, the 82d Airborne, and elements of the 5th and 7th Divisions and Ranger units. It was expected that the 19,000-man Panama Defense Force (PDF) would put up strong resistance. The marine contribution was to be minor, being only one part of five task forces that would be involved in striking at 27 targets simultaneously. The marine contingent, aptly code-named Semper Fi, was made up of K Company of the 6th Marines, D Company of the 2d Light Armored Infantry, a brigade service group, and an antiterrorism security unit. Combined with the security forces already in Panama, the total number of marines deployed was approximately 600 men.

H-hour was 0100 on 20 December 1989. One major objective of the army Special Forces team, code-named Task Force Black, was to seize a key bridge into Panama City as well as to begin searching for Noriega. They could not locate the dictator. The heaviest fighting in the city was in the vicinity of the *Commandancia*, the headquarters of the PDF, where the army's 193d Brigade with assistance from air units drove out the PDF units by the early afternoon. Other elements of the 193d seized Fort Amador, while units of the 82d took Patilla airfield. Meanwhile, units of the 7th and 82d Divisions comprising the Atlantic Task Force had moved into Colon against very little resistance and later seized other vital objectives near Gamboa and Cerra Tigre. Rangers from Fort Lewis, Washington, and Fort Benning jumped at 500 feet to negate PDF forces at Rio Hato and at Torrijos airfield. The large-scale combined operations designed to secure the city and defeat the PDF had gone according to plan while taking minimal casualties. By 21 December the city was occupied, and only sporadic resistance ensued. Two days later 82d Airborne troops swept the city to eliminate any pockets of resistance. Actions of guerrillas outside the city continued for the next few days, but word of Noriega's flight to the Vatican Embassy on the 24th served to moderate this resistance. He left that sanctuary and surrendered on 4 January.

The marines in Task Force Semper Fi were elite forces whose assigned task was to secure a six-square-mile area southwest of Panama City. Within this area were the U.S. Naval Station, Howard Air Force Base, the Arraijan Tank Farm, and the Bridge of the Americas. They had little difficulty securing most of these; the PDF did not choose to defend even the strategic bridge. The only resistance they met was at the Tank Farm, a fuel depot essential to support the aircraft on Howard Air Force Base. This token resistance was soon overcome, and the marines moved in light-armored vehicles to assault a PDF compound in the town of Arraijan and a road block near the town. In the firefight that followed, the marines suffered one killed and two wounded.

From an operational point of view, Operation Just Cause was a glowing success. There were few casualties to U.S. forces, and even the PDF and civilian losses were low considering that much of the action was fought in densely populated Panama City. It was also a political triumph and gave the Bush administration full confidence in all of its military units to perform well in combined operations.

"PANTHER" (F9F). Built by Grumman Aircraft Company, the prototype of this single-seat jet fighter was first flown in 1946. The first of the F9F-2 series was delivered to the corps in late 1948. Ultimately, 437 of this model were delivered to the navy. Three later versions with engine and armament changes were delivered. The F9F-5 was adopted by the corps after 1950, and this became the corps' first-line fighter until replaced by the "Fury" (q.v.) in the mid-1950s. The Panther had a top speed of 625 miles per hour and a service ceiling of more than 50,000 feet. It carried four 20mm cannon and had racks to carry rockets, bombs, or napalm.

PARRIS ISLAND. Located in South Carolina, it is the Marine Corps' major recruit training post in the eastern United States. It was initially the Naval Station at Port Royal, which was renamed Parris Island after the Marine Corps obtained the area in September 1915. It became the major recruit depot for the corps, replacing Norfolk, Virginia. The only access to the island for the first class of recruits was either by navy tug or motor boat. At first the standard training course was 14 weeks. During World War I (q.v.), training time was reduced to eight weeks. In August 1940 the base was almost completely destroyed by a hurricane, forcing the recruits to be transferred to

Quantico (q.v.). During World War II (q.v.), Parris Island was the main recruit training depot east of the Mississippi, a role it has continued in subsequent decades. On 8 April 1956 an overzealous and irresponsible drill instructor ordered an unauthorized night march that led to the drowning of six recruits in Ribbon Creek. The public as well as officials used this tragedy to question the harshness of marine recruit training. After Congressional hearings, the corps implemented numerous changes in basic training procedures.

PATE, RANDOLPH McCALL. 21st commandant, b. Port Royal, S.C., 11 Feb. 1898, d. Bethesda, Md., 31 July 1961. Pate served briefly as an enlisted man in the army in World War I (q.v.) then went to Virginia Military Institute and graduated in 1921 and was commissioned in the Marine Corps Reserve. He was one of 12 junior officers commissioned in 1921 by order of Gen. John Lejeune (q.v.) in a change of policy to accept officers from ROTC military colleges. He served in Santo Domingo (q.v.) during 1923–24 and in China from 1927 to 1929. During the 1930s he served at various posts throughout the United States. By 1941 he was a lieutenant colonel and saw his first action as logistic chief of the 1st Marine Division, responsible for unloading materiel and continuing the supply for the division on Guadalcanal (q.v.). He later became deputy chief of staff, Fleet Marine Force (q.v.), Pacific, and was deeply involved in the planning for Iwo Jima (q.v.) and Okinawa (q.v.). After the war he was appointed director of the reserve and was in charge of the Marine Corps Educational Center at Quantico (q.v.) and was promoted to brigadier general in 1948.

As a major general in June 1953, Pate assumed command of the 1st Marine Division in the Korean War (q.v.) just before the truce went into effect on 27 July, and he held that post until May 1954. He was appointed commandant on 31 December 1955. A traditionalist commandant, he survived the Parris Island (q.v.) scandal that occurred in April 1956. During the Suez crisis in 1956, he sent with the 6th Fleet in the Mediterranean three battalions of the 2d Marines that had landed at Alexandria (q.v.) and supervised the evacuation of 1,500 civilians. Small units of marines also were active in Morocco and during the Venezuelan disturbances in early 1958. Pate retired with the rank of general on 31 December 1959.

PAUL, JOE C. b. Williamsburg, Ky., 23 April 1946. During the Vietnam War (q.v.) on 18 August 1965 units of the 4th Marines, in concert with elements of the 3d and 7th, launched Operation Starlight (q.v.) against the Viet Cong (q.v.) near Van Tuong. Lance Corporal Paul was a member of H Company, 4th Marines, and participated in the capture of a key hill before his unit was caught in a killing crossfire in the open. In the first few minutes his platoon took five casualties from the Viet Cong in positions near Nam Yen. The wounded could not move back because of heavy machine gun and rifle fire, and then the enemy began throwing white phosphorous grenades. Paul moved forward between the wounded and the enemy and delivered devastating fire from his automatic weapon long enough for the wounded to be evacuated. Critically wounded, he stayed in the forward position until he collapsed and was evacuated. Paul was later awarded the Medal of Honor (q.v.) posthumously for his gallant action.

PEARL HARBOR. Located on the island of Oahu in the Hawaiian chain, it was the major U.S. naval base in the Pacific. On 7 December 1941 the Japanese without warning sent two distinct waves of planes launched from six aircraft carriers to attack the naval base and the army and marine stations elsewhere on the island. This sneak attack resulted in a U.S. declaration of war on Japan the following day. The raids were very successful, sinking five battleships and seriously damaging three others. For all practical purposes the Pacific Fleet had been put out of action for a year. Only the two aircraft carriers, a few cruisers, and smaller ships were available during the first few months of the war. The marine airbase at Ewa was heavily damaged, and most of its planes were destroyed or damaged. Marine casualties either on board ship or at Ewa numbered 109 killed and 69 wounded. Pearl Harbor, with its docking facilities and tank farms undamaged, recovered quickly from the raid and with new ships available became the locus of all U.S. offensives in the Central Pacific. It was the headquarters for Adm. Chester Nimitz, commander in chief of the Pacific Ocean areas. Fleet Marine Force (q.v.), Pacific headquarters was also here, and almost all marine units used in the Pacific campaigns staged through Pearl Harbor.

PEKING. Present-day Beijing, Peking was the capital of China during the period of Manchu rule. All the foreign legations were located in one section of the city. In May and June 1900 a revolutionary antiforeign group called Boxers by Westerners showed their hostility by attempting to seize the embassies. A heroic defense by various legation guards (q.v.) fought off multiple attacks. Members of the Marine Corps, although few in number, played a key role in this defense. The Boxer Rebellion (q.v.) failed largely because of this action. Eventually the dowager empress denounced the Boxers, and the rebellion fell apart.

PELELIU. An island in the Palau group of islands in the Western Carolines, which was the target in September 1944 of a major operation ostensibly to seize the airfield there and protect the western flank of the landings in the Philippines. Initially the plans were to seize the larger islands to the north as well, but this phase was canceled. Despite objections from Adm. William Halsey, the southern operations went ahead. These called for the army's 81st Division to seize Angaur Island while the other component of III Amphibious Corps, the 1st Marine Division, invaded Peleliu. The initial estimates of the number of Japanese troops there were terribly wrong. The Japanese commander had over 13,000 troops available to defend the fishhook-shaped island seven miles long and two miles wide at its extreme. The southern part of the island was low-lying flat scrubland, and this was where the airfield was located. The most distinguishing feature of the island was the Umurbrogal heights, limestone cliffs deeply intersected by deep ravines with hundreds of natural caves to which the Japanese had added many man-made caves.

The five-day naval bombardment hardly touched the bulk of the Japanese troops. The commander of the 1st Division, Gen. William Rupertus (q.v.), with one of the most erroneous predictions of the entire war, promised that the quick and dirty campaign would be finished in 72 hours. Even before the first marines reached the reef line, this optimistic forecast was questionable. Artillery and mortar fire took a heavy toll of the LVTs (q.v.) and DUKWs (q.v.). By the end of the day 60 of these had been knocked out. Soon after landing at 0830 on 15 September, the 1st Marines were pinned to the beach and took very heavy casualties from the Japanese on the high ground. The 5th Marines had an easier time and by midafternoon had reached the airfield. Here they fought off a major tank attack. The 7th Marines were being held up by heavy fire from abandoned buildings and a large blockhouse. By evening the marines had only a precarious lodgement and had suffered 1,100 casualties.

In the next four days the marines, aided by awesome air and naval support, slowly expanded the perimeter. The 5th took the Lobster Claw, a jut of land east of the main road, and the

7th cleared the southeastern perimeter. The 1st, with the most difficult task, assaulted the southern section of the Umurbrogol—Bloody Nose Ridge. By 21 September the 1st Marines had suffered over 50 percent casualties, and Gen. Roy Geiger (q.v.), commanding III Corps, decided to replace it with an army Regimental Combat Team (RCT) from Angaur. This unit and the 5th Marines drove up the west road. By 27 September nine-tenths of the island had been captured, but the remaining Japanese had to be rooted out of the caves and ravines, which took time and brought many more casualties. Finally, on 22 October the 7th Marines was pulled out, followed the next week by the 5th.

The quick and dirty campaign promised by the divisional commander had turned into a nightmare, with more than 1,300 marines killed in action. The slow siege of the remaining Japanese ensconced in an ever narrowing fortress was continued by two army RCTs. It was not until 27 November that the last Japanese position was taken. The army units had in their month-long siege suffered 827 casualties. This battle for Peleliu was among the hardest-fought campaigns of the Pacific war, yet the possession of Peleliu proved of little strategic value.

PENDLETON, JOSEPH H. "UNCLE JOE." b. Rochester, Pa., 2 June 1860, d. San Diego, Calif., 4 Feb. 1942. Pendleton graduated from the Naval Academy and was appointed second lieutenant in the corps in July 1884 after serving two years at sea as a cadet. During the next decade he served at marine bases in New York, Mare Island, California, and twice on sea duty—for two years from June 1892 at Sitka, Alaska, and then in Washington, D.C. Promoted to captain, he was once again assigned to Sitka, where he served for five years. Following that assignment he was once more sent to Mare Island briefly before being posted to the Philippines. Now a major, he was given command of the marine base on Guam, and then from 1906 to 1909 he commanded the base at Bremerton, Washington. His second tour in the Philippines began shortly afterward, joining the 1st Brigade there. In May 1912 as a colonel, Pendleton returned to the United States at Portsmouth, New Hampshire. In August of that year he took command of the marine units in Nicaragua (q.v.) where he led them in a number of successful engagements. From February to June of the following year, he was with an expeditionary force at Guantanamo (q.v.) Bay. Later as a colonel he commanded the marine base at Puget Sound, had sea duty, commanded the 4th Marines from December 1914 to

February 1916, and briefly commanded the marine base in San Diego. He took command of all naval forces ashore in Santo Domingo (q.v.) in June 1916 and participated in a series of engagements with the rebel forces. Promoted to brigadier general, he commanded the troops that occupied Santiago. He was then assigned to permanent duty in Santo Domingo, and during part of his service there he was acting military governor.

He returned to the United States in October 1918 and was appointed to command the base at Parris Island (q.v.). One year later he took command of the advanced force base at San Diego and in October 1921 was appointed to command the 5th Brigade. Briefly in 1922 he was commanding general of the Department of the Pacific. Promoted to major general, he was sent on an inspection tour of Central America in 1924 before returning to command the 5th Brigade. He retired in June 1924. The sprawling marine base north of San Diego was named in his honor.

PENOBSCOT BAY. Located at the mouth of the Penobscot River in Maine. During the Revolutionary War (q.v.) a force of 700 British regulars and three warships were sent from Halifax, Nova Scotia, to build a fort and establish a naval base on the western promontory, then a part of Massachusetts. Frightened by this, the State War Board in Boston put together a formidable force of four small warships and 900 men with orders to drive out the British and destroy Fort St. George. The most experienced of the force were the Continental and State Marines, and these landed on 28 July 1779, brushed aside minor opposition, took the high ground in front of the partially built fort, but were halted 500 yards from the low walls by the militia commander. A quarrel between the overall commander and the militia leader resulted in paralysis. The appearance of a heavily armed British frigate frightened the American leaders, who proceeded to scuttle their warships and transports. The marines and militia were forced into a difficult march back to Boston. What should have been a marine triumph had turned into a fiasco. There was little compensation in that a court martial of the overall commander convicted him of dereliction of duty.

PENSACOLA. The site of a naval yard established in 1825 and closed in 1911, Pensacola is best known for its Naval Air Station on the north shore of Pensacola Bay approximately six miles west of the city of Pensacola, Florida. In October 1913 the secretary of the navy appointed a board that was to create a comprehensive plan for a naval air service. On its recommendation in January of the following year, an Aeronautics Center was established at Pensacola. Elementary and advanced flight training was given at the air station until May 1918, when it was designated an advanced training station for navy and marine pilots. World War I (q.v.) witnessed a great expansion of the facilities, with more than 100 new buildings constructed. During the war, 921 heavier-than-air and 63 dirigible pilots were trained at Pensacola. There was little expansion of facilities during the interwar years, although in 1935 Congress authorized an expansion of the air training program. By 1940 the station had over 400 planes. During World War II (q.v.), thousands of naval and marine pilots were trained at Pensacola and its six auxillary fields. One-half of the naval aviators—a total of 28,562 pilots—trained during the war received their wings at Pensacola. During the Korean War (q.v.), more than 6,000 pilots were trained at the station, and advanced jet training was instituted in 1955. In 1971 headquarters for the chief of naval education and training was located there. Naval Air Station Pensacola continued throughout the Cold War to be a key station for the training of pilots and ground crewmen of both the navy and marine air services.

"PERSHING" (M-26) MAIN BATTLE TANK. Developed toward the end of World War II (q.v.), this tank incorporated many updated features based on captured German tanks. A total of 2,400 Pershings were built during the war. An additional 6,400 were manufactured during the 1950s. The Pershing had a crew of five, weighed 42 tons, and was powered by a 500-horsepower gasoline engine that drove it at a top speed of 30 miles per hour. Its frontal armor was four inches thick. The Pershing's main armament was a 90mm gun, and it had as secondary weapons two .50-caliber machine guns. Cutbacks in defense spending after World War II meant that the older "Sherman" tank (q.v.) remained the basis of many army and marine units and was proved in the earlier stages of the Korean War (q.v.) to be outclassed by the Russian-built tanks. When the Pershings were committed as on the Inchon-Seoul (q.v.) operation in September 1950, they were more than a match for the North Korean T-34 tanks.

"PHANTOM II" (F4-B and RF4-B). Built by McDonnell Douglas Aircraft Company, the Phantom was initially developed as a twin-engine, heavy, extremely fast, two-seat, all-weather attack fighter for the navy and later with modifications was adopted by the air force and Marine Corps. These planes included reconnaissance and tactical support functions, and the Phantom F4-G was the key piece of equipment in the "Wild Weasel" Program. The standard F4-B had a top speed in excess of Mach 2 and a combat radius of 900 miles. Its main armament was either six Sparrow III missiles or four Sparrow III and two Sidewinder air-to-air missiles. It could carry various loads of up to eight tons of conventional, napalm, or even nuclear bombs. The first production model of the Phantom was delivered to the navy in December 1960. The plane was in continuous production until October 1979. At that time 5,057 Phantoms had been built. The navy and marines had received 1,264 of the planes. In 1966 the corps received the first model of the F4-J, a modification of the F4-B that gave it full ground attack capability. Fitted with slotted tailplanes, drooping ailerons to slow its approach, and an upgraded fire control system, this model with later retrofits was an even more deadly fire platform than others and proved its capability in the Vietnam War (q.v.).

PHILIPPINE INSURRECTION. During the Spanish-American War (q.v.), the most important Filipino leader, Emilio Aguinaldo, had been used by Commodore Dewey and General Merritt to organize guerrilla forces to operate against the Spaniards. Afterward he felt betrayed by the United States and began a war against his former allies by attacking Manila on 4 February 1899. This "insurrection," which spread to other islands lasted longer and claimed more lives than the short-lived action against Spain. Two battalions of marines arrived later in 1899 and were soon in action against Aguinaldo's forces at Novaleta and in the vicinity of Olongapo.

The Philippine pacification continued into 1900, but most of the marines were transferred to China to confront more pressing threats to U.S. interests. Once the situation in Peking during the Boxer Rebellion (q.v.) had been normalized, the marines were ordered back to the Philippines where the fighting against the insurrectionists was still ongoing. Luzon had been pacified after the capture of Aguinaldo in February, but the Muslim Moros on the southern islands refused to recognize U.S. rule. The island of Samar (q.v.) was the focal point of resistance where earlier an army company had been ambushed. In early October a battalion of marines was sent to the island to operate under overall army control. The prevalent idea of the

U.S. command was to "civilize them with a Krag." Following on the orders to burn and destroy the bases, the battalion in a month-long campaign drove the Moros back into the jungle. By mid-November 1900 all organized resistance on Samar had been crushed. (See also Krag-Jorgensen.)

PLATOON. A title given in the 20th century to a low level infantry unit. Initially before the adoption of the triangular system there were four platoons in a company (q.v.). However, in 1941 with the Marine Corps' reform based on the army's decision to construct its divisions on a basis of threes instead of fours, there were only three platoons in a company. Each infantry platoon was made up of three squads. This system of division remains in effect over 50 years later. A platoon's strength varies depending on the type of unit. The usual size of a rifle platoon during World War II (q.v.) was 76 men.

PULLER, LEWIS B. "CHESTY." b. West Point, Va., 26 June 1898, d. Hampton, Va., 11 Oct. 1972. Puller enlisted in the Marine Corps in August 1918 and was given a reserve commission in June of the following year, but he was soon placed on inactive status because of the downsizing of the corps. He reentered the corps the following week as an enlisted man. He was posted to Haiti (q.v.), and while only a sergeant in the corps he served as a captain in the *Gendarmerie*. He served in Haiti for five years and was often in action against the Caco rebels. In March 1924 he returned to the United States, where he received a regular commission in the corps. He served at the marine base at Norfolk, attended Basic School, and was assigned to the 10th Marines at Quantico (q.v.) before flight training at Pensacola (q.v.) in February 1926. In December 1928 he was ordered to Nicaragua (q.v.) to assist the training of its National Guard and help defend the elected government from the forces of the rebel Augusto Sandino. After a brief exile in Mexico, Sandino returned in May 1930, and once again the marine-led National Guard tried to capture him. In June and July Puller's company fought five actions against superior numbers. For these actions he won his first Navy Cross (q.v.).

Returning to the United States in July 1931, Puller attended the company officers' course at Fort Benning. Upon completion of the course he was ordered once again to Nicaragua, where he again led troops of the National Guard against the Sandinistas. In late 1932 Puller's patrol fought four battles in 10 days and the day after Christmas drove off a rebel attack on a train.

These actions won Puller his second Navy Cross. He left Nicaragua in January 1933 and soon was posted to the detachment guarding the American Legation in Peking (q.v.). Following this duty he commanded the marine detachment aboard the *Augusta* of the Asiatic Fleet. In June 1936 he became an instructor at the basic school in Philadelphia. Three years later he was once again in command of the marines on board the *Augusta*, and in May 1940 he joined the 4th Marines, first as a battalion executive and later as commanding officer. He arrived back in the United States just before Pearl Harbor (q.v.) and took command of the 1st Battalion, 7th Marines, at Camp Lejeune (q.v.) and accompanied it to Samoa (q.v.).

Landing on Guadalcanal (q.v.) on 18 September, this battalion saw action immediately in defense of the perimeter. Beginning on the 27th in conjunction with Raiders and army troops, the 1st Battalion fought a series of actions along the Matanikau River. On the night of 24 October Puller's battalion was the only defense of Henderson Field (q.v.). Attacked by a Japanese regiment, Puller's men fought a desperate battle along a one-mile front for over three hours, and Puller continued in command of the force now augmented by other marines and army troops until late the next day. In a further action along the Metapona River, he was seriously wounded by shrapnel but refused evacuation until the action was complete. This action won him his third Navy Cross. He returned to the United States in January 1943.

After three months touring various U.S. posts and sharing his experiences with the officers and men, Puller rejoined the division as executive officer of the 7th Marines. In January 1944 he was involved in the landings at Cape Gloucester (q.v.). In the ensuing fighting he took over command of two battalions and led a 1,000-man patrol deep into the interior of western New Britain. Just before leaving New Britain in April he was awarded his fourth Navy Cross. Later he took charge of the 1st Marines and led it in the bloody invasion of Peleliu (q.v.). Holding the left flank of the marine line and under direct fire from the Umurbrogol highlands, his regiment suffered 50 percent casualties but secured a lodgement on Bloody Nose Ridge before being withdrawn. After the war he commanded the training regiment at Camp Lejeune and was director of the 8th Reserve District and the marine base in Hawaii. Finally, in August 1950 he returned to command the 1st Marines. He led the regiment in the Inchon (q.v.) landing in Korea and the advance across the 38th parallel to the Yalu River. Struck by invading

Chinese, the marines fell back in the dead of winter from Chosin (q.v.), the flanks of the retreating marines protected by the 1st. For these actions Puller received his fifth Navy Cross. In January 1951 he was promoted to brigadier general and became assistant commander of the division.

In May he returned to the United States to command the 3d Brigade, and after it was upgraded to a division, he was the assistant commander and then took over the troop training command at Coronado, California. Promoted to major general in July 1953, he took command of the 2d Division at Camp Lejeune. He retained that command until appointed deputy camp commander in February 1955. Illness forced his retirement on 1 November 1955, and he was promoted to lieutenant general.

PURPLE HEART. The name normally given to the Badge of Military Merit, so called because of the shape of the medal and the color of its ribbon. It is the oldest U.S. decoration, established by Gen. George Washington in August 1782. After the Revolution it ceased to be issued. The award was revived in 1932. Any member of the U.S. armed forces who receives wounds as a result of enemy action that necessitate treatment in a medical facility is eligible for the award.

PUSAN. The largest and best port in South Korea. After the attack by North Koreans on 25 June 1950, the combined United Nations force, including the hastily assembled army's 24th and 25th Divisions, were pushed back to a defense line roughly a quarter circle with a 100-mile radius from Pusan. Later the 8th Army received further reinforcements of the army's 1st Cavalry and 2d Infantry Divisions and the corps' 1st Provisional Brigade. This latter unit stripped from the 1st Division was what Cmndt. Clifton Cates (q.v.) had promised General MacArthur. Numbering 6,500 men made up mainly of the 5th Marines, it sailed from San Diego on 12 July. Arriving at Pusan on 2 August, the 5th was immediately put into the line on the extreme left attacking the city of Sachon. Supported by Corsairs (q.v.) of two squadrons (VMF 214 and 323), they fought their way into the city by 13 August. The brigade was withdrawn to move 90 miles north to defend the Naktong Bridge. Here it engaged the 4th North Korean Division and battered it so that it retreated across the Naktong River. Then on 3 September it supported the army's 2d Division and helped blunt the North Korean attack in three days of heavy fighting. Two days later the 5th Marines went into reserve in preparation with the rest of the 1st Division for the Inchon (q.v.) operation. That operation in conjunction with the 8th Army's frontal assaults on the North Koreans along the perimeter line all but destroyed the enemy's army. Never again during the Korean War (q.v.) was Pusan threatened.

PYONGYANG-SEOUL CORRIDOR. A part of the sector assigned to the 1st Division in March 1952 after being pulled out of the "Punchbowl" area. This area was on the extreme left flank of the UN line and in part fronted on Panmunjom where the armistice discussions were dragging on. By this time the fighting had become a near stalemate, with each side dug into fortified positions. Attacks were mounted only to maintain control of strategic strong points. Thus, in August 1952 there was a contest for an outpost called "Bunker Hill" and in October a fight for the "Hook." In early 1953 there was particularly hard fighting for three strong points called "Reno," "Carson," and "Vegas." The fighting ceased on 27 July as the truce finally went into effect. By the close of the Korean War (q.v.), the "police action" had claimed the lives of 4,262 marines, with 21,781 wounded and 227 taken prisoner.

Q

QUANTICO. The major marine base in the eastern United States. It extends for five miles along the west bank of the Potomac River; the whole of the base is approximately 100 square miles. It is the home of the corps' Development and Education Command. As long as the corps was small, the bases in Philadelphia and Washington were adequate, but with the increase in its size to 13,700 men just before World War I (q.v.), a larger base was needed. The projected great expansion of the corps during the war spurred the navy to approve a site selection board that eventually fixed upon Quantico, and 5,300 acres were leased from the near bankrupt Quantico Company in April 1917. The first marines to arrive in May were the 5th Marines from Santo Domingo (q.v.).

The weather was hot and humid, and the early contingent had to deal with inadequate services. However, by the end of the year many 50-man wooden barracks had been built as well as mess halls, a power plant, and other services. In the spring of 1918 the Quantico Company agreed to sell the initial acreage and an extra 1,200 acres for $475,000. This deal was approved by Congress in July 1918.

During the interwar years, construction continued, the wooden barracks were replaced, and more land was acquired. Quantico became the site of the Marine Corps schools. It was primarily home of the Advanced Base Force and then its successor, the Fleet Marine Force (q.v.). The landing exercises of the 1930s, which proved crucial for the amphibious operations of World War II (q.v.), were conducted from there. Initially the 1st Brigade was stationed there and after its upgrade to divisional size and departure to the Pacific, Quantico became primarily an instructional base. By January 1942 the size of the corps had increased to over 100,000 and eventually reached almost one-half million men. By 1944 Quantico had become primarily a huge replacement training organization processing recruits for the six active divisions. Throughout World War II (q.v.) and in subsequent decades Quantico remained at the very center of Marine Corps activities.

QUICK, JOHN H. b. Charleston, W. Va., 20 June 1870, d. St. Louis, Mo., 10 Sept. 1922. Quick enlisted in the corps in August 1892 and served on board ship or in various shore stations continuously until his retirement in 1918. He participated in all the campaigns involving the Marine Corps during his period of service. His first serious action was during the Spanish-American War (q.v.) in Cuba (q.v.) on 14 June 1898 where he exposed himself to enemy fire while signaling a naval support vessel that was falling on a small group of marines to lift its fire. For this gallantry he was awarded the Medal of Honor (q.v.). During the Philippine insurrection (q.v.) Quick served from October 1901 until March 1902, further distinguishing himself in the difficult and dangerous campaign on Samar (q.v.). Later during the Cuban troubles of 1906 he served with the Army of Cuban Pacification. Promoted to sergeant major in 1905, he served in a variety of marine posts in the United States until 1914 when he was called on to take part in the Veracruz (q.v.) occupation, where he was commended for gallantry. During World War I (q.v.), Quick participated in every battle fought by the marines—Verdun, Soissons (q.v.), Belleau Wood (q.v.), and the Meuse-Argonne (q.v.) campaigns. For his actions at Belleau Wood he received the Distinguished Service Cross and the Navy Cross (q.v.). He retired in November 1918 and died four years later, one of the most decorated marines of the "Old Breed."

R

REASONER, FRANK S. b. Spokane, Wash., 16 Sept. 1937. On 12 July 1965 as a first lieutenant, Reasoner was leading a patrol of Company A, 3d Reconnaissance Battalion, 3d Division, south of Da Nang (q.v.) in Vietnam. He was with the advanced elements when the patrol came under fire from an estimated 100 Viet Cong (q.v.). He established a firebase and moved from man to man, encouraging those most vulnerable. The main force of marines could not move up, and the enemy machine gun fire began to take its toll. Exposing himself, he provided covering fire and killed at least two Viet Cong and silenced a machine gun. The radio operator was wounded, and Reasoner rushed to give aid. Afterward the man, attempting to move to a better position, was again wounded, and Reasoner once again attempted to go to his aid. He was hit by machine gun fire and mortally wounded. For these actions he was awarded the Medal of Honor (q.v.) posthumously.

REGIMENT. The key large-size component in a divisional organization. For the Marine Corps it is a relatively new operational unit, since before World War I (q.v.) the corps was too small for regimental organization. With its expansion the corps adopted the army divisional organization, that of the square division composed of four infantry regiments. During the war, two brigades (q.v.) of 9,300 men, each composed two infantry regiments, and attached engineering and service units were sent to France. After the war, despite the shrinkage in the size of the corps, two brigades were kept in operation, one at Quantico (q.v.) and the other at San Diego. At the outset of World War II (q.v.), these were upgraded to divisions (q.v.), each organized along a triangular scheme with three infantry regiments comprising a division. By 1944 each division had a targeted size of 16,500 men. Each infantry regiment was composed of approximately 3,100 men. There was also an artillery regiment and headquarters, engineering, and service personnel. This structure remained the basis of the corps' organization even after fundamental changes in the post-Vietnam period were made to create more flexible responses. The infantry regiment remained the key element for the Marine Expeditionary Force (MEF) (q.v.) and the Marine Expeditionary Brigade (MEB) (q.v.). The former is composed of one or more divisions; the latter has one infantry regiment composed of three to five battalions.

REISING GUN. Designed by inventor Eugen Reising and patented in 1940, it was a wartime expedient to meet the increased demand for a submachine gun early in World War II (q.v.). There were two different models, the types 50 and 55. The model 50 had a wooden stock, weighed six pounds, fired standard .45-caliber ball ammunition, and had a compensator attached to the muzzle to reduce the tendency of the weapon to climb. The model 55 was intended for use by paratroops and had a folding metal shoulder stock, a shorter barrel, and no compensator. Although it was reasonably accurate and weighed less than the Thompson submachine gun (q.v.), the weapon had serious flaws. Most of the 100,000 weapons produced between 1940 and 1942 were used by the Marine Corps in the early Pacific operations in wet, humid conditions. The mild steel allowed its magazines to rust easily, dirt could get into the weapon and cause jams, and the safety mechanism was faulty, possibly allowing the weapon to fire while on safety.

"RESCUER" (HRP). Built by the Piasecki Aircraft Corporation in two versions (HRP-1 and -2), this large helicopter (called the "flying banana" because of its shape) was first flown in March 1945 and was in continuous service in the navy and corps for more than a decade. The -1 version was fabric covered, while the -2 was all metal and the shape redesigned to reduce drag. The latter version had a top speed of 105 miles per hour and a service load capacity of one ton. It had twin rotors mounted in front and to the extreme rear, enabling it to climb at a rate of 400 feet per minute. It was used extensively by the navy for rescue work, while the Marine Corps experimented with airborne assault operations.

REVOLUTIONARY WAR. Although some fighting had begun before, the rebellion against British rule officially began on 4 July 1776. The governing body of the fledgling government, the 2d Continental Congress, even before this in the fall of the previous year, moved to create a navy with a small Marine Corps mainly to serve on board its ships. These Continental Marines (q.v.) were thus a part of the ship's complement in every sea engagement during the war. They were also used in amphibious operations. In March 1776 they attacked the town and fort on New Providence Island in the Bahamas. Three companies of marines were with Gen. George Washington in his offensive against Trenton and Princeton. The final major action of the marines was in the flawed attempt to seize a British-held fort at Penobscot Bay (q.v.) in July 1779. Long before the Peace Treaty in 1783 that recognized U.S. independence, the Continental Navy had ceased to exist and with it the need for a Marine Corps.

ROCKEY, KELLER E. b. Columbia City, Ind., 22 Sept. 1888, d. Washington, D.C., June 1970. Rockey was commissioned in November 1913 and was assigned as a student in the officers school at Norfolk. After graduation in 1915, he went to sea serving as a member of the marine detachments first on board the *Nebraska* and later on the *Nevada*. As a member of the 5th Marines, he sailed for France in June 1917. He participated in the action at Chateau-Thierry (q.v.), where on 6 July 1918 he won the Navy Cross (q.v.) for heroic actions along the front lines. Soon after returning to the United States in 1919, he was posted to Haiti (q.v.) and served as a member of the constabulary for two years. Returning to the United States, he served at Marine Headquarters in Washington before attending the field officers course at Quantico (q.v.). Following this in 1925, he attended the Command and General Staff School at Fort Leavenworth. Upon completion of the course, he became an instructor in the Marine Corps' Department of Tactics. In 1928 he was briefly the commanding officer of a battalion of the 2d Brigade in Nicaragua (q.v.). In the 1930s Rockey served at San Diego as chief of staff of the base, in the commandant's department in Washington, and as Force Marine Officer, Battle Force. In 1939 he was assigned to the operations section of the War Plans Division in the Navy Department. As a brigadier general, he chaired a board in March 1941 that dealt with African Americans, recommending that they be enlisted to serve in composite defense battalions. Later that year he became chief of staff of the 2d Division, a position he held until ordered to Washington to become director of plans and policies at Marine Headquarters, and in 1943 he was made assistant to the commandant. In February 1944 he took command of the 5th Division in the Pacific and a year later led it in the assault on Iwo Jima (q.v.), landing on the left on Red and Green Beaches. His 28th Marines captured Suribachi. Advancing up the western side of the island, they drove to the northwest corner and confronted the last remnants of General Kuribayashi's force at Kitoni Point.

After Iwo Jima Rockey was appointed to command III Amphibious Corps. After the deactivation of the corps, he took command of the 1st Division at Tientsin (q.v.). On returning to the United States, he commanded the Department of the Pacific and in January 1947 became commanding general of Fleet Marine Force (q.v.), Atlantic. He retired from the corps as a lieutenant general in September 1950.

ROI-NAMUR. Two islands in the Kwajalein (q.v.) atoll of the Marshall Islands (q.v.) group, these were located 40 miles north of the main island of Kwajalein. The Japanese in January 1944 had approximately 3,500 men on the islands and a major airfield on Roi with an estimated 150 planes. Seizure of these islands along with Kwajalein was planned under the code name Flintlock. The various islands in the atoll had been softened up with continual B-24 raids. On 28 January Task Force 58's four task groups eliminated the Japanese air force on Roi, and three days later a bombardment group of older battleships and cruisers shelled four islands flanking Roi-Namur. Three battalions of the 25th Marines, a part of the untested 4th Division, seized them and brought in Howitzers, which soon began bombarding the main islands. On 1 February the 23d and 24th Marines landed on the southern shores of both islands. There was little opposition on Roi, and within two hours it was declared secure. The 24th Marines encountered heavier resistance on Namur and had not reached the northern areas by nightfall. During the night, several Japanese attacks were beaten off. By the afternoon of 2 February Namur was also declared secure.

Almost all the Japanese defenders were killed. Debris was cleared from the airfield and navy planes were using it by the afternoon of the 3d. Combined with the army's 7th Division capture of Kwajalein Island, the four-day actions gave the navy an excellent harbor that could be used as a forward staging area for future campaigns. Soon a second airstrip was completed on Kwajalein, advancing the U.S. bomber line 600 miles farther into the Japanese defense ring.

ROOSEVELT COROLLARY. Corollary to the Monroe Doctrine was first proclaimed by Pres. Theodore Roosevelt in December 1906. The Monroe Doctrine was designed to prevent intervention by foreign powers in the affairs of the Western Hemisphere. The chronic economic and political instability of what Roosevelt termed the "wretched republics" of the Caribbean and Central America made him decide that when such conditions might invite European intervention, the United States would take the necessary steps to correct the situation. This was used to justify sending the marines to Nicaragua (q.v.),

Haiti (q.v.), Santo Domingo (q.v.), and Mexico in the two decades following Roosevelt's pronouncement.

RUPERTUS, WILLIAM H. b. Washington, D.C., 14 Nov. 1889, d. Washington, D.C., 25 March 1945. Rupertus was educated at the U.S. Coast Guard Academy and commissioned a second lieutenant in the corps in 1913. He was promoted in grade through the rank of major general by 1942. He was the assistant divisional commander of the 1st Marine Division during the southern Solomons actions, leading one regiment in the conquest of Tulagi (q.v.). He continued in that capacity to the end of the Guadalcanal (q.v.) campaign. The division slowly recuperated from Guadalcanal in Australia, and Rupertus succeeded General Vandegrift (q.v.) in command. Under General MacArthur's orders, the division landed in the Cape Gloucester (q.v.) region of western New Britain (q.v.) on 26 December 1943 during a monsoon, and it secured that area in a complex, dirty operation by the end of April 1944.

The next task for General Rupertus and his staff was the seizure of Peleliu (q.v.) in the Western Caroline Islands. D-day was 15 September 1944. This controversial action was meant to secure MacArthur's right flank during the Leyte operation. Rupertus believed that the action would be relatively easy and completed in 72 hours. Instead, the Japanese using natural and man-made defensive positions all but destroyed the 1st Marines and thwarted the other regiments from quickly realizing their objectives. The island was not declared secure until 12 October. After Peleliu, Rupertus gave up command of the division and was soon hospitalized with a fatal illness.

RUSSELL, JOHN H. 16th commandant, b. Mare Island, Calif., 14 Nov. 1872, d. Coronado, Calif., 6 March 1947. Russell graduated from the Naval Academy in 1892 and was commissioned a second lieutenant in July 1894 after serving two years at sea as a midshipman. During the Spanish-American War (q.v.), he served on board the *Massachusetts* blockading Santiago. Afterward he was posted to a variety of stations in Philadelphia, New York, Washington, Hawaii, Guam (q.v.), and Mare Island. He was also on the staff of the Naval War College. Early in 1914 Russell was given command of a battalion of the 3d Marines and landed at Veracruz (q.v.), where he remained for the rest of the year. Subsequently he was promoted to lieutenant colonel and took command of the 3d Regiment in Santo Domingo (q.v.). As a colonel, he commanded the 1st Marine Brigade in

Haiti (q.v.) after October 1919. Marines operated against Cacos insurgents until they were killed or surrendered.

In 1920, promoted to brigadier general, Russell became U.S. High Commissioner, serving as such for nine years. In 1930 he became assistant commandant, and because of many foreign inspections by his superior, Gen. Ben Fuller (q.v.), he had more authority than most assistants had. He persuaded the secretary of the navy to redesignate the Expeditionary Force into Fleet Marine Force (q.v.). He became commandant on 1 January 1935 as a major general and served only two years because he had reached the statutory age limit. Before retiring, Russell established selection boards for promotion of officers.

S

SAINT-MIHIEL. A town in the department of the Meuse, France. From the beginning of World War I (q.v.), the Germans had occupied a deep salient there into allied lines. It covered a sensitive portion of the German front protecting two important rail lines and threatening the entire region from Verdun to Nancy. The reduction of the salient became a prime objective of allied operations in September 1918. The 4th Marine Brigade began the attack in the mud and rain in the sector where the marines were located as reserve. The next day the 5th and 6th Marines were committed, passing through the army's lines. All the major objectives planned by General Pershing's headquarters had been reached by that evening. During the total offensive ending on 15 September, the salient had been taken and 16,000 German prisoners captured. The marine brigade had only a small role in the overall offensive; nevertheless, it secured all objectives assigned to it while suffering 703 casualties.

SAIPAN. The major northern island in the Mariana Islands (q.v.) that in 1944 was a major Japanese military base. The island is small, less than 15 miles long and 7 miles at its widest, narrowing to 3 miles in the center adjacent to Magicienne Bay in the east. The east and north sides of the island have high hills and cliffs dominated by Mount Tapotchau, while the dominant feature of the south and west is a low-lying plain.

Before World War II (q.v.), Japan had transferred approximately 45,000 Japanese there to work the sugar, rice, and corn plantations. Recognizing its importance located only 1,200 miles from the Japanese southern islands, the Imperial High

Command sought to build up its defenses. These attempts were hampered by American submarines. Nevertheless, an estimated 29,000 army and navy personnel were there when the United States, fresh from the conquest of the Marshall Islands (q.v.), decided to invade the island primarily to secure bases for the new B-29 superbombers.

The plan for the Marianas operation, code-named Forager, called for two marine divisions, the 2d and 4th, the main elements of V Amphibious Corps, to land on 11 beaches opposite the town of Chalan Kanoa. Early in the morning of 15 June, covered by the 5th Fleet, the largest assemblage of warships of the Pacific war, the marines landed against stubborn resistance by the Japanese. Information that the Japanese fleet was on its way to the Marianas caused two regiments of the reserve division, the army's 27th, to be hastily landed. Both marine divisions took heavy casualties along the beach areas, but marine and army units within two days had driven across the island, capturing the airfield and then changing the axis and the offensive to a north-south orientation. Here they encountered the hilly areas where the Japanese had dug into caves and fought a fanatical series of small-unit actions.

Generally successful to that point, the campaign was marred by the relief of the 27th Division's commander on highly questionable grounds on 25 June. This action precipitated the most serious interservice quarrel of the war. The 2d Marines captured the main town, Garapan, and clambered up the slopes of Mount Tapotchau, while the army cleared the central pass area called Death Valley and the 4th advanced along the Kagman Peninsula in the east. Army and marine units on the left of the advance survived one of the largest banzai charges of the Pacific war on the night of 7 July. Two days later Marpi Point, the northernmost part of the island, was reached. By that time hundreds of Japanese civilians had committed suicide by leaping from the cliffs.

On 9 July the island was declared secure, but sweeps through the island in the following month killed over 1,900 Japanese soldiers. It had cost V Corps 3,119 killed and 10,992 wounded. However, the conquest of Saipan, combined with the stunning naval victory at the Philippine Sea, was a key to an earlier ending of the war. Within six months B-29s from two major bomber fields on Saipan were pounding Japanese cities to pieces.

SAMAR. A southern island in the Philippines, in 1901 it was the base for the most troublesome of the Muslim Moros who did not accept U.S. rule after the Spanish-American War (q.v.). After service during the Boxer Rebellion (q.v.), the 1st Regiment had been ordered to Cavite to assist the army in pacifying the Moros. On 16 September a company of the army's 9th Infantry was surprised and massacred on Samar. The marines, numbering 314 officers and men under the command of Maj. Littleton Waller, were ordered to the south. Waller took two companies to Basey on Samar. Ordered by the army commander to use terror tactics, burning villages and taking no prisoners, the marines for two months ranged throughout Samar forcing the hard-core resisters into the interior. On 15 November Waller led three columns against the Moros in a night attack and ostensibly wiped out the last organized resistance. The marines were then ordered to survey a telegraph route from Basey to the east coast.

On 28 December 1901, 55 marines with interpreters and more than 30 bearers began the journey. They followed trails leading to nowhere, the men became exhausted, and many were sick. Waller took the strongest, leaving most of the marines behind, and finally arrived on 17 January 1902 at Basey. With additional men he then went back for the ones left behind. They had not waited but retreated back to the east coast. In all, 10 marines were lost during this operation. Convinced that the natives had betrayed him, Waller convened a drumhead trial and then had 11 natives shot. Brought to trial himself at Cavite on a charge of murder, he eventually was acquitted, but the Samar action was a black mark on both army and marine units. (See also Philippine Insurrection.)

SAMOA. Fourteen islands comprise Samoa, located 2,000 miles south of Hawaii, of which only four are important. The others are administered by New Zealand. The key harbor in American Samoa is Pago Pago, located on the island of Tutuila. During World War II (q.v.), the Samoan Islands were a major supply base for the allies, particularly in the early stages. Elements of the 1st Division were staged to Samoa before the invasion of Guadalcanal (q.v.).

SAN PASCUAL. A battle fought on 6 December 1846 between American dragoons commanded by Brig. Gen. Stephen Kearny and Mexican lancers at the present-day site of Camp Pendleton (q.v.). Marine Lt. Archibald Gillespie, who had been named military commandant of southern California, had joined Kearny before the battle. The Mexicans left the field, but Kearny's force was later surrounded. A relief column that included the marine detachment from the frigate *Congress* broke through the Mexican lines. Later the combined force of approximately 600 men moved north and occupied Los Angeles.

SANTO DOMINGO. A large Caribbean island discovered first by Columbus, Santo Domingo was settled by the Spanish in the early 16th century. Their rule over the island continued until the western part was ceded to France and renamed Haiti (q.v.). During the 19th century after the slave rebellion in Haiti, the eastern part of the entire island was ruled at times by Spain and at times by Haiti. In 1844 that portion was declared a republic and afterward endured a succession of weak governments and revolutions. Unstable political and financial conditions beginning in 1902 threatened to bring European intervention to Santo Domingo, and the United States took charge of the state's finances.

Despite this arrangement, revolutions were endemic until a U.S.-brokered constitution allowed for a new provisional republic. Peace lasted for only 18 months, and Pres. Woodrow Wilson decided to intervene militarily. Two companies of marines totaling 350 men were sent from Haiti, and on 15 May 1916 accompanied by 225 sailors they moved into the capital city without incident. Two weeks later a landing was made on the northwest corner of the island at Montecristi, and the marines routed a large party of rebels. On 1 June another landing was made at Puerto Plata on the north coast in the face of considerable rebel resistance. However, the rebels were forced from the city. Reinforcements brought the marine strength up to regimental size, with over 1,700 men on the island, approximately 1,000 on the north coast near Montecristi. Colonel Joseph Pendleton (q.v.), commanding the marines, then began a march toward Santiago, 60 miles away. The marines encountered the rebel forces holding a blocking ridge line at Las Trencheras. After using their artillery and machine guns to soften up the defenders, the marines on 27 June cleared the ridge by a bayonet charge. A later rebel counterattack was beaten off. Another ridge line was taken at Guayacanes, with the marines' machine guns doing deadly work. Reinforced by another battalion, Pendleton's force entered Santiago on 6 July. A military government was then established under a U.S. admiral, and the marines thus began an eight-year stay. They garrisoned a number of towns and trained a police force, the *Guardia Nacional Dominicana*. In 1922 an agreement with Dominican political leaders was reached, the country's name changed to the Dominican Republic, and two years later all U.S. forces were withdrawn. (See also Banana Wars and Dominican Republic.)

SCHMIDT, HARRY. b. Holdrege, Nebr., 25 Sept. 1886, d. San Diego, Calif., 10 Feb. 1968. Schmidt attended Nebraska State Normal School at Kearney and the Washington Navy Preparatory School before being commissioned a second lieutenant in August 1909. He advanced through grades as he served in Guam (q.v.), China, the Philippine Islands, and at sea on cruiser duty during World War I (q.v.). Later he served in Nicaragua (q.v.) where he won the Distinguished Service Medal. In 1933 he became assistant paymaster of the corps, a position he held until 1941. By 1942 he was a major general when he took command of the 4th Marine Division. Schmidt led the division in the very successful three-day operation in February 1944 that secured Roi-Namur (q.v.) in the Marshall Islands (q.v.). Later the 4th Division landed on the beaches north of Chalan Kanoa on Saipan (q.v.) on 15 June. Cutting across the island against heavy opposition, the division assumed the right flank of the U.S. forces, cleared the Kagman Peninsula, and reached the north coast by 9 July. By that time Schmidt had relinquished command of the division and moved up to command V Amphibious Corps. Later this corps under his command planned and carried out the successful conquest of Tinian (q.v.) in July. Schmidt then led V Corps, composed of three divisions, in the bloody invasion of Iwo Jima (q.v.) in February 1945. He continued to command V Corps during the early occupation of Japan.

Returning to the United States, Schmidt was promoted to lieutenant general in March 1946 and took command of all marine forces in the San Diego area. He retired as a lieutenant general soon afterward. In July 1949 he was given his fourth star as a full general.

"SEAHORSE" (UH-34 and VH-34, formerly HUS-1). First produced by Sikorsky Aircraft Company in 1954, the utility version UH-34 was ordered in September. In addition to the pilots, it could accommodate 16 to 18 passengers on inward-facing troop seats, 12 on airline seats, or 8 stretchers. It had a service ceiling of 9,500 feet and a top speed of 97 miles per hour with a very short range of only 250 miles. The UH-34 saw extensive service in the Vietnam War (q.v.). The VH-34 had the same flight characteristics but was a transport version for senior officials.

"SEA KNIGHT" (CH-46). A large, twin-rotor helicopter built by Boeing-Vertol, the first experimental model was flown in April 1958. The corps received its assault transport version three years later. It carried a crew of three with 17 to 25 fully equipped troops or two tons of cargo over a radius of 115 miles at a top speed of 150 miles per hour. Four marine squadrons were operating CH-46As by mid-1965. Introduced into the Vietnam War (q.v.) in March 1966, the CH-46 was in continuous operations there throughout the conflict. By the end of 1970, the corps had taken delivery of 600 of the various models. Older versions of the Sea Knight were modernized (CH46-E) beginning in 1975 with more powerful engines, combat-resistant fuel systems, improved rescue systems, and fiberglass rotor blades.

"SEA STALLION" (navy designation). Marine Corps designation CH53A/D. Sikorsky Aircraft Company was selected in August 1962 to produce a heavy transport helicopter for the Marine Corps. It was first flown in 1964, and deliveries were made beginning in mid-1966. It was powered by two turbo-shaft engines. It carried a crew of three and either 37 combat equipped troops or 24 stretchers. The improved version (CH-53D), first delivered in early 1969, had a service ceiling of 21,000 feet and a maximum speed of 175 miles per hour. In 1968 a modified CH-53A established an unofficial payload record carrying 28,500 pounds. Later in 1968 another Sea Stallion performed a series of rolls and loops for the Joint Naval Air Systems Command. The later versions were equipped with an integral cargo system that enabled one man to load or unload a ton of pallet-sized cargo in one minute. Other version enabled the marines to use the helicopter for airborne minesweeping.

SEMINOLE WAR. The longest and most costly action fought by army and marine units against Indian tribes during the first half of the 19th century. The government of Pres. Andrew Jackson had decided in the spring of 1836 to transport the Seminoles from Florida and Georgia to Arkansas. The Seminoles and their parent nation, the Creeks, rebelled. Two battalions of marines arrived in Georgia in June and immediately went into action against the Creeks. By the end of the summer the Creeks had been defeated. The campaign in Florida against the Seminoles was begun immediately. The marine commandant, Col. Archibald Henderson (q.v.), was given one of the two brigades in action there. The brigade was made up of marine, army, and volunteer troops and won a major victory in January 1837 at Hatchee-Lustee. A peace treaty was signed in March, and Henderson, believing the war to be over, took most of the marines with him when he returned to Washington. Only a two-company battalion was left behind, and it was continually involved in action against those Seminoles who had refused to surrender after the capture of their chief, Osceola, in mid-1837. The guerrilla phase of the war dragged on without a positive decision, and the government, after transporting over 4,000 Seminoles to Oklahoma, simply allowed those remaining in Florida to stay in the Everglades.

SEMPER FIDELIS (Always Faithful). The Marine Corps' motto adopted in 1883 to replace the older one, *Per Mare, Per Terram*, which had been borrowed from the British Royal Marines. The motto is on a ribbon held in the beak of the eagle on the Marine Corps Emblem.

SEOUL. The largest city and capital of South Korea. It was one of the major objectives of Gen. Douglas MacArthur in his plan in September 1950 to break out of the Pusan (q.v.) perimeter and drive the North Koreans back across the 38th parallel. The seizure of Inchon (q.v.) by the 1st Division was the prelude to the capture of Seoul. By 21 September the 5th Marines had crossed the Han River, while the 1st began a three-day battle for the industrial suburb of Yongdungpo. Reinforced by the army's 31st Regiment, a Republic of Korea (ROK) regiment, and the 7th Marines, the final push into the city began. The commander of X Corps began the main drive to liberate the city. The North Korean forces, bolstered by reinforcements from the south, fought for every street. Not since Manila in World War II (q.v.) was there such heavy street fighting. The 1st Marines attacked directly up the main street of Seoul toward the palace. On the night of the 27th the North Koreans mounted their last tank-infantry counterattack, which failed. Although the city was declared liberated on the 25th, over 60 percent of Seoul was then still in enemy hands, and not until after the 28th was the capital free of North Korean troops. The day before, troops of the 8th Army moving up from Pusan made contact with the 7th Division, signaling the total defeat of the North Korean army south of the parallel. The casualties, which had been light at Inchon, had mounted during the week's fighting for Seoul. The UN forces, mostly marines, suffered 600 killed and 2,750 wounded while inflicting over 14,000 casualties on the enemy. (See also Korean War.)

SHAPLEY, ALAN. b. New York, 9 Feb. 1903, d. Washington, D.C., 13 May 1973. Shapley attended schools in Vallejo, California, and Hagerstown, New Jersey. After graduation, he entered the Naval Academy in 1922 from which he graduated in June 1927 as a second lieutenant in the Marine Corps. After duty at Quantico (q.v.) and at the basic school, he was ordered to Hawaii in January 1931 and served three years at the marine base on Oahu. His next assignment was for a two-year tour of sea duty. Returning to the United States in June 1936, he was assigned as aide-de-camp to the commanding general at Quantico. After attending the junior course at Quantico, he became the aide-de-camp to the commanding general of the Pacific Department until mid-1939. Later he became operations and training officer of the department before being assigned to command the marine detachment on the *Arizona*. During the Japanese attack, Shapley, who managed to escape from the stricken ship, saved one of his men from drowning. For this he was awarded the Silver Star.

Later in December Shapley was ordered to San Diego to become personnel officer for the Amphibious Corps. As a lieutenant colonel, he left with the 1st Amphibious Corps for the Pacific, where he took command of the 2d Raider Battalion. He later commanded the 2d Raider Regiment and led it in the landings at Empress Augusta Bay on Bougainville (q.v.) in November 1943. The Raiders on the right of the attacking force met the brunt of the Japanese counterattacks. After Bougainville, he was given command of the 1st and 2d Raider Regiments, which after disbanding became the 4th Marines. Shapley led this regiment on the D-day assault (21 July 1944) on the designated White Beaches on Guam (q.v.) as a part of the 1st Provisional Brigade. The 4th was responsible for the left flank advance on the trapped Japanese on the Orote Peninsula, and later the regiment was the first to reach Ritidian Point, the northernmost part of the island. Colonel Shapley received the Navy Cross (q.v.) for his actions. On 1 April 1945 he led the 4th Marines, now a part of the newly formed 6th Division, in the invasion of Okinawa (q.v.). The 4th Marines operated at first in the north helping to secure the Ishikawa Isthmus. Shifted south, they assaulted the Mobutu Peninsula and continued active operations until 19 June. For his leadership he earned his second Legion of Merit.

Ordered to the United States, Shapley served in the Inspection Division at Marine Headquarters, attended the National War College, and beginning in 1947 served for two years as assistant chief of staff, operations, for Fleet Marine Corps (q.v.), Atlantic. Later he was on the International Planning Staff of the Standing Group in NATO until 1953. His next service was in the Korea War (q.v.), where he was chief of staff of the 1st Division and later senior adviser for the Korean Marine Corps. He was promoted to brigadier general while serving in Japan. On his return to the United States, he was appointed assistant commander of the 1st Division in July 1955. The following year he was promoted to major general and took over command of the 3d Division on Okinawa (q.v.). In 1957 he relinquished command of the division to become director of the Marine Corps Reserve, following which he became commander of Camp Pendleton (q.v.). His last command was as commanding general of Fleet Marine Force, Pacific. Shapley retired in July 1962 and was advanced to the rank of lieutenant general.

SHEPHERD, LEMUEL C. JR. 20th commandant, b. Norfolk, Va., 10 Feb. 1896, d. La Jolla, Calif., 6 Aug. 1990. Shepherd graduated from Virginia Military Institute and was commissioned a second lieutenant in April 1917. Two months later he was on his way to France as a member of the 5th Marines. He served at Chateau-Thierry (q.v.) and was twice wounded at Belleau Wood (q.v.). Returning to action, he participated in the Saint-Mihiel (q.v.) and Argonne offensives, being wounded once again. For this service he received the Navy Cross (q.v.), the Army Distinguished Service Cross, and the *Croix de Guerre*. After serving in the occupation, he returned to France in 1920 to aid in mapping areas over which the marines fought. In the 1920s he was aide-de-camp to the commandant and later had sea duty and was in command of the Sea School at Norfolk. In 1927 he left for China where he served at Tientsin (q.v.) for two years. He was then posted to Haiti (q.v.) until 1934. In 1936 as a lieutenant colonel, he attended the Naval War College and the following year commanded a battalion in the Fleet Marine Force (q.v.), Atlantic, and later served as assistant commandant at Quantico (q.v.). In March 1942 he took command of the 9th Marines and took them to the Pacific as part of the 3d Division. Promoted to brigadier general, Shepherd participated as assistant divisional commander of the 1st Division in the Cape Gloucester (q.v.) campaign.

In May Shepherd became commander of the 1st Marine Provisional Brigade. The brigade, put together at Guadalcanal (q.v.) and made up of two regiments, the 22d and 4th Marines, landed at Agat beaches on Guam (q.v.) on 21 July 1944 and cleared the Orote Peninsula and later southern Guam before taking part in the final actions in the north. Shepherd then became commander of the 6th Division when the 29th Marines were added to the brigade. The 6th Division landed on the northern part of Blue Beaches on Okinawa (q.v.) on 1 April 1945 and operated at first in the north, took Motubu Peninsula, and moved later to confront the western sector of the Shuri line. The 6th Marine Division took Oroku Peninsula. At the conclusion of the war, the 6th Division occupied Tsingtao in China.

Shepherd returned from China in December 1946 to become assistant commandant of the corps. He, along with Gen. Clifton Cates (q.v.), was a major contender to succeed Gen. Alexander Vandegrift (q.v.) as commandant. President Harry Truman chose Cates because of seniority but promised the position to Shepherd after four years. As a lieutenant general and commander of Fleet Marine Force, Pacific, he met with General MacArthur on 10 July 1950 and promised that the 1st Marine Brigade would be in Korea by September. He accompanied Generals MacArthur, Ned Almond, and Oliver P. Smith (q.v.) to Inchon (q.v.) to observe the landings. He became commandant, as promised, on 1 January 1952. He reorganized Marine Corps headquarters along general staff lines (G-1, G-2, G-3, G-4). Congress ended the long debate on the fate of the corps by law, providing for three active divisions and three air wings. As commandant, Shepherd became coequal with the Joint Chiefs when matters related to the corps were under discussion. He retired on 1 January 1956 but was recalled to active duty to serve as chairman of the Inter-American Defense Board.

"SHERMAN" TANK (M4). The standard medium battle tank for the United States and many allied nations during World War II (q.v.), and it remained so through the early months of the Korean War (q.v.). It was redesigned to take the place of the M3 Grant tank and shared some of the features of that earlier medium tank. The Sherman, however, had an all-welded body and a heavily cast-steel turret that gave the main gun a 360-degree potential. Ultimately 48,000 Shermans were produced in 11 different factories during the war. The M4 went through a series of modifications from the earliest M4 through the

M4A6. Most of the differences were in upgrading the engines and drive trains. The main armament for most of the tanks remained a 75mm gun with secondary armament of three .30-caliber machine guns. One version used by the British had a high-velocity 76mm gun that made it more competitive with German armor. The M4 weighed 33 tons, and most had multi-banked 425 horsepower power plants. It had main armor of 81mm and could reach a maximum speed of 25 miles per hour. While no match for the best German tanks in individual battle, its speed and numbers enabled the M4 in Europe to become a major factor in ultimate victory.

In the Pacific there were few examples of tank-to-tank conflict. When these did take place, the Sherman proved superior to any Japanese tank. Its major function in the various island campaigns was as mobile artillery to support infantry operations and destroy fixed Japanese positions. The corps never had a great number of tanks for any operation. By May 1944 the Table of Organization and Equipment assigned a division three tank companies and a headquarters and repair company. In all, each division thus had 46 tanks and 270 men directly assigned to operate the medium tanks.

SHOUP, DAVID M. 22d commandant, b. Battle Ground, Ind., 30 Dec. 1904, d. Arlington, Va., 13 Jan. 1983. Shoup attended De-Pauw University, graduating in 1926, and was a member of ROTC. He served briefly as a second lieutenant in the army before being commissioned in July 1926 in the Marine Corps. His basic school was interrupted by a tour with the 6th Marines at Tientsin (q.v.) in 1927. Completing the school the following year, he then served at San Diego, Pensacola (q.v.), and Quantico (q.v.).

Shoup had sea duty on board the *Maryland* for two years after 1929. During the 1930s, he had a variety of duties including temporary duty with the Civilian Conservation Corps and duty in China at Shanghai and Peking (q.v.). As a captain in 1937, he completed the junior course at Quantico and then served for two years as an instructor there. In June 1940 he joined the 6th Marines and in May 1941 accompanied the unit to Iceland (q.v.), ultimately becoming operations officer for the brigade. Returning from Iceland, he became operations officer for the 2d Division and accompanied it to New Zealand in October 1942. He served as an observer with the 1st Division on Guadalcanal (q.v.) and the army's 43d Division during the New Georgia (q.v.) campaign where he was wounded.

Promoted to colonel, Shoup assumed command of the 2d Marines just before the Tarawa (q.v.) operation in November 1943. In that action, despite being wounded, he displayed extraordinary courage and control during the early desperate hours. For this he was awarded the Medal of Honor (q.v.). In December he became chief of staff of the 2d Division and as such participated in the Saipan (q.v.) and Tinian (q.v.) invasions.

Returning to the United States in October 1944, he served in Washington at marine headquarters until 1947, when he became commanding officer of Service Command, Fleet Marine Force (q.v.), Pacific. In 1949 he became chief of staff of the 1st Division and later in 1950 was commander of the basic school at Quantico. As a brigadier general he later became fiscal director of the corps. In 1956 he investigated deaths of six marines at Parris Island (q.v.). His recommendations changed the nature of boot training. Subsequently, as a major general he served as commander of the 1st Division in June 1957 and later the 3d Division on Okinawa (q.v.) in March 1958. After a brief tour in command of Parris Island, he was promoted to lieutenant general and served as chief of staff at marine headquarters in Washington.

Shoup was appointed commandant by Pres. Dwight Eisenhower on 1 January 1961 ahead of five other more senior lieutenant generals. He disagreed with the forward policy during the Vietnam War (q.v.). Shoup brought the garrison at Guantanamo (q.v.) up to regimental strength and deployed the 5th Marine Expeditionary Brigade (MEB) (q.v.) to the Caribbean in October 1962 to support Pres. John Kennedy's ultimatum on Soviet missiles in Cuba. The Marine Corps adopted the 7.62mm M-14 rifle in place of the M-1 Garand (q.v.) and the M-60 machine gun (q.v.) to replace the Browning (q.v.) during Shoup's tenure. He retired on 31 December 1964 just before the United States became deeply involved in Vietnam.

SILVERTHORN, MERWIN H. b. Minneapolis, Minn., 22 Sept. 1896, d. Washington, D.C., 14 Aug. 1985. Silverthorn attended the University of Minnesota before enlisting in the corps in April 1917. In August of that year he sailed for France as a member of the 5th Marines. He saw action at Chateau-Thierry (q.v.), Soissons (q.v.), Pont-a-Mousson, and the Meuse-Argonne (q.v.). He received a commission in June 1918. He remained in Europe after the Armistice as a member of the Army of Occupation. Returning to the United States in September

1919, he was assigned to duty in Washington and later Mare Island and Quantico (q.v.). In the spring of 1924 he was ordered to Haiti (q.v.) as a member of the 1st Brigade. He was transferred to the *Gendarmerie* and served as a district commander of *Aux Coyes* and later as chief of police at Port au Prince. After this tour he was assigned to Quantico, where he served for four years before being transferred to Guam (q.v.) in April 1930.

Over the next eight years Silverthorn held a number of positions, including completing a course in the Army Quartermaster School, instructing at Quantico, finishing the course at the Naval War College, and serving sea duty aboard a number of different ships. In late 1941 as a lieutenant colonel he was attached to the War Plans section at the Navy Department. Later he was assigned to Headquarters, Commander of U.S. Fleet. In June 1943 he became chief of the Amphibious Warfare section of the Army-Navy Staff College. In January 1944 as a colonel he was appointed chief of staff of the 1st Amphibious Corps and later when the designation was changed to III Amphibious Corps. In this capacity he participated in the planning for and operations of the Guam invasion and those of Peleliu (q.v.) and Okinawa (q.v.). In June 1945 he became chief of staff of Fleet Marine Force (q.v.), Pacific, as a brigadier general, a post he held until September 1946. Then he took command of the Troop Training Command, Amphibious Forces, Atlantic. His next position was a liaison officer to the office of the Chief of Naval Operations, a post he held until named as director of the Marine Corps Reserve.

Holding the rank of major general, Silverthorn was given the temporary rank of lieutenant general in July 1950 when appointed assistant commandant. In February 1951 he reverted to the lower rank when he took charge of Parris Island (q.v.). Upon his retirement in June 1954, he was once again appointed lieutenant general.

"SKYHAWK" (A-4, A-4M, and A-4Y). A lightweight, low cost, single-seat attack and ground support plane. The first flight of the experimental version took place in June 1954. Adopted by the navy and marines, 1,845 planes of the A-4A through E were built by 1973. Many subsequent versions were supplied to Australia, New Zealand, and Israel. A major modification was the A-4M, which had more powerful engines, a braking parachute enabling the plane to operate from short runways of 4,000 feet, and much better electronic equipment. The Marine Corps version (A-4Y) had a redesigned cockpit and a Hughes Angle Rate Bombing System. The later versions of the Skyhawk were continued in production through 1977. The A-4Y had a top speed of 650 miles per hour. There were many variations of the armament that the Skyhawk could carry on inboard and outboard wing racks. Weapons included bombs, air-to-surface and air-to-air missiles, ground attack pods, and torpedoes. In addition, two 20mm cannon were placed in the wing roots.

"SKYRAIDER" (AD-1 through 7). This single-seat monoplane was built by Douglas Aircraft Company. The prototype was flown in March 1945. During the next 15 years, 40 versions of the seven basic models of this versatile attack bomber were created. Originally it was conceived to carry a 1,000 pound bomb. By the Korean War (q.v.), it was carrying loads of over five tons, more than the four-engined B-17 of World War II. Depending on the version, the Skyraider could carry up to 14 rockets or bombs under the wings. It had a service ceiling of more than 25,000 feet and a top speed of 365 miles per hour. At the beginning of the Korean War (q.v.), the corps had only two attack squadrons. Two years later there were 11 squadrons of ADs. The plane's versatility, particularly its heavy armament and relatively slow speed, prolonged its useful life well into the Vietnam War (q.v.).

"SKYRAY" (F4D). A single seat jet aircraft built by Douglas Aircraft Company designed mainly for carrier operations but also used by the Marine Corps. It could be used as a general purpose fighter or fighter-bomber. The experimental model XJ4D with an afterburner set the world's speed record of 752.9 miles per hour in October 1953 and then set records in time to heights. The first production Skyray was flown on 5 June 1954. It had four 20mm wing guns and six external armament stations under the wing that could carry a wide range of missiles, rockets, or bombs. The last Skyray was delivered to the navy in December 1958.

"SKYTRAIN" (DAKOTA) (army designation C-47, Marine Corps R4D). The basic transport aircraft for all the services as well as all allies in World War II (q.v.). Built by Douglas Aircraft Company, it was the military version of the DC-3 that was first flown in December 1935 and before the war was standard equipment for most U.S. airlines. The most important military versions were the R4D-1 and R4D-5. These had large cargo-loading doors, reinforced metal floors, tie-down fittings, and fold-up wooden seats. The major difference in the two versions was the electrical system. Both were powered by two Pratt and Whitney R-1830 engines developing 1,050 horsepower. They had a cruising speed of 230 miles per hour, a service ceiling of 10,000 feet, and a range of 1,500 miles. All DC-3s that were taken over by the military were converted for various functions and modified accordingly. All these had been returned to civil control by 1944. A further version of the Skytrain was designated the "Skytrooper" (R4D-3) with similar characteristics to the basic model except it had no loading door, fixed metal seats for 28 airborne or paratroops, and had a towing cleat for glider towing. It was used by the marines in all Pacific operations mainly for airborne supply and transport.

SMITH, HOLLAND M. "HOWLIN' MAD." b. Seale, Ala., 20 April 1882, d. San Diego, Calif., 12 Jan. 1967. Smith graduated from Alabama Polytechnic in 1901 and two years later received a law degree from the University of Alabama. He practiced law until his entry into the Marine Corps as a second lieutenant in March 1905. His early service included two tours in the Philippines and one in Panama (q.v.) and stateside service at Annapolis, San Diego, and Seattle. In April 1914 he commanded the marine detachment on the *Galveston* while it was in Asiatic waters. In June 1916 as a member of the 4th Marines, Smith was ordered to Santo Domingo (q.v.) to help restore the deposed president to power and as such took part in the few engagements on the march to Santiago. He then became military commander of the Puerto Plata District before returning to the United States in May 1917, and within two weeks he was on his way to France as the commander of a machine gun company in the 5th Regiment. He was soon detached from line duty to attend the army's War College in France. On return to regular duty in February 1918, Major Smith joined the 4th Brigade and took part in the Aisne-Marne defenses. In July he became liaison officer for the 1st Corps and took part in the Saint-Mihiel (q.v.) and Meuse-Argonne (q.v.) campaigns and later served as assistant operations officer for the 3d Army. After returning to the United States, he served in Norfolk, attended the Naval War College, and served in Washington as a member of the joint Army-Navy Planning Committee. Later in 1923 he had sea duty followed by further duty in Haiti (q.v.) as the brigade's chief of staff and in 1925 he became chief of staff of the 1st

Brigade at Quantico. In 1927 he was quartermaster at the marine base in Philadelphia.

During the 1930s, Colonel Smith held a variety of posts, including senior marine officer and aide to the commander of the U.S. Fleet's Battle Force, chief of staff, Department of the Pacific, after which in 1937 he began a two-year tour as director of operations and training. In this capacity, as with seaborne exercises, he was instrumental in formulating concepts for amphibious warfare and in interesting the navy in the designs of a New Orleans shipbuilder, Andrew Higgins, the forerunners of a series of World War II landing craft. It was during this period that Smith earned the title "Howlin' Mad" because of his defense of the corps against naval superiors and his convictions of the need for better amphibious equipment.

Briefly, in 1939, Smith was assistant commandant before taking command of the 1st Brigade in September, and he led it in extended amphibious operations. In February when the brigade was redesignated the 1st Division, Smith became its first commander. In June 1941 he was detached from the division to help organize what eventually became Amphibious Force, Atlantic. In August 1942 as a major general, he took command of the Amphibious Corps, Pacific, headquartered in San Diego, which was responsible for the training of the bullk of marine and army amphibious units early in World War II. In September 1943 General Smith was appointed to command the 5th Amphibious Corps in the Central Pacific. He was an observer during the Aleutian landings and also an observer during the Gilberts operations after his headquarters planned the assaults on Tarawa (q.v.) and Makin (q.v.). He commanded the assaults on Saipan (q.v.) in June 1944 and a month later the invasion of Guam (q.v.).

The key victory at Saipan was clouded by controversy as Smith relieved a subordinate, the army general, Ralph Smith. This action caused the army leadership to pledge that H. M. Smith would never command army troops in the future, and thus he was never considered for the command of 10th Army during the Okinawa (q.v.) operation. Instead, as a lieutenant general, he was given command of Fleet Marine Force (q.v.), Pacific, and as such was technically in command of the Iwo Jima (q.v.) operation although another marine general, Harry Schmidt (q.v.), conducted the operations.

In July 1945 he returned to the United States to head the Training and Replacement Center at Camp Pendleton (q.v.). On 15 May 1946 he retired and was given a promotion to general.

SMITH, JULIAN C. b. Elkton, Md., 11 Sept. 1885, d. Washington, D.C., 5 Nov. 1975. Smith graduated from the University of Delaware and was commissioned a second lieutenant in the corps in January 1909 and underwent basic training at Port Royal, South Carolina. After service at the Philadelphia Navy Yard until January 1914, he was ordered to Panama (q.v.) as a part of the expeditionary force and then to Veracruz (q.v.). Afterward he once again served briefly at Philadelphia before being ordered to Haiti (q.v.) in August 1915. Later he was transferred to Santo Domingo (q.v.). After attending the Naval War College in 1917, he spent World War I at Quantico (q.v.) as an instructor and later was posted to Cuba (q.v.). During the 1920s he served at sea and at Marine Headquarters in Washington, attended the Army General Staff school, and captained the corps' Rifle and Pistol Team. In 1930 he was ordered to Nicaragua (q.v.) and spent three years there and then was promoted to colonel and became director of personnel. In June 1938 he assumed command of the 5th Marines. Later promoted to brigadier general, he served in the American Embassy in London as a naval observer during the early stages of World War II (q.v.).

After this duty and a further promotion, Smith briefly commanded the training schools at New River and then took command of the 2d Division in the spring of 1943. He was a key figure in planning for the invasion of the Gilbert Islands (q.v.) and led the division in the bloody assault on Tarawa (q.v.) in September. The following year as commanding general of III Amphibious Corps, he was in overall charge of marine and army troops at the invasion of Peleliu (q.v.) and Angaur and the occupation of Ulithi. In December 1944 he took command of the Department of the Pacific with headquarters in San Francisco. His last command was that of Parris Island (q.v.). He retired on 1 December 1946 and was advanced to the rank of lieutenant general.

SMITH, OLIVER P. b. Menard, Tex., 26 Oct. 1893, d. 25 Dec. 1977. Smith graduated from the University of California at Berkeley in 1916 and entered the corps as a second lieutenant in May 1917 and was posted to Guam (q.v.) for two years. During the 1920s he served at sea, in Washington, D.C., and as a part of the *Gendarmerie* in Haiti (q.v.). In 1931 he completed the army field officers course at Fort Benning and later was an instructor and assistant operations officer of the 7th Marines at Quantico (q.v.). In 1934 he was assigned duty at the American Embassy in Paris and later attended the prestigious *École de Guerre*. Returning to the United States in 1936, he served as an instructor at Quantico until July 1939 when he was transferred to the Fleet Marine Force (q.v.) in San Diego, and in June of the following year he became a battalion commander in the 6th Marines and sailed with the regiment when it was ordered to Iceland (q.v.) in May 1941. In May 1942 he assumed a position in the division of Plans and Policies in Washington until ordered to take command of the 5th Marines in the Cape Gloucester (q.v.) operation. In April he was appointed assistant divisional commander of the 1st Division and participated in the bloody operation on Peleliu (q.v.) in September and October 1944. Later appointed marine deputy chief of staff of the 10th Army, he was deeply involved in the three-month Okinawa (q.v.) campaign. Briefly after his return to the United States, Smith served as commandant at Quantico before becoming assistant commandant in April 1948.

In June 1950 Smith became commander of the 1st Division and led the marines in the successful assault on Inchon (q.v.) and the capture of Seoul (q.v.) which helped destroy the North Korean forces south of the 38th parallel. Shifted to Wonson as a part of X Corps, the marines and 7th Division troops drove north to the Yalu River. In freezing weather the marines at the Chosin Reservoir (q.v.) in November 1950 were struck by an overwhelming force of Chinese. Smith led the heroic 13-day retreat against the Chinese who threatened to envelop his forces. After a 70-mile retreat to Hungnam harbor, the 1st Division was rescued and moved south by sea.

In May 1951 Smith returned to the United States and took over command of Camp Pendleton (q.v.). He assumed command of Fleet Marine Force, Atlantic, In July 1953, a post he held until his retirement as a four-star general in September 1955.

SOISSONS. A city in northern France located on the Aisne River that in 1918 was the western part of the Marne salient created by the last German offensive. The Germans began the offensive in this area on 15 July and were briefly successful, driving a wedge 25 miles deep and reaching the Marne River at Chateau-Thierry (q.v.). By 18 July it had been contained, and the Allied High Command then launched a well-planned major counteroffensive with four armies. The 4th Marine Brigade, a part of the U.S. 2d Division, was attached to XX Corps of General Mangin's 10th Army, which held the defense line southwest of Soissons. This army was to deliver the first counterblow to the

Germans. The 5th Marines were scheduled to be a part of the initial assault; the 6th was to follow in reserve. After having assembled in the forest of Retz, the 5th Marines along with other units of the 10th Army attacked without artillery preparation at 0430 on 18 July. By noon they had seized their objectives two miles within the salient. The next day the 6th Marines passed through the 5th's lines and continued forward a further one and a half miles before being halted by a counterattack by a German corps. By that evening a fresh army division replaced the brigade in the line. The marines then rested at a camp near Nancy before moving to buttress the attack on the Saint-Mihiel (q.v.) salient.

SOLOMON ISLANDS. A chain of islands lying northeast of Australia occupied by the Japanese during the first months of World War II (q.v.). Fears of Japanese interdiction of U.S. supply lines to the South Pacific led to the first allied offensive of the Pacific war with the 1st Division invading Guadalcanal (q.v.), one of the major islands in the southern Solomon Islands, in August 1942. The land and naval battles there forced the Japanese to evacuate Guadalcanal. Afterward the Japanese were forced on the defensive. Later in mid-1943 army and marine units captured New Georgia (q.v.) in the central Solomons. Finally, in November 1943 the 3d Division landed at Empress Augusta Bay on the island of Bougainville (q.v.). By the beginning of 1944 bomber fields on Bougainville had been constructed and were a key factor in the negation of the great Japanese naval and air base at Rabaul, New Britain (q.v.).

SOMALIA. A large state in northeast Africa bordering in the east on both the Red Sea and Indian Ocean. Extremely poor, the society was also deeply divided into a number of warring clans. Political unrest evolved into full-scale civil war in 1992. Combined with a devastating drought, it threatened starvation for more than a million persons. In response to the needs of the refugees who were dying by the thousands in makeshift camps, the United Nations launched a major effort to supply food and medicine to Somalia. Various factions continued to fight for control of the impoverished state and it was obvious that any significant relief effort depended on providing the UN workers with security. The UN sent in peacekeepers, but at first they were too few to provide the kind of protection necessary. In December 1992 the United States decided to provide just enough troops to secure these limited goals. This operation was a joint operation with the U.S. Navy and Air Force, but the majority of the ground troops during the first phase were marines of the 1st Expeditionary Force. Ultimately, almost 9,000 marines were deployed to Somalia, with the largest number in the capital, Mogadishu, although elements were sent to Baidoa in the west and Kismayu in the south.

The major problem with the operation was apparent from the beginning. Although the United States provided the bulk of the forces, it was a UN operation, and despite the presence of armed hostile groups within Mogadishu and Kismayu, the marines at first were not permitted to attempt to disarm them. Rules of engagement were that the troops were to shoot only when fired upon. Later when the U.S. command did begin an attempt to disarm the clans and arrest their leaders, the Somali population turned on the troops, who were absolutely necessary to keep the food supplies going to the camps. Eventually Pres. William Clinton in May 1993 decided that to keep the ground troops in Somalia would involve them even deeper in the civil war, and most were withdrawn, with only a minimal number kept there. The last U.S. troops were not withdrawn until March 1995.

On one level this operation was a success; thousands of lives in the camps were saved by the relief supplies. Therefore, the military operation that made this possible was also a success. However, Somalia was an embarrassment to the United States since the marines and other forces were committed with no clear objective and little knowledge of the clan system and the Somali warlords. Problems of joint command also hampered the military operations. Nevertheless, as in all previous wars, police actions, and peacekeeping ventures for 200 years, the marines acquitted themselves honorably and lived up to their watchwords, *Semper Fidelis*.

SOUSA, JOHN PHILIP. b. Washington, D.C., 6 Nov. 1854, d. Reading, Pa., 6 March 1932. Sousa's father, Antonio Sousa, was a carpenter who worked on the commandant's quarters in Washington and also played in the Marine Band. Believing that his son, then age 13, needed discipline, he convinced the commandant to enroll him as an apprentice enlisted to learn music. That enlistment lasted for over seven years, during which Sousa was educated and trained in the military and also perfected his knowledge of the violin. He reenlisted and until 1875 played in the band, as did his father. Receiving a discharge, he became a civilian bandmaster and held various positions until

1880 when he was appointed the 14th leader of the Marine Band.

Sousa's musicianship and executive ability were soon apparent as the band gave more concerts at the Marine Barracks and the Plaza as well as participating in parades and celebrations. Reacting to requests for the band to perform throughout the country, he gained permission from Pres. Benjamin Harrison in 1891 to take the band on tour. From that time onward the band has made an annual tour.

Sousa left the corps in 1892 to organize his own band. In the years that followed, he composed a series of marches whose popularity earned him the title of "The March King." The most played of these marches was *Semper Fidelis*, which later was adopted by the Marine Corps as its official march, the *Washington Post, Liberty Bell*, and the stirring *Stars and Stripes Forever*.

At the onset of the Spanish-American War (q.v.), Sousa attempted to rejoin the corps, but there was no vacancy as a bandmaster and he joined the army. Illness prevented him from serving. Sousa continued his very busy schedule, leading his band in concerts at home and abroad. During World War I (q.v.), he joined the navy, and as a lieutenant commander and musical director at the Great Lakes Training Center, he led that band in a long series of Liberty Bond concerts. Discharged in 1919, he returned to his active career.

Sousa's last appearance with the Marine Band was early in 1932 at a celebration in Washington, D.C., where he led it in a rendition of his *Stars and Stripes Forever*. He died at Reading, Pennsylvania, where he was scheduled to lead a band the following day. He was returned to Washington where he lay in state at the Marine Barracks before interment in the Congressional Cemetery.

SPANISH-AMERICAN WAR. Growing nationalism in the United States combined with newspaper accounts of the presumed cruelties of the Spanish in putting down a three-year revolt in Cuba (q.v.) brought on the Spanish-American War in April 1898. Ill prepared for a land war, the United States hastily expanded the army and prepared to invade Cuba. By the close of the month the 2d Marine Battalion was on its way to Florida ultimately to reinforce the detachments on board Adm. William Sampson's fleet blockading Santiago. The need for a secure coaling station for the fleet convinced the admiral to use the marines to seize Guantanamo (q.v.). On 10 June the battalion landed against slight opposition, but as the perimeter was widened, the marines were under constant sniper fire. Two companies on 14 June were ordered to take Cuzco Well, the major source of water for that area of southeastern Cuba. Despite taking fire from U.S. naval vessels that should have been giving support, the marines drove the 500 Spanish defenders from the well. Later troops of Gen. William Shafter's V Corps relieved the marines at Guantanamo, and they saw no further action in the Cuban war, which climaxed with the surrender of Santiago on 10 July.

In the Pacific on 1 May Commodore Dewey had destroyed the small antique Spanish fleet at Manila Bay. He then ordered a marine detachment ashore to seize the naval station at Cavite. Too few marines and sailors were available for further land action, and Dewey simply blockaded the harbor and waited for the arrival of Gen. Wesley Merritt's army units, which in August made quick work against the demoralized defenders of Manila. Little fighting had taken place during the land operations, and it was assumed that the peace treaty with Spain, which ceded the Philippines to the United States, would bring peace to the islands. This was far from the case, since Filipino patriots had assumed from the prewar political rhetoric that the war had been to create an independent state. Soon there was an uprising more dangerous than any action demanded of the corps during the war. (See also Cuba and Philippine Insurrection.)

SPRINGFIELD (M1903) RIFLE. Adopted by the armed forces as a replacement for the .30-caliber Krag-Jorgensen (q.v.) rifle, which had shown a number of serious problems during the Spanish-American War (q.v.), the 03 was a modification of the German Mauser 1896 rifle. The original .30-caliber cartridge was replaced in 1906 by the 30.06 round, which was to be standard for a half-century. With the coming of World War I (q.v.), the production of the M1903 was increased, but there never were enough of this model to supply the rapidly expanding forces. This meant that the M1917 Enfield was manufactured in great quantities. After the war the dependable 03 once again became the standard weapon for the Marine Corps as well as the army. It was highly prized for its ruggedness, relatively light weight, and accuracy.

Although the M-1 Garand (q.v.) was the standard weapon for the armed forces, when World War II (q.v.) began production of the rifle was accelerated, manufactured by the Remington Arms Company. A few modifications were incorporated in

1942, particularly with redesigning those items that took a large amount of machining. These guns were designated M1903A3. A few sniper rifles were also manufactured, and these became M1903A4. The early campaigns in the Pacific were fought by marines using the 03, and not until 1943 were enough M-1 Garands available to displace most of the older rifles, which, nevertheless, remained in use in front-line combat throughout the war. This was particuarly true of those that had been fitted with grenade launchers.

STALLINGS, LAURENCE. b. Macon, Ga., 25 Nov. 1894, d. Santa Barbara, Calif., Feb. 1968. Stallings was educated at local schools and received a B.A. degree from Wake Forest in 1915 and an M.S. from Georgetown University in 1922. Before World War I (q.v.), he was a writer for the *Atlanta Journal*. Stallings joined the Marine Corps soon after war was declared, and he was commissioned. He was assigned to the 5th Regiment and arrived in France in May 1918. As a captain in the 3d Battalion, he was deeply involved in the fighting at Belleau Wood (q.v.). He was seriously wounded by an enemy machine gun and spent many months convalescing, eventually losing his leg. During this period, he wrote a fine novella and returned to journalism at the *New York World*.

As an editor, Stalling became a force in the American literary scene. Among those he aided was a fellow marine officer, John Thomason (q.v.), who wrote *Fix Bayonets*. In 1924 Stalling collaborated with Maxwell Anderson to write and produce *What Price Glory* for Broadway. The play was a hit, introducing "Old Breed" marines, Sergeant Quirt and Captain Flagg. Later he helped adapt the play for the motion pictures. An even greater success at the time was his play *The Big Parade*, which was based in part on his experiences in the war. This, too, was made into a film. In 1933 Stalling published another work, *The First World War*, a collection of magnificent photographs with descriptive captions. In later years he was deeply involved in the film industry. During World War II (q.v.), he was an officer in the Army Air Force. His legacy to the corps was undoubtedly *What Price Glory*.

STREETER, RUTH C. b. Brookline, Mass., 2 Oct. 1895. Streeter attended schools abroad and later Bryn Mawr, graduating in 1918. During the 1930s she worked in the public health field and old age assistance in New Jersey. Attending New York University, she completed a course in aeronautics and learned to fly in 1940, becoming adjutant of a Civil Air Patrol group. In 1942 she received her commercial pilot's license. She served as a member of the New Jersey Defense Council and the Citizen's Committee for the Army and Navy.

With some reluctance, Gen. Thomas Holcomb (q.v.) approved the creation of a Women's Reserve Force, and this group was approved in November by Pres. Franklin Roosevelt. Streeter was selected to head the program and was the first woman to hold the rank of major. She was promoted to lieutenant colonel in November 1943 and to full colonel in February 1944. By the close of World War II, Colonel Streeter commanded 18,460 women marines serving in over 200 job classifications as far west as Hawaii. She left the corps in December 1945.

"STUART" TANK (M3/M5). A light tank designed in the spring of 1940 incorporating lessons learned from the European war, particularly in increased armor. It had 51mm in the nose area, 38mm elsewhere. It went into production in March 1941. The earliest models had riveted plate bodies but this design was soon changed to all-welded construction. Problems in supply of the Continental gas engines led to modification to take diesel engines, and by 1942, 500 of this type had been built. The M5 version was first introduced in late 1942 with two Cadillac engines and a hydramatic transmission. The Stuart weighed 12 tons, had a crew of four, and could travel at a maximum speed of 37 miles per hour. The 37mm main gun and two .30-caliber machine guns were barely adequate for operations in Africa and Europe against older German tanks. However, the few light tanks, which became a part of the corps' operations in the Pacific, performed well early in the war primarily to support infantry actions against fixed Japanese defenses.

SUBMACHINE GUN (M3 and M3A1). Aptly named the "grease gun" for its appearance, it was constructed mainly of stamped parts; thus, it was cheap and easily manufactured. It fired the standard .45-caliber ammunition from a 30-round magazine at 400 rounds per minute. It had a folding stock and was relatively light-weight. Tests showed that it was equal or superior to all other .45-caliber guns and performed well under adverse combat conditions. The M3 was adopted by the U.S. Army in December 1942 and by the Marine Corps soon afterward to replace the Thompson submachine gun (q.v.). The M3A1 became available in early 1945. More than 600,000 guns were produced before World War II (q.v.) ended. Both models were available and used during the Korean (q.v.) and Vietnam Wars.

SURIBACHI. The most prominent feature on the small, lamb chop-shaped volcanic island of Iwo Jima (q.v.) which was assaulted by the 4th and 5th Marine Divisions on 19 February 1945. This mountain was strategically important because Japanese observers from there could see every part of the island. On the 21st after heavy fighting, the Japanese had been cleared from their defenses at Surabachi's base. Two days later the 28th Marines of Gen. Keller Rockey's (q.v.) 5th Division made the final attack on the mountain, reaching the top early in the morning. At first a small flag was raised, but then a second and larger flag was found and affixed to a longer piece of pipe. This second flag raising was immortalized by a news photographer in what was undoubtedly the most famous photograph of the Pacific war. The flag raising has in the years since become a symbol for marine valor during World War II (q.v.).

T

TANK M60A3. The most widely used Main Battle Tank (MBT) during the two decades after 1960. Its antecedents dated to the M26 Pershing (q.v.) heavy tank, which was widely used during the Korean War (q.v.). The M60, weighing 45 tons, was powered by a 12-cylinder diesel engine and had a crew of four. Its maximum speed was 30 miles per hour with a road range of 400 miles. It had very advanced fire control systems that incorporated stabilization, passive night vision equipment, a laser range finder, and a ballistic computer. Some earlier versions (A2) that the army ordered for use in Europe mounted the Shilleigh weapons system, which allowed for use of traditional high explosive rounds in addition to antitank missiles. However, most tanks had as main armament the standard NATO 105mm gun and two .50-caliber machine guns. The various models of the M60 remained the mainstay of U.S. armored units until replaced by the M1 Abrams (q.v.). The Marine Corps continued to use the M60s long after the army armored units had adopted the M1, and some were used during Desert Storm (q.v.).

TARAWA. An atoll in the Gilbert Islands (q.v.), 2,085 miles southeast of Pearl Harbor (q.v.), the main island of which is Betio.

Betio is less than three miles long and only 800 yards at its widest. From the air the island seems to resemble a bird with the head located to the west. No elevation is higher than 10 feet above sea level.

Following the 2d Raider Battalion strike at Makin (q.v.) in 1942, the Japanese had reinforced and strengthened its main bases in the Mariana (q.v.), Marshall (q.v.), and Gilbert Islands (q.v.). By mid-1943 they had on Betio eight-inch naval guns, coastal defense artillery, light tanks, and a bunker system replete with automatic weapons. The garrison was composed mainly of Naval Special Landing Forces, in all numbering 4,800 men. The admiral commanding had boasted that the Americans could not take the fortress island in a hundred years. The decision was made in mid-1943 to capture the island primarily for its airfield, which dominated the small island. The unit selected for this task was the 2d Division, and the date set for the invasion was 20 November. At the same time, an army regiment was to seize Makin.

From the beginning the operation was compromised by restrictions. Fears of the Japanese navy attacking the covering naval force resulted in only a minimal bombardment. There was also little air interdiction, although at the time both naval and air support appeared adequate. Further, one regiment, the 6th Marines, was to be held in reserve. Fortunately for the success of the operation the marine command had insisted on more amphibians (LVTs [q.v.]) rather than using only the wooden navy landing craft.

Despite a mixup of landing craft in the dark, the troops of two regiments went in on schedule and landed on three beaches on the north side shortly past 0900. Despite the heavy fire, which sank 23 LVTs in the first three waves, 1,500 men had been landed in the first 10 minutes. Japanese counterattacks pinned the marines down on the beaches, particularly the central one code-named Red One. The situation at one time was so bad that one of the division's reserve battalions was committed, but most of the amtracs had been put out of action, and the troops had to wade in for over 700 yards and thus had very heavy losses. Despite suffering 1,500 casualties, by nightfall the marines had secured a strip 700 yards long by 300 yards deep in the center and to the west another lodgement 150 yards long by 500 yards deep. The next afternoon the corps reserve was sent in, landing at the extreme western end of the island. By then tanks and artillery had been landed, and the Japanese garrison had been split in half. On the third day the marines cleared most of the southern section of the island except the area around the big bombproof structure. The advance to the east continued with a noticeable slackening of Japanese resistance. The riflemen that evening repulsed three desperate counterattacks. On the 23d the marines continued to take casualties from the entrenched enemy, but by afternoon the eastern part of the island had been reached. Two battalions were committed at the same time to the reduction of the bunker complex.

With the capture of those interlocking positions, all organized Japanese resistance ceased. All that was left was hunting down individual Japanese. In the United States reports of the heavy losses, 980 marines and 29 sailors in just 70 hours, shocked the nation and made it clear how costly the ultimate victory would be. For the Japanese only 146 men, mostly Koreans, survived. The vaunted naval battalions had lost 4,690 men killed.

TET OFFENSIVE. This was a major shift in North Vietnamese strategy at the beginning of 1968. Its planners believed their forces were strong enough to openly challenge the South Vietnamese Army (ARVN) and U.S. forces for control of the major cities and towns in the south. By tricking the allied leaders into believing they would honor an announced truce for the Tet religious holiday, they gained almost total surprise.

Beginning on 30 January, the offensive at first seemed successful. Even the U.S. Embassy in Saigon was briefly occupied. The heaviest fighting occurred in the ancient imperial city of Hue (q.v.), where the North Vietnamese forces took control of most of the city. Three battalions of marines of the 1st and 5th Marine Regiments, in conjunction with ARVN units, conducted 10 days of house-to-house fighting before the area south of the Perfume River was pacified. Another 10 days were required to end the North's control of the rest of the city. The North Vietnamese were no more successful elsewhere as the allied forces quickly responded.

Tet was a major defeat for the North Vietnamese. They had lost heavily and had not gained any of their objectives. Nevertheless, Tet was viewed by large segments of the American public and the media as a defeat. Thus, it became the turning point of the Vietnam War (q.v.) as opposition to continuing the conflict mounted in the United States and political leaders began to search for a way out of the war.

THOMASON, JOHN JR. b. Huntsville, Tex., 28 Feb. 1893, d. San Diego, Calif., 12 March 1944. Thomason attended schools in

Huntsville and later was certified as a teacher and taught in rural schools. Already an accomplished artist, he attended the Art Students League in New York in 1914. Two years later he was hired as a reporter for the *Houston Chronicle*. The day after war was declared in April 1917 he joined the Marine Corps and was commissioned a second lieutenant in the reserve. This was soon converted to a regular commission. Promoted to first lieutenant, he attended the Basic School at Quantico (q.v.). He arrived in France in May 1918 as a part of the 5th Marines and commanded a platoon at Belleau Wood (q.v.). Later in action at Soissons (q.v.), Captain Thomason was instrumental in destroying a machine gun nest, killing 13 Germans. For this action the army awarded him the Silver Star, and much later the navy belatedly awarded him the Navy Cross (q.v.). Thomason was involved in all subsequent actions—Blanc Mont, Saint-Mihiel (q.v.), and the Argonne (q.v.).

After the Armistice, Thomason drew occupation duty at Coblenz until late 1919. During the interwar years he served in Cuba, Dover, New Jersey, at sea aboard the *U.S.S. Rochester*, at Fort Humphreys, as a member of the Peking Legation Guard (q.v.), and he was an aide to the assistant secretary of the navy. In 1937 he attended the Naval War College and the following year was assigned to command a regiment at Camp Pendleton (q.v.). In June 1940 he was ordered to Washington to serve in the Office of Naval Intelligence. Admiral Chester Nimitz requested his assignment to the Pacific, and Thomason served on his staff as inspector of marine bases. He was hospitalized for pneumonia in mid-1943 and was transferred to Camp Elliot. Again hospitalized early the following year, Colonel Thomason died in March at the age of 51.

However distinguished Thomason's regular service was, it was eclipsed by his writing and artwork, which made him the best known marine of the interwar period. His book *Fix Bayonets*, published in 1926, was a major success, described by reviewers as the best and most realistic account of the trials of the average soldier in World War I (q.v.). His work was further enhanced by his sketches of men and locales in France. Thomason later wrote a biography of Jeb Stuart and a book about frontier life in Texas. In addition, he contributed many articles on military life to a variety of publications.

THOMPSON SUBMACHINE GUN (M1921 and M1928A1). Designed by Col. John Thompson after his retirement from the army, the gun fired .45-caliber ball ammunition from either a

50-round drum or a 20-round magazine at a rate of 800 rounds per minute. The M1921 was tested by the Marine Corps, and although not officially adopted, it was impressive enough that several hundred were ordered for use in Nicaragua (q.v.). The 1928 model was a redesign of the earlier gun to meet the suggested modifications by the navy, which purchased 500 guns. This was sufficient to meet the needs of the navy and corps during the interwar years. By 1940 War and Navy Department orders and requests from Britain boosted production. Ultimately over 300,000 M1928s were produced. Further changes were made in 1942 in the M1 model, particularly in the blowback design, and some more slight variations were made in the M1A1 Thompsons. Over 800,000 of these models were produced.

The weapon was particularly prized by Marine Raiders for its reliability, high rate of fire, and ready availability of the .45-caliber ammunition. It was officially replaced by the M-1 Carbine (q.v.), which had more range and power, before World War II (q.v.) ended. However, a few Thompsons were available for use in the Korean War (q.v.) and even the Vietnam War (q.v.).

TIENTSIN. A city in China on the Peiho River southeast of Peking (q.v.). In 1900 it was connected to the Manchurian Railway at the head of the Grand Canal. Its possession gave the Boxers a considerable advantage in their attempts to drive the Europeans out of China. The action of the small marine contingent of the multinational relief force at Tientsin drove out the rebels and relieved pressure on the troops defending the legations at Peking. (See also Boxer Rebellion.)

TINIAN. A sparsely settled island in the Mariana Islands (q.v.) located only three miles south of the larger island of Saipan (q.v.). It was the last of the Marianas to be targeted for occupation during World War II (q.v.). The island is 13 miles long by 6 miles wide, with cliffs rising directly from the coast, making any landing hazardous. The best beaches were adjacent to the only settlement, Tinian Town, and the Japanese commander of approximately 6,000 troops had concentrated his forces to repel any attempt to land there. However, the commander of V Amphibious Corps decided to land the 4th Division on two narrow beaches on the northwest coast on 24 July 1944. The 2d Division, covered by the navy, demonstrated off Tinian Town, which convinced the Japanese that the invasion there was imminent. Before discovering the ruse, the 4th Division by evening of D-day had over 15,000 men ashore and had begun to move south against weak resistance. After the demonstration, the 2d Division was landed in the north to take position on the left flank of the 4th. Advancing rapidly over difficult terrain, the marines were on the outskirts of Tinian Town by the 29th, having survived a number of banzai attacks. The Japanese garrison, reduced by one-third, retreated into the wooded hilly area of southern Tinian. However, the combination of marine firepower supplemented by naval gunnery and air attacks broke organized resistance on the island, and it was declared secure on 1 August.

Described by the marine commander as an almost perfect operation, the conquest of Tinian had cost the marines 317 dead. Numerous Japanese civilians, like their counterparts on Saipan, chose suicide rather than surrender. Continued sweeps throughout the island by the 8th Marines, the one regiment left for occupation duty, killed an additional 542 Japanese by 1 January 1945. Construction of the massive North Field bomber strips began almost immediately, and by early 1945 the B-29s located there were bombing Japan regularly. The *Enola Gay* and *Bock's Car*, the two atom bomb–carrying planes whose actions ended the war, were based on Tinian.

TRIPOLITANIAN WAR. The war with the Barbary pirates controlled by the bey of Tripoli once again allowed the marines to prove their usefulness in amphibious warfare. They were a part of the ship's company of the *Constitution* that bombarded Tripoli and in February 1804 accompanied Commo. Stephen Decatur in his attack on the harbor to burn the captured frigate *Philadelphia*. Even more daring was the action of Lt. Presley O'Bannon (q.v.). Supporting a rival of the bey of Tripoli, the United States authorized an expedition from Alexandria (q.v.) to capture the city of Derna (q.v.). O'Bannon and seven marines were a part of a force made up of Greek mercenaries and soldiers of fortune that marched along the coastal route for 600 miles. Attacking the city from the southwest under protective guns of a small U.S. fleet on 27 April 1805, O'Bannon's small army of "Christians" took the town in two hours. O'Bannon had the bey's flag taken down and the Stars and Stripes was raised, the first time the U.S. flag flew over a foreign fort. Six weeks later a peace treaty was concluded with the bey favorable to the U.S. maritime interests in the Mediterranean.

TULAGI. A small island in the southern Solomon Islands (q.v.) across the Sealark Channel from Guadalcanal (q.v.) and adjacent to Florida Island. Before World War II (q.v.), the New Zealand government made it the seat of administration for the area. The Japanese occupied Tulagi in late April 1942 and later decided to expand their control over northern Guadalcanal, which brought on the first offensive ground action by the United States in the war. On 7 August 1942 at the same time that the 1st Division landed on Guadalcanal, the 1st Raider Battalion landed on Tulagi. They were met with heavy mortar and rifle fire, and it was not until evening of the next day that Tulagi was secured. Because of the more healthful conditions on Tulagi, it became once again an administrative center, and its harbor became a main staging ground for the continued allied offensives in the Solomons.

TURNAGE, ALLEN H. b. Farmville, N. C., 3 Jan. 1893, d. Tide Water, Va., 22 Oct. 1971. Turnage was educated at Homer Military School, Oxford, North Carolina, before being commissioned a second lieutenant in the corps in 1913. He was promoted through grades to major general in 1943. He served sea duty and was involved in the marine campaigns in Haiti (q.v.) and Nicaragua (q.v.). In July 1943 he took command of the 3d Division. Planning for the initial assault on Bougainville (q.v.) was completed in New Zealand, and on 1 November 1943 Turnage led the division in its landing at Empress Augusta Bay. The division, along with army troops, moved inland and established a defensive perimeter to allow the building of two bomber airfields. The division was relieved in December.

Its next action was on 18 July on Guam (q.v.) where it made the major assault on the Asan beaches and bore the brunt of the early fighting against the Japanese, who held the high ground. The final conquest of the north was made by a three-division assault with the 3d in the center of the drive. For his leadership, Turnage was awarded the Navy Cross (q.v.). After the Guam conquest he was ordered to Washington to become director of personnel and assistant commandant, a position he held until his retirement as a lieutenant general in 1946.

U

UNIFORMS. In September 1776 the Naval Committee of the Continental Congress authorized a standard uniform for the newly created Marine Corps. This uniform had white trousers and a green coat with white facings. The hat was round with a turned up brim on which was a cockade. A leather collar was provided, presumably to protect the wearer from sword slashes. This item became standard for all subsequent enlisted mens' uniforms until 1875. When the Marine Corps was reconstituted, the uniform changed drastically.

In 1798 the corps was provided with leftovers from Gen. Anthony Wayne's army. These were the marines' first dress blues, a blue coat with red facings. The hat continued to be round, black, and with a part of the brim turned up. In 1804 a minor change was made. The coat continued to be blue but of a lighter hue and had scarlet facings. The round hat was abandoned for a tall shako with a large brass eagle in front.

In 1834 Pres. Andrew Jackson, who was not a supporter of the corps, directed a major change. The coat was to be grey-green in color with buff facings. The pants were grey. This unpopular uniform was worn for only a short time. It was discovered during the Seminole War (q.v.) that the green color faded badly. Thus, in 1841 the corps' uniform became blue again with a dark blue coat and light blue trousers. For general use there was provided a dark blue cap with a leather visor. On this was a device of a brass anchor encircled by a wreath. For dress there was a tall shako. In 1859 enlisted men and officers were allowed to wear fatigue caps resembling the French kepi.

In 1869 a major change was made, particularly in the dress uniform. A new-style blue-black shell jacket with a standing collar was authorized with lighter blue trousers. For officers there was considerable gold braid on both. The Mameluk Sword (q.v.) was once again authorized for officers, while the noncommissioned officers wore the army-type sabre. With some modifications, this uniform style was carried over to the 20th century and remains the famous dress blues of today. Further changes in headgear was made in 1875 by adoption of a forage cap for the undress uniform. A new-style jacket was also issued to enlisted men. The unpopular leather stock was abandoned for the first time. In the 1890s several changes were made in the field uniform. A blue flannel shirt replaced the coat, and high leggings were first issued. These remained standard until the early 1950s. A white broad-brimmed hat creased fore and aft replaced the kepi. It had the marine emblem on the side.

During the Spanish-American War (q.v.), khaki had become the standard, and tropical service and field uniforms became lighter in weight. A mustard-colored shirt replaced the blue in 1904, and a khaki blouse was also issued. The spiked dress helmet adopted after the Franco-Prussian War was finally abandoned and replaced by a visored hat. In 1912 the corps adopted a forest green service uniform with dull bronze buttons. A new campaign hat was adopted. It was also a shade of green and had a narrow brim and a four-dent crown—the same style hat is still worn by drill instructors. Under pressure of rapid mobilization, the corps' leadership accepted the standard army woolen khaki uniforms during World War I (q.v.), complete with leggings and the steel helmet modeled on the British style.

Further changes were made in all the uniforms during the interwar years. In 1928 a roll-collar coat with a khaki shirt and green tie for the service uniform was authorized. For a time Sam Browne belts were popular with officers. By World War II (q.v.) the fatigue uniform was green and made of relatively lightweight material. This was the standard combat uniform for marines during the war. The steel helmet of World War I vintage was soon replaced with a standard army-style pot helmet covered with camouflage cloth and netting.

Aside from a few changes in headgear, the uniform of World War II continued until the early 1960s. The heat of Vietnam (q.v.) dictated lighter-weight combat clothes, and the corps adopted camouflage colors for the basic fatigue uniform. The last major change for the corps was the adoption of the Kevlar helmet for all combat units.

UPSHUR, WILLIAM P. b. Richmond, Va., 28 Oct. 1881, d. Sitka, Alaska, 18 Aug. 1943. Upshur graduated from Virginia Military Academy in 1902 and joined the corps as a second lieutenant in February 1904. Subsequently he served at sea, and in 1906 and the following year he served in Cuba (q.v.). Later he was posted to Panama (q.v.) and in 1912 served in the Philippines and two years later at the American Legation in Peking. In August 1915 he assumed command of a company at Port au Prince, Haiti (q.v.). In the operations against the Cacos insurrectionists, he distinguished himself, earning the Medal of Honor (q.v.). During World War I (q.v.), he served in France with the 13th Marines from September 1918 until August 1919. He was in command of an American military prison and also the guards at the French docks.

After the war, Upshur held a number of responsible positions, including duty in the Virgin Islands and Haiti, and he took part in Fleet Marine exercises. In the 1930s Upshur attended the corps' School of Application, the Army Command and General Staff School, and the Army and Navy War Colleges. He commanded the Marine Corps station at Quantico (q.v.) and was the director of the corps' reserve while serving in the office of the chief of naval operations. Promoted to major general in January 1942, he assumed command of the Department of the Pacific with headquarters in San Francisco and covering the western United States, Alaska, and Hawaii. His tragic death in 1943 near Sitka, Alaska, while on a routine inspection trip, removed from the corps one of the best-trained and experienced senior officers whose service would have been sorely needed during the last two years of World War II (q.v.).

V

VANDEGRIFT, ALEXANDER A. 18th commandant, b. Charlottesville, Va., 13 March 1887. Vandegrift attended the University of Virginia and was commissioned a second lieutenant in January 1909. Following schools and shore duty, he was posted to the Caribbean, where he was involved in action in Nicaragua (q.v.) and later in the occupation of Veracruz (q.v.). As a lieutenant with Maj. Smedley Butler (q.v.) in Haiti (q.v.), he helped capture General Rameau, an insurgent leader, in September 1915 and became a member of the Haitian Constabulary before returning to the United States. Later in July 1919 he became inspector of the constabulary at Port au Prince. Further duty in the 1920s and 1930s included service at Tientsin (q.v.) and Peking (q.v.) in China and administrative posts in Washington, D.C.

In March 1940 Vandegrift became assistant to the commandant, a post he held until appointed to command the 1st Marine Division, which left the east coast in May 1942 for New Zealand. Two weeks after arrival he was alerted for the attack on Guadalcanal (q.v.) and Tulagi (q.v.). He commanded all forces on Guadalcanal from landings on 1 August until 9 December 1942, when he turned over responsibility to Maj. Gen. Alexander Patch. Vandegrift was appointed lieutenant general commanding I Amphibious Corps (3d division and 37th army division) which landed on Bougainville (q.v.) on 1 November 1943.

Soon after the invasion, Vandegrift turned over command to Maj. Gen. Roy Geiger (q.v.) and returned to Washington to become commandant on 1 January 1944. He presided over the expansion of the corps to a total of six combat divisions as well as continuing the policy begun by Gen. Thomas Holcomb (q.v.) of encouraging enlistment of women marines. By 1945, 18,240 women were in the corps. As a stalwart defender of the corps, he testified many times to Congress protesting the 1946 plan for unification of the armed services. Nevertheless, the National Security Act passed after his retirement left the corps' future uncertain.

For his stalwart defense of the Guadalcanal perimeter, General Vandegrift received the Navy Cross (q.v.) and later the Medal of Honor (q.v.). He left active service on 31 December 1947.

VERACRUZ. Located on the Bay of Campeche, Veracruz is one of two major Mexican eastern seaports. It is the key to the valley of Mexico and Mexico City located 200 miles to the west. During the Mexican War (q.v.), it was bombarded between 22 and 25 March 1847 by U.S. forces under the command of Gen. Winfield Scott. After occupation it served as the main supply base for that part of the Mexican campaign. The 1st Marine Battalion landed there in August on its way to join the expedition.

Much later Veracruz became a major pawn in the diplomatic game being played by Pres. Woodrow Wilson, who in 1914 refused to recognize the regime of Gen. Victoriano Huerta. On 9 April a minor incident at Tampico resulted in the brief imprisonment of American sailors. The U.S. admiral in command of the Gulf squadron demanded an apology and a 21-gun salute for the U.S. flag. The bad feelings between the two states were intensified by the discovery that a German ship carrying arms to Huerta was bound for Veracruz. Wilson ordered the city seized. The 2d Marine Regiment went ashore on 21 April against only slight resistance. Soon, however, Mexican army units began a strong defense of the city. The initial marine component was soon reinforced by the Panama Battalion and a naval brigade, bringing the total force up to 7,000 men, of whom 3,100 were marines. There was sharp house-to-house fighting before the city's garrison surrendered on the 24th. The seizure of the port and subsequent blockade was sufficient to oust Huerta, who resigned as head of state on 15 July.

VIET CONG. The antigovernment guerrilla force in South Vietnam that with the aid of the Communist North Vietnamese threatened the Saigon regime for a decade. By the end of 1966 most of the Viet Cong units had been destroyed. Their place was taken by an increasing number of North Vietnamese army units. (See also Da Nang, Con Thien, Khe Sanh, and Vietnam War.)

VIETNAM WAR. A serious problem for the United States had been slowly unfolding in the decade following the Korean War (q.v.). The French had attempted to restore their control over Indo-China after World War II (q.v.), and this had resulted in a massive nationalist opposition. The most important of the anticolonial groups was the Communists led by Ho Chi Minh. After seven years of attempting to restore their control over Vietnam, the French finally in 1954 agreed to leave and to the partitioning of the country along the 17th parallel. They left behind a divided Vietnam, with the North controlled by the Communists and the South in a state of near anarchy. From this internecine struggle in the South, the faction led by Ngo Dinh Diem emerged triumphant.

Following its dictum of containment, the U.S. government had assisted the French and in the late 1950s gave unstinting support to Diem, at first only with money and equipment. Diem continued to rule South Vietnam primarily because he controlled the army, which he used to crush opposition parties, but he was unable to wipe out the growing menace of the Viet Cong (q.v.) guerrilla forces. A major factor in the attitude of the United States toward Diem in the spring of 1963 also was the opposition of the Buddhists, whose leaders detested the harsh measures of Diem, a Catholic. In May and June this opposition became more open and forced even more repressive measures, and civil war began in the South. By November there was fighting between factions in Saigon.

At this juncture the U.S. withdrew its unequivocal support of Diem. He was arrested and subsequently murdered by the military. A parade of generals in command of the government followed: Big Minh, Little Minh, Khan, Ky, and Thieu. The United States continued to support each of these in turn and, because of the unstable nature of the government and the increasing presence of the North Vietnamese, escalated its commitment. At first it sent military advisers and then after an apparent North Vietnamese strike against naval ships in the Gulf of Tonkin, the United States became a full-fledged partner in the war against the Viet Cong and the North Vietnamese.

The Marine Corps' presence in Vietnam began in April 1962 when a helicopter squadron arrived in the delta south of Saigon. This unit was later moved to Da Nang (q.v.), Vietnam's second largest city, in I Corps area. The helicopters were used to transport South Vietnamese Army (ARVN) troops into battle. Operations were expanded so much that by 1965 half of the corps' helicopter squadrons had served in Vietnam. By 1964 the corps was also providing advisers to ARVN. An attack on the American outpost at Pleiku in early February 1965 produced an escalation of the war, with Washington approving massive air attacks. As a result of this, the corps' 9th Expeditionary Brigade was landed at Da Nang in March, the first large-scale U.S. ground combat force in Vietnam. Very soon it was moved westward to protect the Da Nang airfield, one of only three that could handle jet aircraft. There was a sudden massive buildup during the late spring and summer. A squadron of Phantoms (q.v.) arrived in April, and III Amphibious Force was constituted, with its main strength being the 3d Division. A second jet airfield was constructed at Chu Lai, and a squadron of A-4 Skyhawk (q.v.) bombers were brought in. By the end of summer the corps had four regiments—the 3d, 4th, 7th, and 9th Marines—in Vietnam in addition to four air groups. The regrouping of the Viet Cong in central Vietnam reinforced by four North Vietnamese regiments led Pres. Lyndon Johnson and his advisers to decide to further escalate and Americanize the war.

Intelligence reports indicated that a Viet Cong regiment approximately 2,000 strong was concentrating on the Von Tuong Peninsula south of Chu Lai. Operation Starlight (q.v.) was designed to clear them from this potentially dangerous region. On 18 August 1965 the 7th Marines, using helicopters from the west and landing one battalion from the sea and another crossing a river to the north, boxed in the enemy and killed a reported 1,000 troops. Elsewhere the 9th Marines had cleared the coastal areas as far as Hoi An. This action enabled the marines to begin their policy of pacification by clearing villages of the Viet Cong, providing security for the villagers, and then beginning civic action programs. The marines also provided for better training for popular and regional forces. First tried in the nine villages of Hoa Vang, the concept was later applied to all areas held directly by the marines. One of the major disagreements between marines and higher command was the decision to all but adandon the pacification programs and rely almost entirely on search-and-destroy missions targeting suspected Viet Cong strongholds without prior reference to the loyalty of villagers.

Marine participation in the long, drawn-out conflict was an important but minor part of the overall American efforts. Most of the key officers in the Military Assistance Command Vietnam (MACV) headed by Gen. William Westmoreland were army, and the bulk of all troops were army units. Before the end of 1966 the buildup ordered by President Johnson included the army's 1st, 1st Air Cavalry, 9th, and 25th Divisions and two large brigades. It must also be understood that the war was a highly political one, with major decisions being made in Washington by civilian authorities far removed from the combat zones. It was fundamental that the South Vietnamese government be supported even though it was ineffective and many of its units were far from effective. Battle losses, corruption, inefficiency, and high desertion rates plagued many of the South Vietnamese units throughout the war, meaning that U.S. ground forces had to assume an ever increasing offensive burden. The marine efforts had to be within the context of an overall strategic and tactical structure determined by MACV or higher authority. The corps became a part of the land army, and its peculiar skills were only seldom utilized.

By June 1966 the rest of the 1st Division had arrived in Vietnam and was firmly emplaced in the vicinity of Chu Lai. Finally, III Marine Amphibious Force (MAF) commanded by Lt. Gen. Lewis Walt (q.v.) had the two-division ground force with which it would fight almost six years of war. Marine activities in 1966 centered on defense of three bases in I Corps' area—Chu Lai, Phu Bai near Hue (q.v.), and Da Nang—and guarding the Demilitarized Zone (DMZ) (q.v.) in Quang Tri Province against the North Vietnamese Army (NVA) moving south. In the Chu Lai area the Viet Cong were supported by two North Vietnamese divisions. In early January 1966 an offensive against the enemy south of Chu Lai was launched with an amphibious assault by three battalions cooperating with an ARVN division. Launched in foul weather, the marines moved inland, attempting to pin the elusive enemy down. The operation was eventually called off after weeks of frustration as the Viet Cong continually eluded the marines. Another operation begun in February was more successful. A composite battalion of the 1st Division was called on to support ARVN units in a heavy firefight near Hue (q.v.). In scenes reminiscent of World War II, the marines methodically reduced the Viet Cong bunker defenses and inflicted heavy losses on them, forcing a withdrawal. Another localized victory was Operation Texas in which marine and ARVN troops were moved by helicopter to hold the outpost of An Hoa on 20 March. Subsequently, in cooperation with ARVN forces to the south, they sandwiched the Viet Cong between them and largely destroyed the enemy.

Meanwhile, a North Vietnamese division had crossed the Ben Hai River into Quang Tri, the northernmost province of South Vietnam. This move forced the marines to shift their major activity 250 miles north near the DMZ. For months there was continual confrontation between large-scale forces, with the marines using their air mobility to send units into action to check specific incursions. A major base was established at Dong Ha. In early July a sea and air assault was preliminary to Operation Hastings in which six marine and five ARVN battalions were landed in the Ngan Valley and were immediately engaged with the enemy. Without gaining full control of the area, the marines prepared to leave. However, on 28 July two companies of the 4th Marines were attacked by more than 1,000 regular NVA troops. Despite inflicting heavy casualties on the attackers, the outnumbered marines were forced to retreat into the safe regimental perimeter. Small scale actions continued and then abated during August. Then in September the NVA renewed major actions. The marines responded by a coordinated offensive of four battalions. The most serious action was fought by the Special Landing Force of the 26th Marines in the Cua Viet River area. The marines drove the NVA back across the Ben Hai River and destroyed their prepared positions of trenches, tunnels, and bunkers. But as with most successful actions in Vietnam, the troops were too few to hold the ground, and they were evacuated on 25 September, leaving the area to be reoccupied by the enemy.

In other areas throughout September, violent small-scale actions occurred in various places in central and western Quang Tri Province. One of the most serious operations was the attack on the highlands of Nui Cay Tre dominated by a ridge called by the marines Mutter's Ridge and defended by NVA regulars. On 15 September two companies of the 1st Battalion, 4th Marines, moving toward the ridge were ambushed and were in danger of being wiped out before reinforcements from the 2d Battalion, 7th Marines, linked up with them on the 18th. Four days later in conjunction with the 3d Battalion, 4th Marines, brought in on the NVA flank, the ridge line was assaulted. By the 26th only a part of the ridge was secured, and on the 27th the NVA launched a major counterattack. Heavy fighting continued for days as the marines slowly took the surrounding hills and the ridge was cleared by 4 October. Nevertheless, contact with the enemy continued in this area throughout the rest of the year.

The 1966 campaign in the north had proved the tactical superiority of marine combined arms in a series of hard fought actions. With mobility supplied by helicopter units and support from marine air, the regular NVA troops were systematically driven northward after sustaining heavy losses. However, the policy of restricting the war to South Vietnam enabled the battered NVA units in their safe haven to regroup and refit to come back and once again challenge the marines. The two marine divisions, with minimal support from ARVN units, were not large enough to hold all the ground, and thus they would foray from established bases over and over to contain the invaders. This pattern continued in the DMZ area throughout the war.

By 1967 Gen. William Westmoreland had seven U.S. divisions, two parachute and two light infantry brigades, one armored cavalry regiment, and a special forces group in addition to the ARVN forces. That year would be known as the time of the big battles; none of the 14 were won by the enemy, who nevertheless at the end of the year remained a force to be reckoned with. The no-pursuit doctrine gave sanctuary to the NVA not only in Vietnam but also in Laos and Cambodia. That policy also hamstrung the marines near the DMZ. The marines there hinged their action on the possession of a series of strong points along the major highway, Route 9. Two new positions were established closer to the DMZ at Con Thien (q.v.) and Gio Linh. These were the locus of much of the 3d Division action during the year as the North Vietnamese launched attack after attack on these and on Khe Sanh (q.v.).

In April a series of actions undertaken by the 3d Marines in the Khe Sanh area were aimed at clearing the enemy from the hills that dominated the marine base. These were successful, and on 5 May the 26th Marines took over defense of Khe Sanh. Con Thien took on added significance when the Defense Department ordered the construction of a bulldozed infiltration barrier strewn with mines and protected by barbed wire and sensors to stretch ultimately across Vietnam. The test section was to extend from the western terminus of the DMZ to Gio Linh. Con Thien was to be one of the major strong points along this line. Much of the activity of the 3d Division during the summer was constructing this McNamara Line (q.v.) despite the opposition by all senior marine commanders to this project. Con Thien had already begun to be an objective for the North Vietnamese and was shelled on 8 May followed by a heavy frontal attack by the NVA. This was beaten back by the 4th Marines. A counterattack in combination with ARVN forces ten days later led to the capture of the NVA's bunker complex north of Con Thien. The NVA then pulled back.

During the summer and fall, Con Thien continued to be a magnet for the NVA. The most serious fighting occurred during Operation Buffalo when two battalions of the 9th Marines and one of the 3d engaged a North Vietnamese regiment on 5–6 July. The enemy sustained horrendous casualties, and the marines suffered 100 dead and 270 wounded. A major regimental-size attack on Con Thien on 10 September against the 26th Marines was broken by marine artillery. The North Vietnamese finally gave up the siege of Con Thien in early October. The last major action along the DMZ in 1967 was a seaborne attack on 28 December on several villages harboring the NVA. After brief resistance, the NVA once again escaped north.

In early 1968 the North Vietnamese decided to challenge the 26th Marines' hold on the main bastion and hills surrounding Khe Sanh and concentrated two divisions to reduce the station. The second battle for Khe Sanh began on 21 January. On 5 February after having established control of Route 9, they overran a special forces base at Lang Vei. Khe Sanh, although a key base on the McNamara Line, became important to both sides for political rather than strict military reasons. The marine and ARVN forces in the vicinity were supported by massive tactical and strategic air strikes. By the time of its relief, over 110,000 tons of bombs and 142,000 rounds of artillery shells had been used on the North Vietnamese. Although the enemy's Tet offensive (q.v.) in 1968 forced a focus of attention on the main cities, there was a quick buildup of forces in I Corps' zone. Lieutenant General Robert Cushman (q.v.), now commanding III MAF, had by March the equivalent of a land army composed of 24 marine and 28 army battalions, and he began the relief of Khe Sanh in an operation code-named Pegasus on 1 April. The 1st Marines and three ARVN battalions moved west along Route 9, clearing that vital communications link of the enemy. At the same time the 1st Air Cavalry and ARVN airborne troops were flown forward. The 26th Marines attacked southwest of Khe Sanh and made contact with the airborne troops on 4 April. The 77-day siege of Khe Sanh was over. The North Vietnamese plan to replicate Dienbenphu had been foiled.

Following the relief of Khe Sanh, the 1st Air Cavalry and the 101st Division descended on the A Shau Valley and delivered a smashing defeat on the NVA, inflicting the greatest losses suffered by the enemy in I Corps' zone. On 20 April a NVA division attacked 3d Division troops at Dong Ha and were beaten back in a fierce six-day battle. At the same time, the 7th Marines conducted a large-scale sweep southwest of Da Nang near Hoi An, and in May the 1st and 4th Marines were involved in a fast-moving operation against a NVA salient south of Khe Sanh near the Laotian border. After two weeks of fighting, the NVA division retreated to its sanctuary north of the DMZ.

The most important strategic and political set of events had begun on 30 January 1968. The Viet Cong announced a truce in fighting during the Tet religious holiday, and as a result ARVN and American forces relaxed their vigilance. The North Vietnamese and Viet Cong in a change of tactics used this time to infiltrate their forces into all the major cities. The NVA high command was confident that their troops would be able to seize all five provincial capitals and thus deal a death blow to the South Vietnamese government. The operation at Da Nang began when the infiltrators, catching the marines by surprise, almost reached I Corps headquarters before being stopped. At the same time a full NVA division attacked from the west and south. These main elements were caught by marine air and artillery and cut to pieces before being engaged and driven back by marine ground troops.

The heaviest fighting during the Tet offensive occurred in the beautiful old city of Hue. Several thousand ARVN troops had infiltrated into the city and by the evening of the 30th had established control over most of Hue. The following morning the 1st Battalion, 1st Marines, had fought its way from Phu Bai through to the southern suburbs and later established contact with ARVN division headquarters. On 1 February the marines began the difficult task of recapturing that part of Hue south of the Perfume River. Joined by the 2d Battalion, 5th Marines, they engaged in house-to-house fighting not experienced since the capture of Seoul in 1950. By 9 February all of southern Hue had been cleared. Elsewhere, beginning on the 12th ARVN units, aided by the 1st Battalion, 5th Marines, attacked from the north into the city proper. The heavy fighting lasted 10 more days before the bulk of the city was retaken. Mopping up consumed the rest of the month, and Hue was declared secure on 2 March.

The North Vietnamese had made a major miscalculation, and they paid heavily for it; nowhere were their open attacks successful. At Hue alone they lost an estimated 13 battalions. In every previous U.S. war such a tactical victory would have been followed by a general offensive to secure ultimate victory. But Vietnam was not like other wars. Micromanagement from Washington and severe restrictions on the military had produced a virtual stalemate even after Tet. In the United States a coalition of citizens who at first supported the war now demanded its end, and ultimately their opposition would bring an end to the Johnson presidency. To the American public, the Tet offensive, far from being a victory, showed how complex Vietnam was and how far the North was from being subdued. The major goal in the coming years then was how to get out of the war. To the army and marine leaders, this aim ultimately meant a scaling back of operations.

After Tet the war entered a new phase. Although the war continued, actions tended to be on a smaller scale. General Creighton Abrams, who succeeded Westmoreland in July 1968, came under increasing pressure from Washington to measure offensive operations against the attempts of the government to find a way out of the Vietnam morass. President Johnson had decided in March not to stand for reelection in November, and the civilian protests against the war mounted. In part, the general dissatisfaction resulted in the election of Pres. Richard Nixon, who claimed he had a way to end the war. The first contacts between the U.S. and North Vietnamese diplomats occurred in late 1968, and National Security Adviser Henry Kissinger began secret meetings with Vietnamese representatives in Paris in February 1970. Despite the intensification of the bombing of North Vietnam and underwriting the incursion into Cambodia, it was obvious that the Nixon administration's main goal was to find an honorable way out.

For the marines the war continued much the same as in the previous years. This meant an active defense of Da Nang, operating in the "Dodge City" area to the south, and westward toward the Laotian border. In November 1968 six marine battalions trapped and destroyed over 1,200 North Vietnamese in that region. In early 1969 elements of the 1st Division struck deep into the hill country west of Da Nang, and the largest Special Landing Force operation was launched into the Batangan Peninsula. To the north the 3d Division in Quang Tri Province, in a model for mobile warfare, cleaned out enemy bases in Da Krong Valley in Operation Dewey Canyon. The marines continued with their Combined Action Program with four battalion-sized action groups designed to cooperate with Regional Force units to give quick response to Communist threats.

The decision by the Nixon administration to reduce conventional forces and turn back to the South Vietnamese the responsibility for conducting the war resulted in the phased withdrawal of U.S. troops. The first of these for the marines was the relief of the 9th Marines as well as elements of the 1st Air Wing. Late 1969 saw the 1st Division beginning operations in the Que Son Valley, replacing army units there. The fighting to clear the troublesome "Dodge City" region began once again in June and continued for the rest of the year. By 1970 it was estimated that over 90 percent of the population of five northern provinces were living in safe areas and the enemy had been reduced to guerrilla operations.

The second troop withdrawal began in September, and within a month the rest of the 3d Division had been relocated in Okinawa and Camp Pendleton. This reduction of force continued in early 1970 with more than 12,000 troops brought out of Vietnam. In March the army took over the defense of the areas near Da Nang, and the area of responsibility for III MAF, now basically the 1st Division, was primarily in Quang Nam Province. One of the last major offensives was begun in August with the 7th Marines supporting an ARVN offensive code-named Pickens Forrest. This thrust westward was indicative of the changed nature of the war. Now the South Vietnamese were expected to take on the major responsibility for defending themselves. By October more than 18,000 more marines were ordered home. The 7th Marines participated in one more offensive in the Que Son area before being transferred to Camp Pendleton (q.v.). Marine Air Group 13 turned Chu Lai over to the army before returning to the United States.

The reduction of forces continued in 1971, and the conduct of the war became more and more an ARVN responsibility. In February General Lam led a major incursion into Laos to interdict the Ho Chi Minh Trail. This was backed by U.S. forces, although these did not enter Laos. Marine participation was limited to air and engineering support. The 5th Marines began to leave Vietnam in February, leaving only the 1st Marines in Vietnam, and even this regiment soon rejoined the other two at Camp Pendleton. All remaining combat elements were briefly combined into an amphibious brigade, which also had been redeployed by midyear. By then the numbers of marines in Vietnam were approximately 500 men acting as embassy guards and advisers to ARVN forces. The North Vietnamese Easter offensive of 1972, when 120,000 NVA overran the northern provinces, brought more marine air units into the country to try to counter the NVA successes. Marine Air Group 15 with four squadrons of F-4 Phantoms (q.v.) arrived at Da Nang, and in May Group 12 brought in two squadrons of Skyhawk (q.v.) bombers. Other marine squadrons flew off aircraft carriers. These were extremely important in aiding the ARVN units in stopping the NVA before their units reached Hue.

The long, drawn-out peace talks in Paris finally brought about accord, and the Peace Agreement was signed in January 1973. The agreement allowed the United States to withdraw from the conflict without appearing to abandon the South Vietnamese. Although politically defensible, it was tactically a mistake since it left the NVA in possession of a large section of Vietnam. Without U.S. aid, the South Vietnamese were no match for the regular NVA troops. The final North Vietnamese offensive began in March 1975 and within two months had conquered the South. The 9th Amphibious Brigade in April stood by to evacuate U.S. citizens. On the 29th elements landed at Ton Son Nhut airport to provide security for civilian and military planes carrying civilians. After 395 Americans and 4,000 other civilians had been evacuated, the marines burned the buildings at this giant airfield. Meanwhile, the embassy guards reinforced by men of the 9th Marines guarded the embassy while helicopters took off the remaining U.S. personnel and designated Vietnamese and foreign citizens. In all, 978 U.S. and more than 1,100 foreign nationals were evacuated. The last marines were airlifted from the embassy on the morning of 30 April. In this fashion the marines' direct involvement in Vietnam ended three years after the main force of marine ground and air units had returned home.

The longest war in U.S. history had tested the corps as much as any previous conflict but was unique in that the final result was not victory. Constrained by rules dictated far from the scenes of action, members of the corps distinguished themselves in every action. The war had demanded new tactics to which the corps responded with the use of helicopters to increase mobility and even closer cooperation between ground and air forces than in World War II. More than 800,000 men had been brought into the corps during the seven years of its involvement, and the peak strength reached 317,000. The largest complement to serve in MAC III was almost 86,000 men. The corps had suffered 12,926 men killed in action and 88,582 wounded. (See also Con Thien, Da Nang, Hue, Khe Sanh, McNamara Line, Robert Modrzejewski, and Tet Offensive.)

VLADIVOSTOK. The chief Russian Pacific port. During the Bolshevik Revolution, the various allied powers supported the opposition White forces. Taking advantage of the chaos, the Japanese occupied the city in December 1917. Partially to prevent Japan's seizure of territory, the United States decided to send troops there, eventually two army regiments. One reason was to facilitate the evacuation of thousands of Czech soldiers caught in the middle of the civil war. The first U.S. element landed there in June 1918 was the marine contingent from the cruiser *Brooklyn*. After landing, they joined French and British units already there. The marines patrolled the Imperial Navy Yard until the arrival in August of the first of the army regiments.

W

WAKE ISLAND. In actuality, Wake Island is a group of three coral islets in the Pacific Ocean 2,300 miles west of Honolulu and 1,500 miles northeast of Guam (q.v.). Claimed by the United States in 1899, it was uninhabited until 1935 when Pan American Airways established a base there. The United States decided later to build rudimentary defenses on Wake, and by 1941 a garrison of 449 marines of the 1st Defense Battalion was stationed there. A late addition was 12 Wildcat (q.v.) fighters flown in from the carrier *Enterprise*. The Japanese first attacked the island on 11 December 1941 but were beaten off. Operating the island's five-inch guns, the marines sank two destroyers, damaged another, and scored hits on three cruisers. After this failure, the Japanese returned on the 22d with a much larger force, neutralized Wake's big guns, and landed 2,000 men of the Special Landing Force. By then all the Wildcat fighters had been destroyed. Despite heroic actions, the marine garrison was overwhelmed by the evening of the 22d. The conquest of Wake was very costly to the Japanese. In addition to the ship losses, approximately 1,500 of their infantry were killed. The defense of Wake along with the attack on Pearl Harbor (q.v.) became events that rallied the American people in the early phases of World War II (q.v.).

WALSH, KENNETH A. b. Brooklyn, N.Y., 24 Nov. 1916. Walsh enlisted in the Marine Corps in December 1933 and spent two years as an aviation mechanic and radioman. Selected for flight training at Pensacola (q.v.), he won his wings in April 1937 although still a private. He served four years in scout planes aboard three navy carriers. During this period he was advanced in rank to gunnery sergeant. In October 1942 he was commissioned while a member of Fighting Squadron 124 slated for duty in the Solomon Islands (q.v.). Flying from Vella Lavella in a Corsair (q.v.), he soon became one of the corps' most deadly fighter pilots. His most daring exploit occurred on 15 August 1943. While defending marine positions on the island, he led his division against six-to-one odds, personally destroying three Japanese planes. Landing his disabled plane at Munda, Walsh replaced it with another Corsair. Once aloft he encountered a force of Zero fighters estimated at 50 planes. Attacking alone, he destroyed four more aircraft before being shot down. He was later rescued off Vella Lavella. For this exploit 1st Lt. Walsh received the Medal of Honor (q.v.).

Before being ordered back to duty in the United States at Jacksonville, Walsh had scored 21 victories. In April 1945 he returned to the Pacific and took part in the Okinawa (q.v.) campaign as operations officer of Fighting Squadron 222. In March 1946 he was assigned to the Bureau of Aeronautics, a position he held for three years. He then served at Quantico (q.v.) and El Toro. The latter assignment was with Marine Air Group 25, and he went to Korea with this organization in July 1950, returning to El Toro after one year. Promoted to lieutenant colonel in October 1958, he served in a number of assignments in both Atlantic and Pacific Fleet areas. He retired from active service in January 1962.

WALT, LEWIS W. b. Wabaunsee County, Kans., 16 Feb. 1913, d. 26 March 1989. Walt graduated with a degree in chemistry in 1936 from Colorado State where he was an enlisted member of the National Guard and the ROTC program. He was briefly a commissioned officer in the Army Field Artillery before joining the Marine Corps as a second lieutenant in July 1936. He attended basic school in Philadelphia before being assigned to the 6th Marines in San Diego. He was posted to China in August 1937, where he spent six months in Shanghai. Returning briefly to the United States, he was then sent to join the small marine detachment on Guam (q.v.) in mid-1939. Fortunately, he had been ordered back to the States before the Japanese overran that island on 8 December 1941.

As a captain, Walt volunteered for service with the 1st Raider Battalion in early 1942 and accompanied the battalion to Samoa (q.v.) later that year as a company commander. He led a company in the assaults on Tulagi (q.v.) and Florida Islands in August, winning a Silver Star. After those areas were secured, he joined the 5th Marines, first as a battalion operations officer and then commander of the 2d Battalion on Guadalcanal (q.v.), and led them in the pursuit of the Japanese westward from Henderson Field (q.v.). In October he was wounded but remained in command of his battalion. In December he was promoted to lieutenant colonel and was hospitalized. He led the 2d Battalion in the invasion of Cape Gloucester (q.v.), New Britain (q.v.), in December 1943. He briefly served as executive officer of the 5th Marines before assuming command of the 3d Battalion in its assault on Aogini Ridge. For this action he was awarded the Navy Cross (q.v.).

Walt returned in February for further hospitalization in the United States and returned to the Pacific in June as the executive officer of the 5th Marines. In September he landed with the battalion in the center of the assault forces against the entrenched Japanese on Peleliu (q.v.). He took brief command of the regiment when its commander was wounded and received his second Navy Cross for his heroism during this bloody action. Later that year he was ordered to the United States, where he assumed command of the tactics section of the officers candidate school at Quantico, and in July 1946 he became a Battalion Landing Team instructor.

After the war, Walt served in a variety of positions, including operations officer of the 3d Brigade, then of the 1st Division, and he served in a special training regiment and attended the senior course of amphibious warfare, remaining on the staff until November 1951. Promoted to colonel, he served on the staff of the commander of the Amphibious Forces, Pacific, before taking command of the 5th Marines in Korea in November 1952 and later as operations officer of the 1st Division. Decorated by the Korean government, he also won the Legion of Merit and Bronze Star. After Korea he served at Quantico in a number of capacities before being ordered to Washington to be the head of the Detail Branch, Personnel Department, and later in November 1957 he was assistant director of personnel before attending the National War College. In 1960 he began a one-year appointment as the corps' representative to the Joint Advance Study Group, and afterward as a brigadier general, he served as assistant divisional commander of the 2d Division. In September he returned to Washington as director of Landing Force Development.

As the Vietnam War (q.v.) escalated, the commandant chose Walt, then the most junior major general, to command III Marine Amphibious Force there. By mid-1966 he had 55,000 men under his command. He and his immediate corps commander, Lt. Gen. Victor Krulak (q.v.), disagreed with the overall command decisions related to strategy, preferring pacification policies while still conducting day and night sorties against the enemy. He was against the tactic later agreed to by his successor to concentrate forces in I Corps' area at Khe Sanh (q.v.). Promoted to lieutenant general, he was rotated back to the United States in June 1967.

WAR OF 1812. In 1804 Capt. Daniel Carmick with 122 marines was sent to New Orleans (q.v.) which had just been obtained from France. They were responsible for helping provide law and order for the next decade before being called on for an active combat role at the close of the War of 1812. That war, the result of many misunderstandings with Britain, was at first fought on the sea where the fledgling U.S. fleet challenged the most powerful navy in the world. Most of the corps, numbering fewer than 500 men in 1812, were stationed on board ships and thus took an active part in the early successful sea battles. These included the *Constitution* versus the *Guerrière*, the *Wasp* versus *Frolic*, *Constitution* versus *Java*, and the *United States* versus *Macedonian*. One of the most successful cruises was that of the *Essex* commanded by Capt. David Porter operating in the Pacific against British whalers and privateers. He kept six of these captured ships to add to the strength of the 32-gun *Essex*. With few naval officers, he turned over command of one of the privateers, the *Greenwich*, to the senior marine officer, Lt. John Gamble (q.v.) who promptly used it to capture the heavy 22-gun British vessel, the *Seringapatam*.

Gamble's exploits provide one of the more exotic events in Marine Corps history. Porter had retired to Nuku Hiva (q.v.) Island in the Marquesas Islands to refit. While there he paraded the marines before an assemblage of natives and then took possession of the island in the name of the United States. Some of the natives proved troublesome and were quelled only when the marines and sailors burned down a number of villages. Porter then decided to continue his raiding and sailed off with most of his ships. However, he left Gamble behind with only 22 men. Very soon Gamble was threatened by another native uprising, followed by a mutiny of his own men on 17 May 1814. The mutineers took Gamble aboard the *Seringapatam* and set him loose in a longboat with a few loyal supporters. They made their way back to the island, fought off a native attack, and sailed in another small ship for the Hawaiian Islands. Arriving there, Gamble and his crew were made prisoners of the British, who informed them of the fate of the *Essex*, which had been destroyed in Valaparaiso harbor in March 1814. Let ashore under parole by the British at Rio de Janeiro, Gamble and his men eventually made their way to New York.

Elsewhere marines served on board the *Hornet* and the *Chesapeake* during its losing battle with the *Leopard* and were with Commodore Oliver Perry on Lake Erie. Despite the heroics of the fledgling U.S. Navy, by mid-1813 the Royal Navy controlled the sea lanes. Based on this dominance, Rear Adm. George Cockburn landed a large force in June 1813 on Craney Island in Chesapeake Bay, only to be beaten off by American militia stiffened by 50 marines. However, the next year the British were back. General Robert Ross landed 4,000 troops at Benedict, Maryland, and reinforced by Royal Marines, moved northward toward Marlboro, southeast of Washington. By 24 August they were five miles east of the capital at Bladensburg (q.v.). The American force under Gen. Henry Winder consisted of a large number of untrained militia bolstered by 400 seamen and 103 marines. The British crossed the Anacostia River under the cover of rockets and scattered the bulk of the militia. The seamen and marines held a defensive line across the main road with five naval guns and repulsed three charges. Both the naval commander and marine captain, Samuel Miller, were wounded, and the British forced a withdrawal by flanking the American position. With that retreat, the road to Washington was open. Ross then proceeded to the capital, and the government officers along with the commandant of the corps fled, and the British proceeded to burn most of the major buildings in the city. After bombarding Fort McHenry, the British naval force sailed for Halifax, Nova Scotia, while the troops retired to Jamaica, where the Duke of Wellington's brother-in-law, Sir Edward Pakenham, took command and planned an attack on New Orleans.

Major Carmick's marine force, now swelled to 300 men, had been involved until late 1814 in attempts to destroy the pirate Jean Lafitte's bases. However, Gen. Andrew Jackson, in charge of the defenses of New Orleans, offered Lafitte a full pardon in return for his aid. The British advance through Lake Borgne was blocked temporarily by five American gunboats manned by 182 men, of which 35 were marines. The defense cost the British time and 300 casualties. Jackson arranged his defense line behind a canal with both flanks protected by water, forcing the British to attack directly ahead. The marines were positioned in the center of the line. On 28 December Packenham ordered a probing attack in the center, which was contained, and Carmick led a counterattack, during which he was severely wounded. The British main attack was launched on 8 January 1815, with the bulk of the force, approximately 3,500 men, advancing in regular formation, so typical of European operations, toward the American breastworks. In 20 minutes the attack was repulsed, with the British suffering 2,300 casualties, including Pakenham. No pursuit was ordered; the British were allowed to bury their dead, numbering approximately 700 men, before departing. This battle in which the marines had taken a significant part and which played an important role in creating Jackson's legend, was fought two weeks after the peace treaty had been signed at Ghent.

WHARTON, FRANKLIN. 3d commandant, b. Philadelphia, Pa., 23 July 1767, d. Washington, D.C., 1 Sept. 1818. Wharton was commissioned a captain in the marines on 3 August 1798 and served on board the frigate *United States* until the close of the French troubles in 1801. He commanded the Philadelphia garrison until he became lieutenant colonel commandant on 7 March 1804 on the resignation of Cmndt. William Burrows (q.v.). He continued the work to develop the Marine Barracks at 8th and I Streets in Washington, completing the commandant's house. He was commandant during the difficulties with the Barbary pirates (q.v.). A new uniform based on European models was adopted during his tenure with a tall shako topped by a red plume. He sent a unit of 122 marines in 1804 to garrison recently acquired New Orleans (q.v.). During the War of 1812 (q.v.), marines were again active on board all U.S. ships and were in action at Annapolis, Fort McHenry, and Craney Island. At the battle of Bladensburg (q.v.), 103 marines joined with 400 seamen to deliver the only resistance to the British on their way to Washington. Wharton stayed behind and fled the capital with the president and the government before it was taken. His failure to take the field brought criticism from senior officers of the corps, and he was charged with neglect of duty and conduct unbecoming an officer. A court martial in September 1817 exonerated him. Although urged to resign by Pres. James Monroe, Warton continued in office until his death the following year.

"WILDCAT" (F4F and FM). A single-seat, low-winged monoplane first ordered by the navy from the Grumman Aircraft Company in 1940. The F4F-3 became the staple fighter for the

Marine Corps from 1941 to 1943. In 1942 the manufacture of the Wildcat was transferred to General Motors Corporation, which built over 2,500 of the planes designated FM-1 and FM-2. These two were nearly identical except for the power plant. In addition to producing the planes for the U.S. Navy and Marine Corps, Grumman and General Motors also provided them for the British. The F4F-1 and FM-2 had a top speed of 315 miles per hour, a service ceiling of 34,000 feet, and a range of 925 miles. Armament consisted of six .50 caliber wing guns. The plane could also carry two 250-pound bombs mounted under the wings. The Wildcat distinguished itself in all the Pacific actions, from the defense of Wake Island (q.v.) to the Marianas Islands (q.v.) operations. It was particularly important during the Guadalcanal (q.v.) actions. Marine aces John Smith, Marion Carl, and Joe Foss (q.v.), all multiple aces, flew the Wildcat against the Japanese with their overwhelming superiority in numbers at Guadalcanal.

WILSON, LOUIS H. JR. 26th commandant, b. Brandon, Miss., 11 Feb. 1920. Wilson enlisted in the Marine Corps Reserve in May 1941 and went on active duty the next month. Then he attended Officers Candidate School and was commissioned in November and assigned to duty in San Diego with the 2d Division. In April 1942 Wilson accepted a regular commission. In February 1943 as a member of the 9th Marines of the 3d Division he performed routine duty on Efate and Guadalcanal (q.v.). Promoted to captain, he participated in the landings on Bougainville (q.v.) and soon after was given command of F Company of the 2d Battalion. He led the company in the initial landings on the Asan beaches of Guam (q.v.) on 21 July 1944. The ferocious banzai attack on 25 July against the marines on the Fonte Plateau struck directly at the 9th Marines. Despite being wounded in the ensuing 10-hour action, Wilson rallied his men, defended the line, and eventually led the charge that seized vital ground necessary for the eventual advance on the plateau. For his actions on Guam he was awarded the Medal of Honor (q.v.).

Evacuated to the United States after the action, Wilson served in Washington for the remainder of the war. He later was aide-de-camp to Lt. Gen. Watson commanding Fleet Marine Force (q.v.), Pacific. After returning to the States in 1949, he became officer in charge of New York's recruiting station before beginning a three-year tour at Quantico (q.v.) in November 1951. In September 1954 he was assigned to the 1st Division in Korea and in August 1955 took command of a battalion of the 5th Marines. In 1958 he was again assigned to Quantico, where as a colonel he commanded the Basic School, and in July 1962 he was posted to Washington as a member of the Plans and Programs section of Marine Headquarters.

During the 1960s Wilson attended the National War College, served a tour with the 1st Marine Division during the Vietnam War (q.v.), and was promoted to major general. Before becoming commandant on 1 July 1975, he served as commander, Fleet Marine Force, Pacific. As commandant, he presided over the 200th-year celebrations of the corps. His major problem was to maintain the level of the corps at its authorized size of 190,000 men. Negative reactions to the Vietnam conflict limited recruitment, and General Wilson even recommended reinstatement of the draft. This problem was not solved even during the tenure of his successor, Gen. Robert Barrow (q.v.), who took command of the corps on 1 July 1979.

WOMEN MARINES. The corps was the last branch of the services to organize a women's force during World War II (q.v.). The commandant, Gen. Thomas Holcomb (q.v.), under pressure from his superiors reluctantly agreed to the establishment of a Women's Reserve. The plan was approved in November 1942, and enlistments began early the following year. Total strength was to be 1,000 officers and 18,000 enlisted women under the command of Maj. Ruth Streeter (q.v.). Initially training for officer candidates was at Mount Holyoke College in South Hadley, Massachusetts, and enlisted recruits at Hunter College, New York City. Very soon training for both shifted to Camp Lejeune (q.v.). Most became clerks and stenographers. Within a year 85 percent of enlisted personnel at headquarters in Washington were women marines. By the end of the war, the goals of the planners had almost been reached, with over 17,000 enlisted personnel, some serving as far west as Hawaii. The plan to discharge all women marines after the war was modified to keep a small cadre on active duty. In June 1948 the secretary of the navy ordered the integration of women into the regular corps.

WORLD WAR I. While the Marine Corps was involved in the various police actions around the world, the First World War, which began in August 1914 involving all but a few of the nations of Europe, ground on in stalemate on all fronts. The United States, ostensibly neutral, had from the start been pro-

British and anti-German. Allied propaganda had firmly fixed in the minds of most Americans the specter of the Hun, the Boche, the rapists of Belgium. The appearance of the submarine, a new weapon, gave the Germans hope of breaking the British blockade, but its use also worked against the Germans. Submarines attacked merchant vessels, and with the increasing U.S. trade with Britain, this strategy meant the loss of American property and lives. After the tragedy of the *Lusitania*, Pres. Woodrow Wilson negotiated a halt to unrestricted submarine warfare. This agreement lasted almost a year but when the Germans resumed their attacks, Wilson believed, despite his election promise, that the United States had no choice but to enter the war on the side of the Allies, a decision that meant that the war-weary Allies would eventually win the war. On 6 April 1917 Congress concurred and declared war on Germany.

Long before this point, the administration had moved to improve the military. The National Defense Act of 1916 was an important step in preparing the armed forces for the coming conflict. It authorized the expansion of the corps from 10,000 to 15,500 men. Within a month of the declaration of war, volunteer enlistment brought this number to 31,000. As with the army, there had been no long-range planning for the utilization of the Marine Corps in the European war beyond the traditional roles of shipboard duty and defense of bases. However, the commandant argued successfully that the corps should be a part of the American Expeditionary Force (AEF), and President Wilson authorized the deployment of a regiment to France in May. The 5th Regiment sailed in early June and on arrival was ordered to guard duty at Saint-Nazaire. Another regiment, the 6th, was formed, as was a machine gun battalion. Early in 1918 these units were joined into the 4th Brigade. Despite the suspicions of Gen. John Pershing and the army high command, it joined with the army's 3d Brigade to make up the 2d Division, commanded by Gen. James Harbord. In May 1918 the brigade was sent into the lines with French units for seasoning. The first major action came at Belleau Wood (q.v.).

The Germans, freed from maintaining a huge force on the Russian front, shifted those divisions to the west and in May 1918 launched an all-out offensive designed to restore movement and finally win the war. In the front area near Chemins des Dames, 30 German divisions aimed at the heights along the Aisne River. They drove 30 miles through the French army, captured Soissons, and reached the Marne River and Chateau-Thierry. Moving up, the 2d Division took a blocking position in front of a rocky, wooded area called Belleau Wood located west of Chateau-Thierry. At first only a few Germans were in the woods, but as the battle progressed several divisions became involved. The Germans attacked the 2d Division positions for three days without breaking the line. They then took up defensive positions inside the woods. On 6 June the 2d Division, with the 4th Brigade leading, attacked across a wheat field and into the woods, thus beginning a 20-day battle to take the area. By the close of the action, the woods were cleared and several German divisions had been mauled. The brigade suffered 55 percent casualties, the most costly action of any American brigade during the war. The action at Belleau Wood was instrumental in halting the German drive on Paris. The Germans who had earlier downgraded American troops gave the name "devil dogs" to the marines who fought there. The French, too, recognized the valor of the marines by renaming the woods "Bois de la Brigade de Marine."

The Germans were not yet ready to give up the offensive, and on 15 July they began the last great offensive of the war, with 52 divisions in the attack. The 2d Division was moved up to Forêt de Retz and prepared to join with the French XX Corps in the counterattack against the German advances near Soissons. Three days later after a very heavy artillery bombardment, the marines attacked and within a short time had overrun the enemy's-front line positions. Before they were relieved two days later, they had almost reached their final objective, the Soissons–Chateau-Thierry road, after suffering 2,000 casualties. The division was removed to a rest area near Nancy. While there General Harbord was appointed chief of the AEF's Services and Supply, and the marine brigade's commander, Brig. Gen. John Lejeune (q.v.), moved up to command the 2d Division. The next action for the marines took place on 12 September aiding the army's 3d Brigade in pinching off the Saint-Mihiel (q.v.) salient. Attacking in the mud and rain, the marine brigade passed through the army's lines on the 13th and within two days had achieved its objectives. Compared with previous actions, the battle at Saint-Mihiel was slight, although it cost over 700 casualties.

General Ludendorf's gamble had failed; the German offensive had been halted and the Allies had begun to advance on all fronts. The American 1st Army on the right of the allied line faced the strongly entrenched enemy in the Hindenburg Line. Adjacent to most of the U.S. troops was the French Fourth Army, and the 2d Division was attached to it for the Meuse-

Argonne (q.v.) offensive. French forces had been halted by the end of September in the Champagne sector whose key defensive position was Blanc Mont. The 2d Division was assigned the task of capturing this position held by the Germans since 1914. On 2 October the marine brigade launched a frontal attack, while the 3d Infantry struck at the right flank and the French moved to drive the Germans from a salient called the Essen Hook. By noon the 6th Marines had secured Blanc Mont; the French drive, however, was stalled. The 5th Marines passing through their lines turned left and drove the Germans from the hook. The marines continued the attack and, despite German counterattacks, secured Saint-Etienne three miles from the original point of attack on the 6th. The 2d Division was then withdrawn and reassigned to the U.S. V Corps. The action had cost the brigade over 2,500 casualties. Their heroism was recognized by the French who awarded the two regiments the *Croix de Guerre* streamer for their colors and allowed members to wear the red and green *fourragère*.

The 2d Division was deployed on a narrow front in the center of the 1st Army line for what became the final offensive of the war. Confronting it was a veteran German division supported by two others in reserve. On 1 November after a very heavy artillery concentration, the division advanced in a column of battalions and shortly had broken the German defenses; by the close of the day they had advanced more than six miles. The Germans then pulled back across the Meuse. Although their front was collapsing everywhere else, the Germans maintained a stubborn defense against the Americans in the Argonne sector. On 10 November the 5th Marines crossed the Meuse at night and was still attacking when the Armistice was announced. At the 11th hour of the 11th day of the 11th month, the war that in Wilson's terms was to make the world safe for democracy came to a quiet end. The French and German armies had each suffered 1.7 million dead, while the British Empire had lost almost one million men. American casualties also were very high considering the brief time of engagement. Over 32,000 marines had served in France; of these, 2,459 were killed in action and 8,900 were wounded.

The brigade had won universal respect even from army commanders who at first viewed the marines with suspicion. In all, members of the corps won 12 Medals of Honor (q.v.), 34 Distinguished Service Medals, and 393 Navy Crosses (q.v.). After the war the brigade was posted to Coblenz for occupation duty in the Rhineland until the fall of 1919. It was returned to the United States and after a march past the White House in August was disbanded soon after at Quantico. By 1920 the size of the corps had been reduced to 17,000 men.

The war had seen the rapid expansion not only of the ground units but also of the aviation force. The first marine qualified as a pilot in 1911, and soon after the corps authorized the creation of an Aviation Detachment sited at Pensacola. However, there were only 6 officers and 44 enlisted men in the detachment operating only four aircraft when the United States declared war on Germany. By October the service had expanded to the point where it was divided into two parts: the 1st Marine Aviation Squadron (land planes) and the 1st Marine Aeronautic Company (sea planes). The latter was posted in January 1918 to the Azores where flying Curtiss R-6 planes, they fruitlessly searched for German submarines. The Aviation Squadron was reassigned to Curtiss Field in Miami, expanded, and redesignated the 1st Aviation Force. It was composed of four squadrons. The size of the air services quickly expanded to 2,480 men and by the close of the war to 340 planes. Three of the squadrons were ordered to France, arriving at the end of July 1918. While waiting for the American-made De Havilland-4s (DH-4), the pilots were assigned to two RAF bombing and one fighter squadrons. Either as attached members of the RAF or flying their own planes, the Aviation Force participated in the final actions of the war where the pilots took part in 57 bombing missions and shot down 12 German planes. (See also Belleau Wood, Chateau-Thierry, Meuse-Argonne, and Soissons.)

WORLD WAR II. In September 1939 the Germans invaded Poland and within a year had conquered most of western Europe, and Britain was fighting a losing battle to keep the Atlantic sea lanes open. Just emerging from isolationism, the United States committed the navy to assist although still officially neutral. One base considered necessary to win the battle of the Atlantic was Iceland (q.v.). Prime Minister Winston Churchill convinced Pres. Franklin Roosevelt to send U.S. troops there to relieve the 25,000-man British force. Thus, in June 1941 the 6th Marine Regiment was posted to Reykjavik. Relieved by army units, the last marine battalion left Iceland in March 1942. Marine activity in the European theater during the remainder of the war remained minimal; the main focus for the corps was the Pacific.

The entry of the United States into the war was a result of

the Japanese attack on Pearl Harbor (q.v.) on 7 December 1941, climaxing a year of tensions between the two countries. The attack was preliminary to Japanese expansion throughout Southeast Asia and the South Pacific. Most of the U.S. capital ships were either sunk or damaged. The two carriers that escaped were the only offensive threat to Japan in the following months. The attack had also caught the Marine Defense Battalion unaware, and almost all the planes at Ewa airfield were destroyed. The first six months of the war witnessed a series of Japanese victories as its armies conquered Malaya, Singapore, Burma, the East Indies, and the Philippines and pushed to within striking distance of Australia. The allied response was generally ineffective, and the Japanese navy and air forces were dominant in all areas. Small-sized marine units were involved from the beginning in this disastrous phase of the war. The 4th Marines, helping to defend Corregidor in the Philippines, were forced to surrender in May 1942. Earlier the Japanese had occupied Guam (q.v.), forcing the surrender of the small naval and marine garrison there. Sustaining heavy losses from the marine garrison, the Japanese nevertheless occupied Wake Island (q.v.) on 23 December. By early spring of 1942 the Japanese had succeeded far beyond what they believed possible.

The Japanese juggernaut was soon dealt stunning blows by twin naval engagements. The Coral Sea battle in May 1942 resulted in a strategic American victory and probably saved the Allied base of Port Moresby, New Guinea. The following month the Japanese launched their long-awaited attack on Midway (q.v.) Island. The island was defended by a marine defense battalion, and the marines had a few outdated fighters. In the opening phase of the attack most of these planes were destroyed. However, with great skill and considerable good fortune, the navy intercepted and sank four Japanese aircraft carriers. Japan never recovered from these losses.

During the early phases of the war, Japanese forces had leisurely taken possession of New Britain (q.v.) and the Solomon Islands (q.v.). Their decision to build an airfield on Guadalcanal (q.v.) resulted in the greatest encounter battle of the Pacific war. Fearing that the Japanese from this base could threaten the vital shipping lanes to New Zealand, the navy decided to seize the island by committing the only available force, the 1st Marine Division, in August. Once the marines had landed, the Japanese reacted by committing their navy, air force, and ultimately a large portion of their available land force to its recapture. From August to December the 1st Division held off numerous attacks by superior numbers. Marine pilots took a deadly toll of the enemy, and the embattled outnumbered naval units forced a draw in repeated battles. Reinforced by the 2d Division and army units, the island was finally secured in early February 1943. The course of the war in the South Pacific turned on the Guadalcanal battles. Taken together with the defensive victories in Gen. Douglas MacArthur's Southwest Pacific theater, it marked the end of Japan dictating the pace of the war.

The Allied offensives began in mid-1943 and followed two different courses. In the southwest Pacific the Allied advance was up the 1,000-mile north coast of New Guinea and ultimately the invasion of the Philippines in late 1944. Marine Corps major units were utilized only once in MacArthur's offensive. The first was at Cape Gloucester (q.v.) on New Britain, where in January 1944 the 1st Division secured the flank of the army's advance across the straits in New Guinea. The second line of advance was first in the South Pacific where marine ground and air secured the central and northern Solomons. The invasion of Bougainville (q.v.) by the 3d Division in November 1943 helped to negate Japan's major southern base of Rabaul. At the same time Adm. Chester Nimitz used the marines in conjunction with his increasingly powerful navy to carry out the general outlines of the prewar Orange Plan. This called for an advance westward into the Gilbert (q.v.), Marshall (q.v.), and Mariana Islands (q.v.), seizing bases and forcing the Japanese navy into a showdown battle.

The first breaching of Japan's outer defense ring in the Central Pacific was the capture of Betio Island in the Tarawa (q.v.) atoll in November 1943. The 2d Division in a bloody 72-hour engagement took the small, heavily fortified island at the same time an army unit seized Makin atoll. The next step in Admiral Nimitz's plan was to capture forward air and naval bases in the Marshall Islands. By the end of 1943 his great blue-water fleet had wrested naval superiority from the Japanese, and thus the landings at Kwajalein (q.v.) atoll in January 1944 were made with little fear of Japanese naval forces. The V Amphibious Corps, composed of the 4th Division and the army's 7th Division, had little trouble taking the islands of Roi-Namur (q.v.) and Kwajalein. Emboldened by the Kwajalein success, Admiral Nimitz moved up the next offensive to 18 February. A regiment of the 4th Division landed on Engebi Island and later Parry Island in the Eniwetok (q.v.) atoll, while an army regiment assaulted Eniwetok Island. After short, heavy fighting, all three islands were secured. The excellent harbors at Kwajalein and Eniwetok became major marshaling points for further U.S. advances into the Mariana Islands. At the same time as the Eniwetok invasion, the massive U.S. 5th Fleet struck the major Japanese Central Pacific bastion of Truk and rendered it all but useless.

Still following the outlines of the Orange Plan, Admiral Nimitz planned to capture three major islands in the Marianas to provide bases for the B-29 bombers. By this time all Japanese garrisons had been almost completely isolated by U.S. submarine attacks on Japanese ships. The key island was Saipan (q.v.) located only 1,500 miles from Tokyo. On 15 June the 2d and 4th Divisions were landed on the western beaches and after sustaining heavy casualties, supported by the army's 27th Division, drove across the island. Turning northward, the U.S. forces pushed the Japanese back to the northern part of the island by 9 July. Practically the entirety of the Japanese garrison, approximately 30,000 men, was destroyed. The marine casualties amounted to almost 13,000. Of equal importance to the land action was the naval battle of the Philippine Sea. Recognizing that if Saipan was lost, Japanese cities would soon become targets, the long-quiescent Japanese navy challenged the 5th Fleet with disastrous results. Japan lost the bulk of its naval air force in this battle, which came to be known as the Marianas Turkey Shoot. Soon after Saipan was secured, the 2d and 4th Divisions invaded neighboring Tinian (q.v.) and within less than two weeks controlled the entire island. On 21 July the long-delayed liberation of Guam (q.v.) was begun. The 3d Division and 1st Brigade supported by the army's 77th Division landed on the eastern beaches. Despite fanatical Japanese resistance, the island was secured by 10 August. Ultimately three bomber fields were constructed on Guam, two on Saipan, and one on Tinian. By January 1945 the B-29s from these islands began their devastating raids on Japan proper.

Further to the west General MacArthur's forces landed on Leyte in October. This brought the remnants of the Japanese fleet out in a desperate attempt to counter the landings. In a series of confrontations in Leyte Gulf and off Samar, the U.S. 3d and 7th Fleets destroyed the remaining Japanese fleet elements. From this point onward the Japanese were reduced to kamikaze suicide attacks. Ostensibly to protect the eastern flank of the Leyte operation, Admiral Nimitz's headquarters planned to seize two small islands in the Palau group. The army's 81st Division landed on Angaur two days after the 1st Division assaulted the main objective, Peleliu (q.v.), on 15 September. Japanese resistance on Peleliu was logical and efficient. Within five days the division had suffered almost 50 percent casualties. What was believed to be a quick and easy operation became a campaign of attrition. The marines had secured nine-tenths of the island before turning over the final campaign to the army. Organized resistance ceased only on 27 November.

The two prongs of the Allied offensives, those of the southwest Pacific and the Central Pacific, converged in early 1945. The various army units had invaded Luzon Island defended by one-third million Japanese in January 1945. Heavy fighting continued there in the mountains until the war's end. However, long before this point the Philippines had become a major base for the final assault, if needed, on Japan. The most pressing problem for the Central Pacific command early in 1945 was to provide for emergency landings of B-29s damaged in their bombing runs over Japan. This concern, combined with the need for airfields closer to Japan to enable fighter aircraft to accompany the big bombers, led Nimitz's headquarters to target Iwo Jima (q.v.), a small lamb-chop-shaped island, for the marines' next action.

Iwo Jima was only five miles long and two and one-half miles wide. Much of the island was black volcanic sand. The highest point in the southwest was Mount Suribachi (q.v.), slightly over 500 feet high. The Japanese garrison was over 23,000, men and the commander had seven defense lines anchored by 650 blockhouses. Capture of this island was the most costly action of the entire war for the marines. V Amphibious Corps composed of the 4th and 5th Divisions in the assault stormed ashore on 19 February. Pinned down on the beach, the marine casualties were very heavy, but by nightfall they were firmly ashore. On the second day marines on the extreme left began the assault on Suribachi. The crest was reached on the 23d and the second flag raising was captured on film and became the most famous symbol of marine actions during the Pacific war. Meanwhile, the heaviest fighting was occurring on the flat land in the center and right of the line. Two regiments of the 3d Division were landed and assumed the center position in the slow, murderous advance. The loss of key hills on 7 March broke the concerted Japanese resistance, and they were reduced to individual defense of isolated positions. The final well-defended position at Pitano Point was taken on 26 March, the same day the island was declared secure. Bloody Iwo had cost the corps over 26,000 casualties in the worst sustained fighting in its history.

Even before Iwo, MacArthur's and Nimitz's staffs had been working on the plans for the invasion of Japan. The end of the war in Europe in May allowed the transfer of army and air force units to the Pacific. Elements of the 8th Air Force and 1st Army had already begun to arrive. The plan for the invasion called for four armies to attack first southern Kyushu in November and then Honshu in the spring of 1946. For this massive set of operations a forward base was needed for staging. The base chosen was the heavily populated island of Okinawa (q.v.), 60 miles long and 14 miles wide, located only 850 miles from Tokyo. The Japanese commander had more than 60,000 regular army troops, a large naval contingent, and many Okinawan units, in all more than 100,000 men. The Okinawa campaign, although three marine divisions participated, was primarily an army affair. The corps contributed 81,000 of the total of 182,000 men of X Army. The army, divided into two corps, landed on the western beaches north of the main city of Naha on Easter Sunday, 1 April 1945.

The landings were generally unopposed, and the marine divisions quickly moved across the island and then cleared the northern part of the island while the army units captured the airfields and then moved south against the main Japanese defenses. The Okinawa campaign was a land battle, and the enemy defenses were as formidable as any encountered in Europe. Thus, the 1st and 6th Divisions were used in the same way as the army units in a slow, at times frustrating, advance southward against the three main Japanese defense lines. The main defense line, the Naha-Shuri line, was not breached until late May. Elements of the 1st Division captured Shuri Castle on 29 May. Torrential rains slowed the advance even further, but the Japanese, greatly reduced in number, fell back to their last defensive positions. One of these key positions, Kanishi Ridge, fell to the 1st Division on 15 June. On 18 June the X Army commander, Gen. Simon Buckner, was killed, and marine Lt. Gen. Roy Geiger (q.v.) briefly assumed command, the only marine ever to command an Army. Three days later the island was declared secure. Total U.S. losses were 12,520 killed, of which 2,938 were marines. The navy had given unqualified support and had also suffered greatly from the kamikaze suicide bombers. The Japanese sank 36 ships and damaged 368, and the navy's killed in action in the six-week engagement surpassed losses sustained by either army or marine units.

Marine air squadrons were active in all Central Pacific campaigns, generally in tactical support roles. After the Solomons actions, marine fighter squadrons also assumed the primary function of close support. However, the corps developed specialized units such as the night fighter squadron, which was based on Peleliu and later shifted to Leyte. By mid-1944 there were five wings composed of 28 groups containing 112,000 men, of whom 10,500 were pilots. Although the complex Philippine operation was primarily an army operation, marine squadrons played an important tactical role. By the close of December 1944, five squadrons were operating from Tacloban. To support the Luzon operation, an additional two air groups were deployed. Marine dive bombers and fighters continued operations on Luzon and later were involved when the 8th Army invaded the southern islands. In early 1945 Admiral Nimitz agreed that marine aircraft should operate from carriers. Flying the improved Corsair (q.v.), marine pilots at first were posted only to light carriers, but just before Okinawa they were assigned to four fleet carriers and took part in the defensive air battles against the kamikazes. Marine fighters and dive bombers began operating from Kadena airfield on Okinawa soon after its capture. By the close of the campaign, 22 marine squadrons were sited on Okinawa.

In the waning months of the war, all military units prepared for Operations Coronet and Olympic, the invasion and occupation of the Japanese home islands. Coronet, the assault upon Kyushu, was scheduled for November 1945, and III and V Amphibious Corps as part of the 6th Army were to be among the first to land and form the right wing of the force. The dropping of the two atom bombs on Hiroshima and Nagasaki made this potentially costly venture unnecessary. On 10 August Emperor Hirohito announced acceptance of the Potsdam Declaration, and on 2 September the formal surrender on board the *Missouri* brought the war officially to an end. The war had added even more luster to the Marine Corps' already distinguished record, but it had been costly. Casualties amounted to 86,940 killed and wounded. (See also Bougainville, Cape Gloucester, Choiseul, Eniwetok, Guadalcanal, Guam, Iwo Jima, Mariana Islands, Marshall Islands, Midway, New Britain, New Georgia, Okinawa, Pearl Harbor, Peleliu, Roi-Namur, Saipan, Tarawa, Tinian, and Wake Islands.)

Z

ZEILIN, JACOB. 7th commandant, b. Philadelphia, Pa., 16 July 1806, d. Washington, D.C., 18 Nov. 1880. Zeilin was appointed a second lieutenant on 1 October 1831. In the years before the Mexican War (q.v.), he served primarily on board such naval vessels as the *Erie, Columbus,* and *Congress.* During the Mexican War, as a lieutenant, he commanded the marine detachment on board the frigate *Congress,* and when the war began he was on the west coast. He led his marines in capturing San Pedro and was recruited by Kit Carson to lead a relief column to reinforce Gen. Philip Kearny besieged by Californians near San Bernardino in December 1846. On 10 November 1847 as a captain, Zeilin led a force of marines supported by sailors to land at Mazatlan and remained as military governor there until June of the following year. In 1853, now a major, he commanded the 200-man marine contingent in Commodore Perry's visit to Japan and China.

At the beginning of the Civil War (q.v.), Zeilin commanded a company at the Battle of Bull Run (1st Manassas), defending two batteries of guns on Henry Hill. Forced to retreat when Union forces broke, Zeilin was very seriously wounded in the engagement. In August 1863 he led a detachment of 300 marines to reinforce marine and army units attempting to take Charleston. He became seriously ill before the abortive attack on Fort Sumter (q.v.) in September. Later he became commanding officer of Marine Barracks at Portsmouth, New Hampshire. Although others were senior, the secretary of the navy on 9 June 1864 appointed him the seventh commandant and promoted him to the rank of colonel. During his 12-year tenure, the marines were involved in landings in China, Formosa, Korea, Japan, Nicaragua (q.v.), Uruguay, Mexico, Panama (q.v.), and Hawaii. Also during this time the corps survived an attempt by the House of Representatives to abolish it.

Bibliography

For serious researchers, the best sources for Marine Corps history are the archives located in the Washington, D.C., area. The Marine Corps History and Museum Branch sited at the Washington Navy Yard has an extensive library of books and journals related to the corps. If the director is notified as to the subject being pursued, he can order a great amount of primary documents from the storehouse in Virginia. These include after-action reports from division to company size units, radio messages, correspondence, and other original documents. Located also at the Navy Yard is the U.S. Naval Historical Center. Serious researchers are also welcomed, although the rules for using materials there are more strict than at the marine archives. Both the marine and naval centers have extensive oral histories. The Marine Oral History Division has dozens of long detailed conversations with senior officers. Most of those interviewed had served in high command capacities during World War II. The reference section of the marine archives also has detailed biographies of each commandant of the corps.

Another major source of information is the National Archives. Some materials are located in the main archive building in Washington, D.C., the most important being the thousands of photographs that were transferred from the corps' own photo archive at Anacostia. Most documents, however, are located at the Modern Military Records Branch in Suitland, Maryland. The archives are open not only to academic researchers and writers but to the general public.

The staff at the History and Museum Branch includes a number of very competent historians. Some of these are civilians, but many are career officers. Their main task over the past 50 years has been to survey the mass of documentary material related to each conflict involving marines and to produce official accounts of the campaigns. These have been uniformly well done and provide very readable and accurate accounts of the specific action. These are uncritical histories. The writer's main purpose was to tell what happened and not to critique the campaign or the decisions made at the time by individual commanders. For a critical view, one must go beyond the official histories to other books or articles written by writers not directly connected with the military. Nevertheless, the official histories are the keys for readers to understand what the corps did in a particular campaign. They are also the starting point for any serious researcher.

The following list has first a general section that includes books and articles that apply to all periods of Marine Corps history. Following this the bibliography is organized into two main sections, one for official and the second for unofficial histories. Each of these is further divided into five parts: Pre–World War II, World War II, Korea to Vietnam, Vietnam, and finally post-Vietnam.

General Works

Aldrich, M. Almey. *History of the United States Marine Corps*. Boston: Shepherd, 1875.

Angelucci, Enzo (ed.). *The Rand McNally Encyclopedia of Military Aircraft, 1914–1980*. New York: Military Press, 1983.

Bailey, Thomas. *A Diplomatic History of the American People*. New York: Appleton-Century-Crofts, 1950.

Costello, John. *The Pacific War*. New York: Rawson, 1981.

Donovan, James A. Jr. *The United States Marine Corps*. New York: Praeger, 1967.

Dyer, George C. *The Amphibians Came to Conquer: The Story of Admiral Richmond Kelley Turner*. Washington, D.C.: Government Printing Office, 1972.

Gailey, Harry A. *The War in the Pacific: From Pearl Harbor to Tokyo Bay*. Novato,Calif.: Presidio, 1995.

Gayle, Gordon. "Commandants of the Corps." *Marine Corps Gazette*, November 1950.

Heinl, Robert D. *Soldiers of the Sea: The United States Marine Corps, 1775–1962*. Annapolis, Md.: Naval Institute Press, 1962.

Krulak, Victor H. *First to Fight: An Inside View of the U.S. Marine Corps*. Annapolis, Md.: Naval Institute Press, 1984.

Larrabee, Eric. *Commander in Chief*. New York: Harper & Row, 1987.

Macksey, Kenneth, and John Batchelor. *Tank: A History of the Armored Fighting Vehicle*. New York: Scribners, 1970.

McMillan, George. *The Old Breed*. Washington, D.C.: Infantry Journal Press, 1949.

Manchester, William. *American Caesar*. New York: Dell, 1978.

Megee, Vernon E. "The Evolution of Marine Aviation." *Marine Corps Gazette*, October 1965.

Mersky, Peter B. *U.S. Marine Corps Aviation, 1912 to the Present.* Baltimore, Md.: Nautical and Aviation Publishing, 1983.

Metcalf, Clyde H. *A History of the United States Marine Corps.* New York: Putnam's, 1939.

———, ed. *The Marine Corps Reader.* New York: Putnam's, 1944.

Millett, Allan R. *Semper Fidelis: The History of the U.S. Marines.* New York: Macmillan, 1980.

Montross, Lynn. *Cavalry in the Sky.* New York: Harpers, 1954.

Moran, Jim. "Marine Camouflage Uniforms, 1942–45." 2 parts. *Military Illustrated Past and Present,* January and February 1991.

Moskin, J. Robert. *The U.S. Marine Corps Story.* New York: McGraw-Hill, 1982.

Murphy, Jack. *History of the U.S. Marines.* Greenwich, Conn.: Bison, 1984.

Perkins, Dexter. *The United States and the Caribbean.* Cambridge, Mass.: Harvard University Press, 1947.

Potter, Elmer B., and Chester Nimitz. *Triumph in the Pacific.* Upper Saddle River, N.J.: Prentice Hall, 1963.

Reber, John J. "The Fleet and the Marines." *Naval Institute Proceedings,* November 1982.

Schuon, Karl. *U.S. Marine Corps Biographical Dictionary.* New York: Watts, 1963.

Simmons, Edwin H. *The United States Marines.* New York: Viking, 1976.

Spector, Ronald H. *Eagle against the Sun: The American War with Japan.* New York: Free Press, 1985.

Thomas, Lowell. *Old Gimlet Eye: The Adventures of Smedley D. Butler.* New York: Farrar & Rinehart, 1933.

U.S. Military Academy, History Department. *Campaign Atlas to the Great War.* West Point, N.Y.: U.S. Military Academy, 1980.

———. *Campaign Atlas to the Second World War: Asia and the Pacific.* West Point, N.Y.: U.S. Military Academy, 1981.

Vandegrift, Alexander A., as told to Robert Asprey. *Once a Marine.* New York: Norton, 1959.

Weigley, Russell F. *The American Way of War.* Bloomington: University of Indiana Press, 1973.

Who Was Who in American History—The Military. Chicago: Marquis Who's Who, 1975.

Official Histories: Marine Corps Publications (Washington, D.C.: Historical Division)

Pre–World War II

Clifford, Kenneth. *Progress and Purpose: A Developmental History of the U.S. Marine Corps.* 1973.

Fuller, Stephen M., and Graham Cosmas. *Marines in the Dominican Republic.* 1974.

McClellan, Edwin N. *The United States Marine Corps in the World War.* 1968.

Nalty, Bernard C. *The United States Marines in Nicaragua.* Photocopy. 1961.

———. *The United States Marines in the Civil War.* 1958.

———. *The United States Marines in the War with Spain.* Mimeograph. 1959.

Santelli, James S. *A Brief History of the 4th Marines.* 1970.

———. *A Brief History of the 7th Marines.* 1980.

———. *A Brief History of the 8th Marines.* 1976.

Smith, Charles R. *Marines in the Revolution.* 1975.

World War II: Standard Histories

Bartley, Whitman. *Iwo Jima: Amphibious Epic.* 1954.

Chapin, John C. *History of the Fifth Marine Division in World War II.* 1945.

Frank, Benis M., and Henry Shaw. *History of U.S. Marine Corps Operations in World War II. Vol. V: Victory and Occupation.* 1968.

Garand, George W., and Truman R. Strobridge. *History of U.S. Marine Corps Operations in World War II. Vol. IV: Western Pacific Operations.* 1971.

Heinl, Robert D. *The Defense of Wake.* 1947.

Hoffman, Carl. *Saipan: The Beginning of the End.* 1950

———. *The Seizure of Tinian.* 1951.

Hough, Frank. *The Assault on Peleliu.* 1950.

———. *The Campaign on New Britain.* 1952.

Ludwig, Verle E., and Henry Shaw. *History of U.S. Marine Corps Operations in World War II. Vol. I: Pearl Harbor to Guadalcanal.* 1958.

Lodge, Orlan R. *The Recapture of Guam.* 1954.

McCahill, William P. *The Marine Corps Reserve: A History.* 1966.

Nichols, Charles S., and Henry Shaw. *Okinawa: Victory in the Pacific.* 1955.

Shaw, Henry, and Douglas Kane. *History of U.S. Marine Corps Operations in World War II. Vol. II: Isolation of Rabaul.* 1963.

Shaw, Henry, Bernard Nalty, and Edwin Turnbladh. *History of U.S. Marine Corps Operations in World War II. Vol. III: Central Pacific Drive.* 1966.

Stremlow, Mary V. *A History of Women Marines, 1946–1977.* 1986.

World War II: Commemorative Series (1992)

Alexander, Joseph H. *Across the Reef: The Marine Assault on Tarawa.*
————. *Closing In: Marines in the Seizure of Iwo Jima.*
Chapin, John C. *Breaching the Marianas: The Battle for Saipan.*
————. *Breaching the Outer Ring: Marine Landings in the Marshall Islands.*
Cressman, Robert J. *A Magnificent Fight: Marines in the Battle for Wake Island.*
Cressman, Robert J., and J. Michael Wenger. *Infamous Day: Marines at Pearl Harbor, 7 December 1941.*
Donovan, James A. *Outpost in the North Atlantic: Marines in the Defense of Iceland.*
Edwards, Harry W. *A Different War: Marines in Europe and North Africa.*
Harwood, Richard. *A Close Encounter: The Marine Landing on Tinian.*
Hoffman, John. *From Makin to Bougainville: Marine Raiders in the Pacific War.*
Melson, Charles D. *Up the Slot: Marines in the Central Solomons.*
Mersky, Peter B. *Time of Aces: Marine Pilots in the Solomons, 1942–1944.*
Nalty, Bernard C. *Cape Gloucester: The Green Inferno.*
————. *The Right to Fight: African-American Marines in World War II.*
O'Brien, Cyril J. *Liberation: Marines in the Recapture of Guam.*
Shaw, Henry. *First Offensive: The Marine Campaign for Guadalcanal.*
Stremlow, Mary V. *Free a Marine to Fight: Women Marines in World War II.*

Korea to Vietnam

Heinl, Robert D. *Victory at High Tide: The Inchon-Seoul Campaign.* 1968.
Montross, Lynn, and Nicholas Canzona. *U.S. Marine Operations in Korea, 1950–53.* 1957.
Rawlings, E. W. *Marines and Helicopters, 1946–1962.* 1976.
Shaw, Henry, and R. Donnelly. *Blacks in the Military.* 1975.
Shulimson, Jack. *Marines in Lebanon, 1958.* Washington: 1966.

Vietnam

Cosmas, Graham, and Terence Murray. *U.S. Marines in Vietnam: Vietnamization and Redeployment.* 1986.
Fails, William R. *Marines and Helicopters, 1962–1973.* 1978.

Shore, Moyers S. *The Battle for Khe Sanh.* 1969.
Shulimson, Jack, and Charles Johnson. *The Landing and the Buildup, 1965.* 1978.
———. *U.S. Marines in Vietnam: An Expanding War, 1966.* 1982.
West, Francis J. *Small Unit Actions in Vietnam, Summer 1966.* 1977.
Whitlow, Robert H. *U.S. Marines in Vietnam: The Advisory and Combat Assistance Era, 1954–1964.* Washington: 1977.

Post-Vietnam

Frank, Benis M. *U.S. Marines in Lebanon, 1982–1984.* 1987.
Quilter, Charles J. III. *U.S. Marines in the Persian Gulf, 1990–1991.* 1993.
Spector, Ronald H. *U.S. Marines in Grenada, 1983.* 1987.

Nonofficial Publications

Pre–World War II

Alexander, J. H. "Roots of Deployment—Vera Cruz, 1914." *Marine Corps Gazette* [hereafter referred to as *MCG*], November 1982.
Altoff, Gerard T. "War of 1812: Leathernecks on Lake Erie." *Leatherneck,* November 1988.
Arthur, Billy. "Camp Lejeune—The Early Days." *Leatherneck,* November 1982.
Aruilina, Robert V. "Over There: The Marine Experience in World War I." *Fortitudine,* Spring 1988.
Asprey, Robert B. *At Belleau Wood.* New York: Putnam's, 1965.
———. "Waller of Samar." *MCG,* May and June 1961.
Ballendorf, Dirk A., and Merrill Bartlett. *Earl H. "Pete" Ellis: The Life and Times of an Amphibious Warfare Prophet, 1880–1923.* Annapolis: U.S. Naval Institute, 1996.
Bartlett, Tom. "The Banana War Marine." *Leatherneck,* September 1984.
Boyce, Jim. "Combat Patrol: Nicaragua." *Leatherneck,* October 1982.
Denig, Robert L. "Native Officer Corps, *Guardia Nacional de Nicaragua.*" *MCG,* November 1932.
Donnelly, Ralph W. "Officer Selection in the Old Corps." *MCG,* November 1982.
Edson, M. A. "The Coca Patrol." *MCG,* August and November 1906 and February 1907.

Gibbons, Floyd. *And They Thought We Wouldn't Fight*. New York: Doran, 1918.

Gordon, John W. "General Thomas Holcomb and the Golden Age of Amphibious Warfare." *Delaware History*, Fall/Winter 1985.

Hammond, James W. "Lejeune of the Naval Service." *Naval Institute Proceedings* [hereafter referred to as *Proceedings*], November 1981.

Holmes, Maurice G. "With the Horse Marines in Nicaragua." *MCG*, February 1984.

Johnson, Lucius W. "Guam Before December 1941." *Proceedings*, vol. 72, March 1946.

Lejeune, John A. *Reminiscences of a Marine*. Philadelphia: Dorrance, 1930.

Liddell Hart, Basil H. *The Real War, 1914–1918*. Boston: Atlantic Monthly Press, 1930.

Livesey, Anthony. *The Historical Atlas of World War I*. New York: Holt, 1994.

McClellan, E. N. "The Battle of Blanc Mont Ridge." *MCG*, March 1922.

———. "The Capture of New Orleans." *MCG*, December 1920.

Meader, Equen B. "Birth of the Amphibian: Navy-Marine Operations in the Mexican Gulf, 1846–1848." *Shipmate*, November 1981.

———. "A Marine in California: Archibald Gillespie in the Mexican War, West." *Shipmate*, November 1982.

Meyers, John T. "Military Operations & Defenses of the Siege of Peking." *Proceedings*, September 1902.

Miller, J. G. "William Freeland Fullam's War with the Corps." *Proceedings*, November 1975.

Millett, Allan R. *The Politics of Intervention, The Military Occupation of Cuba, 1906–1909*. Columbus: Ohio University Press, 1968.

Moore, Richard S. "Ideas and Direction: Building Amphibious Doctrine." *MCG*, November 1982.

Musicant, Ivan. *The Banana Wars: A History of United States Military Intervention in Latin America from the Spanish American War to the Invasion of Panama*. New York: Macmillan, 1990.

Rothwell, R. B. "Shanghai Emergency." *MCG*, November 1972.

Russell, John H. "The Birth of the FMF." *Proceedings*, January 1946.

Schott, Joseph L. *The Ordeal of Samar*. Indianapolis: Bobbs-Merrill, 1964.

Shoup, David M. *The Marines in China, 1927–1928: The Chinese Expedition Which Turned Out to Be the Chinese Exhibition*. Hamden, Conn.: Shoe String Press, 1987.

Simmons, Edwin H. "The Federals and Fort Fisher." *MCG*, January–February 1951.

Skelly, Anne. "Dan Daly: The Legendary Marine Devil Dog," *Journal of Military History*, November 1988.

———. "Marines in the Boxer Rebellion." *Leatherneck*, September 1987.

ter Horst, Jerald F. "Our First Korean War." *MCG*, December 1953.

Zimmerman, John. "The Marines' First Spy." *Saturday Evening Post*, 23 November 1946.

Zissa, Robert F. "Nicaragua, 1912." *Leatherneck*, July 1984.

World War II

Aurthur, Robert A., and Kenneth Cohlima. *The Third Marine Division*. Washington, D.C.: Infantry Journal Press, 1948.

Averill, Gerald A. *Mustang*. Novato, Calif.: Presidio, 1987.

Baer, George W. *One Hundred Years of Sea Power*. Stanford, Calif.: Stanford University Press, 1994.

Bartlett, Tom. "Guadalcanal Aces." *Leatherneck*, August 1984.

Berry, Henry. *Semper Fi Mac*. New York: Arbor House, 1982.

Boyington, Gregory. *Baa Baa Black Sheep*. New York: Bantam Books, 1979.

Calvocoressi, Peter, and Guy Wint. *Total War: The Story of World War II*. New York: Random House, 1972.

Campbell, D'Ann. "Servicewomen of World War II." *Armed Forces and Society*, Winter 1990.

Canfield, Bruce N. *Infantry Weapons of World War II*. Lincoln, R.I.: Mowbray, 1994.

Clifford, Kenneth J. "Iceland." *MCG*, November 1965.

Corson, William R. *The Betrayal*. New York: Norton, 1968.

Cunningham, Winfield S. *Wake Island Command*. Boston: Little, Brown, 1961.

Davis, Burke. *Marine! The Life of Lt. Gen. Lewis B. (Chesty) Puller*. New York: Bantam Books, 1962.

Davis, Russell, and Brent Ashabranner. *Marine at War*. Boston: Little, Brown, 1961.

Donovon, James A. Jr. "Saipan Tank Battle." *MCG*, October 1944.

Ellis, Chris. *Tanks of World War 2*. London: Octopus Books, 1981.

Evans, R. A. "Infanitillery on Peleliu." *MCG*, January 1945.

Falk, Stanley. *Bloodiest Victory: Palaus*. New York: Random House, 1974.

Foss, Joe, with Donna W. Foss. *A Proud American: The Autobiography of Joe Foss*. New York: Pocket Books, 1992.

Francis, Arthur A. "The Battle for Banzai Ridge." *MCG*, June 1945.

Frank, Benis. "Vandegrift's Guadalcanal Command." *MCG*, August 1987.

Fuller, John F. C. *Decisive Battles of the U.S.A.* New York: Thomas Yoseloff, 1942.

Gailey, Harry A. *Bougainville, 1943–45: The Forgotten Campaign.* Lexington: University Press of Kentucky, 1991.

———. *"Howlin' Mad" versus the Army: Conflict in Command.* Novato, Calif.: Presidio, 1986.

———. *The Liberation of Guam.* Novato, Calif.: Presidio, 1985.

———. *Peleliu, 1944.* Annapolis, Md.: Nautical & Aviation Publishing, 1983.

Gattis, Austin P., et al. *Third Marine Division's Two Score and Ten.* Paducah, Ky.: Turner, 1992.

Graham, Michael B. *Mantle of Heroism: Tarawa and the Struggle for the Gilberts.* Novato, Calif.: Presidio, 1993.

Griffith, Samuel B. *The Battle for Guadalcanal.* Annapolis, Md.: Nautical & Aviation Publishing, 1979.

Hammel, Eric M. *Ace: A Marine Night-Fighter Pilot in World War II.* Pacifica, Calif.: Pacifica, 1985.

———. "Guadalcanal: 1st Battle of the Matanikau." *MCG*, August 1982.

———. *Munda Trail.* New York: Orion, 1989.

Haynes, F. E. "Left Flank at Iwo." *MCG*, March 1953.

Heinl, Robert. "We're Headed for Wake." *MCG*, June 1946.

Hough, Frank O. *The Island War.* New York: Lippincott, 1947.

Hoyt, Edwin P. *Storm over the Gilberts.* New York: Mason/Charter, 1987.

———. *To the Marianas.* New York: Avon, 1983.

Hunt, George P. *Coral Comes High.* New York: Harper & Row, 1946.

———. "Point Secured." *MCG*, January 1945.

Isley, Jeter A., and Philip Crowl. *The U.S. Marines and Amphibious Warfare.* Princeton, N.J.: Princeton University Press, 1951.

Johnson, Richard. *Follow Me: The Story of the Second Marine Division in World War II.* New York: Random House, 1948.

Josephy, Alvin M. "Iwo Jima." *American Heritage*, June/July 1981.

———. *The Long and the Short and the Tall.* New York: Knopf, 1946.

Ladd, J. D. *Assault from the Sea, 1939–45.* Newton Abbot, England: David & Charles, 1976.

Leckie, Robert. *Challenge for the Pacific: Guadalcanal—The Turning Point of the War.* Garden City, N.Y.: Doubleday, 1965.

————. *Conflict: The History of the Korean War*. New York: Putnam, 1962.

————. *Helmet for My Pillow*. New York: Random House, 1957.

————. *Strong Men Armed*. New York: Bantam, 1962.

Lee, Richard E. *Victory at Guadalcanal*. Novato, Calif.: Presidio, 1981.

Lord, Walter. *The Dawn's Early Light*. New York: Norton, 1972.

————. *Incredible Victory*. New York: Harper & Row, 1967.

Lowry, Timothy S. *And Brave Men Too*. New York: Crown, 1985.

Luckey, Robert B. "Cannon, Mud and Japs." *MCG*, October 1944.

Lundstrom, John. *The First Team: Pacific Naval Air Combat from Pearl Harbor to Midway*. Annapolis, Md.: Naval Institute Press, 1984.

MacArthur, Douglas. *Reminiscences*. New York: McGraw-Hill, 1964.

Manchester, William. *Goodbye Darkness*. New York: Dell, 1979.

Marshall, Samuel L. A. *Island Victory*. Washington: Infantry Journal Press, 1944.

Morris, James M. *America's Armed Forces: A History*. Upper Saddle River, N.J.: Prentice Hall, 1996.

Potter, Elmer B. *Bull Halsey*. Annapolis, Md.: Naval Institute Press, 1985.

————. *Nimitz*. Annapolis, Md.: Naval Institute Press, 1985.

Pratt, Fletcher. "Marines Under MacArthur: Cape Gloucester," *MCG*, December 1947.

————. "Marines under MacArthur: Willaumez." *MCG*, 1 January 1947.

————. *The Marines' War*. New York: Sloan, 1948.

Proehl, Carl W. (ed.). *The Fourth Marine Division in World War II*. Washington, D.C.: Infantry Journal Press, 1946.

Ross, Bill D. *Iwo Jima: Legacy of Valor*. New York: Vanguard, 1985.

————. *Peleliu: Tragic Triumph*. New York: Random House, 1991.

Schmuck, David M. "Battle for Peleliu." *MCG*, February 1945.

Shaw, Henry, *Tarawa, A Legend Is Born*. New York: Ballantine Books, 1969.

————. "That's My Beach." *MCG*, November 1978.

————. "The United States Marines in the Guadalcanal Campaign." *Military History Review*, August 1984.

Sheel, Patrick, and Gene Cook. *Semper Fidelis: The U.S. Marines in the Pacific, 1942–1945*. New York: Sloan, 1947.

Shepherd, Lemuel C. "Battle for Motubu Peninsula." *MCG*, August 1945.

Sherrod, Robert. *The History of Marine Corps Aviation in World War II*. Washington, D.C.: Combat Forces Press, 1952.

——. *On to Westward: War in the Central Pacific.* New York: Duell, Sloan & Pearce, 1945.

Simmons, Edwin H. "Alabama's Holland M. Smith." *Fortitudine,* Fall 1989.

——. "An Appreciation of Lt. Gen. Julian C. Smith." *Fortitudine,* Winter 1988–89.

——. "Marine Corps Logistics in World War II." *Fortitudine,* Spring 1987.

——. "Remembering General Shepherd." *Fortitudine,* Fall 1990.

Sledge, Eugene B. *With the Old Breed at Peleliu and Okinawa.* Novato, Calif.: Presidio, 1981.

Smith, Holland M. "Tarawa Was a Mistake." *Saturday Evening Post,* November 1943.

Smith, Holland M., and Percy Finch. *Coral and Brass.* New York: Scribners, 1948.

Smith, S. E. *The United States Marine Corps in World War II.* New York: Random House, 1969.

Stockman, James R. "The Taking of Mount Tapotchau." *MCG,* October 1948.

Wheeler, Richard. *The Bloody Battle for Surabachi.* New York: Crowell, 1965.

——. *Iwo.* New York: Lippincott & Cowell, 1980.

Wilds, T. "The Japanese Seizure of Guam," *MCG,* July 1955.

Korea to Vietnam

Appleman, Roy. *Escaping the Trap: The U.S. Army X Corps in Northeast Korea, 1950.* College Station: Texas A & M University Press, 1990.

Blair, Clay. *The Forgotten War: America in Korea, 1950–1953.* New York: Times Books, 1987.

Collins, J. Lawton. *War in Peacetime: The History and Lessons of Korea.* Boston: Houghton Mifflin, 1969.

Fehrenbach, T. R. *This Kind of War.* New York: Brassey's, 1994.

Geer, Andrew C. *The New Breed: The Story of the U.S. Marines in Korea.* New York: Harper Brothers, 1952.

Goulden, Joseph C. *Korea: The Untold Story of the War.* New York: Times Books, 1982.

Hammel, Eric. *Chosin: Heroic Ordeal of the Korean War.* New York: Vanguard, 1981.

——. *Victory at High Tide: The Inchon-Seoul Campaign.* Annapolis, Md.: Nautical & Aviation Publishing, 1979.

Hastings, Max. *The Korean War.* New York: Simon & Schuster, 1987.

Hoyt, Edwin P. *On to the Yalu*. New York: Stein & Day, 1984.

Keiser, Gordon W. *The U.S. Marine Corps and Defense Unification, 1944–47*. Washington, D.C.: National Defense University Press, 1982.

Leckie, Robert R. *The March to Glory*. Cleveland: World, 1960.

Lowenthal, Abraham F. *The Dominican Intervention*. Cambridge, Mass.: Harvard University Press, 1972.

Millet, Allan R. "Crisis in Cuba." *MCG*, November 1987.

Pirnie, Bruce R. "Inchon Landing: How Great Was the Risk." *Joint Perspectives*, Summer 1982.

Ridgeway, Matthew B. *The War in Korea*. New York: Doubleday, 1967.

Shaw, Henry "Four at Center Recall 1945 Landing in North China." *Fortitudine*, Fall 1985.

Stanton, Shelby L. *America's Tenth Legion, X Corps in Korea, 1950*. Novato, Calif.: Presidio, 1989.

Summers, Harry G. *Korean War Almanac*. New York: Facts on File, 1990.

Utz, Curtis A. *Assault from the Sea: The Amphibious Landing at Inchon*. Washington, D.C.: Naval Historical Center, 1994.

Whelan, Richard. *Drawing the Line: The Korean War, 1950–1953*. New York: Little, Brown, 1990.

Whiting, Allan. *China Crosses the Yalu: The Decision to Enter the Korean War*. Berkeley: University of California Press, 1970.

Vietnam

Emerson, Gloria. *Winners and Losers: Battles, Retreats, Gains and Losses from a Long War*. New York: Random House, 1977.

Esper, George and the Associated Press. *The Eyewitness History of the Vietnam War, 1967–1975*. New York: Villard, 1983.

Finlayson, A. R. "Vietnam Strategies." *MCG*, August 1988.

FitzGerald, Frances. *Fire in the Lake*. Boston: Little, Brown, 1972.

Hackworth, David H., and Julie Sherman. *About Face*. New York: Simon & Schuster, 1989.

Hammel, Eric M. *Ambush Valley, I Corps, Vietnam, 1967*. Novato, Calif.: Presidio, 1990.

———. *Fire in the Streets: The Battle for Hue, Tet, 1968*. Chicago: Contemporary Books, 1991.

———. *Khe Sanh: Siege in the Clouds*. New York: Crown, 1989.

Herring, George C. *America's Longest War: The United States and Vietnam*. New York: Knopf, 1986.

Isaacs, Arnold. *Without Honor: Defeat in Vietnam and Cambodia*. Baltimore, Md.: Johns Hopkins University Press, 1983.

Karnow, Stanley. *Vietnam: A History*. New York: Viking, 1983.

Nolan, Keith W. *Battle for Hue: Tet 1968*. Novato, Calif.: Presidio, 1983.

Oberdorfer, Don. *Tet*. New York: Doubleday, 1971.

Pike, Douglas. *PAVN: The Peoples Army of Vietnam*. Novato, Calif.: Presidio, 1986.

———. *Viet Cong: The Organization and Techniques of the National Liberation Front of Vietnam*. Cambridge, Mass.: M.I.T. Press, 1966.

Pimlott, John (ed.). *Vietnam: The History and the Tactics*. New York: Crescent, 1982.

Piser, Robert. *The End of the Line: The Siege of Khe Sanh*. New York: Norton, 1982.

Sheehan, Neil. *A Bright and Shining Lie*. New York: Random House, 1988.

Simmons, Edwin H. "Fox Company at Toktong Pass." *Fortitudine*, Fall 1991.

Stanton, Shelby L. *The Rise and Fall of an American Army: U.S. Ground Forces in Vietnam, 1965–1973*. Stevenage, England: Spa Books, 1989.

———. *Vietnam Order of Battle*. Washington, D.C.: U.S. News Books, 1981.

Summers, Harry G. *On Strategy: A Critical Analysis of the Vietnam War*. Novato, Calif.: Presidio, 1982.

Walt, Lewis W. *Strange War, Strange Strategy: A General's Report on Vietnam*. New York: Funk & Wagnalls, 1970.

Westmoreland, William C., and U. S. Grant Sharpe. *A Soldier Reports*. New York: Doubleday, 1976.

Post-Vietnam

Bartlett, Tom. "Operation Just Cause, Marines Fight in Panama." *Leatherneck*, February 1990.

———. "Operation Starlight." *Leatherneck*, August 1985.

Cushman, John H. "Joint, Jointer, Jointest." *Proceedings*, May 1992.

Dare, John A. "Dominican Diary." *Proceedings*, December 1965.

Fleming, Keith. *The U.S. Marine Corps in Crisis: Ribbon Creek and Recruit Training*. Columbia: University of South Carolina Press, 1990.

Gaddo, Randy. "Beirut Bombing." *Leatherneck*, February 1984.

Grace, John J. "The U.S. Marine Corps in 1991." *Proceedings*, May 1992.

Hamel, Eric. *The Root: Marines in Beiruit, August 1982–February 1984.* New York: Harcourt Brace Jovanovich, 1985.

Hof, Frederick, "The Beiruit Bombing of October 1983." *Parameters,* Summer 1985.

Jacobs, Richard H. "A Chronology of the Gulf War." *Arab Studies Quarterly,* Winter/Spring 1991.

Keys, William M. "Rolling with the 2d Marine Division." *Proceedings,* November 1991.

Khalidi, Walid. "The Gulf Crisis: Origins and Consequences." *Journal of Palestine Studies,* Winter 1991.

Krulak, Charles C. Interview, "A War of Logistics." *Proceedings,* November 1991.

Leahy, A. M. "Grenada—In Retrospect." *Fortitudine,* Spring 1984.

Marutoolo, Frank. "Preserving the Marine Corps as a Separate Service." *MCG,* June 1988.

Moore, Royal N. Interview, "Marine Air: There When Needed." *Proceedings,* November 1991.

Mundy, Carl E. "Redefining the Marine Corps' Strategic Concept." *Proceedings,* May 1992.

Myatt, J. M. "The 1st Marine Division in the Attack." *Proceedings,* November 1991.

Pope, John R. "U.S. Marines in Operation Desert Storm." *MCG,* July 1991.

Reynolds, Bradley M. "Guantanamo Bay: A Doubly Important Advanced Base." *MCG,* November 1982.

Rowan, R. *The Four Days of Mayaguez.* New York: Norton, 1975.

Rowe, Peter J. "Interview: Desert Storm." *Proceedings,* May 1992.

Schwarzkopf, H. Norman, and Peter Petre. *It Doesn't Take a Hero.* New York: Bantam Books, 1992.

Simmons, Edwin H. "Getting Marines to the Gulf." *Proceedings,* May 1991.

———. "The Marines and Crisis Control." *Proceedings,* November 1965.

———. "The Marines Now and in the Future." *Proceedings,* May 1975.

Utz, Curtis A. *Cordon of Steel: The U.S. Navy and the Cuban Missile Crisis.* Washington, D.C.: Naval Historical Center, 1993.

Van Riper, Paul K. "Observations during Operation Desert Storm." *MCG,* June 1991.

Watson, Bruce W., ed. *Military Lessons of the Gulf War.* Novato, Calif.: Presidio, 1991.

Watson, Bruce W., and P. G. Tsouras, eds. *Operation Just Cause.* Boulder, Colo.: Westview, 1991.

Yates, Lawrence A. "Joint Task Force: Panama Just Cause—Before and After." *Military Review,* October 1991.

About the Author

Harry A. Gailey was born 4 December 1926 in Kansas City, Missouri. He graduated from high school in McAllen, Texas, in 1943. After working in the engineering department at Douglas Aircraft Company in Long Beach, California, he entered the Army Air Corps in 1945. Later he attended U.C.L.A. receiving his B.A. (1953), M.A. (1955), and Ph.D. (1958) in history. He was chairman of the Humanities Department at Northwest Missouri State University before moving to San Jose State University in 1962, where he was a professor of history and the coordinator of African Studies for over 25 years, during which time he authored 10 books related to Africa. He has received research grants from the Ford Foundation, Social Science Research Council, and San Jose State University. Since 1975 he has been responsible for teaching all graduate and undergraduate military history courses at San Jose State. In 1972 he was named the Outstanding Professor and in 1978 the President's Annual Scholar. He has traveled widely in the Central Pacific area and was a visiting professor at the University of Guam. He has directed symposiums on the Pacific War at the Admiral Nimitz Museum and the University of New Mexico, and he recently directed a year course for the Naval War College at the Naval Post Graduate School at Monterey, California. He is the author of five books on World War II in the Pacific: *Peleliu, 1944; "Howlin' Mad" vs. the Army; The Liberation of Guam; Bougainville, 1943–1945;* and *The War in the Pacific: From Pearl Harbor to Tokyo Bay.*